Saving the
WEST SOMERSET
⤳ RAILWAY ⤲

Saving the
WEST SOMERSET
⇢ RAILWAY ⇠
THE BRANCH LINE
THAT REFUSED TO DIE

John Parsons

Frontispiece: Bishops Lydeard Station after the blizzard in 1978. (Stephen Edge)

First published 2011

The History Press
The Mill, Brimscombe Port
Stroud, Gloucestershire, GL5 2QG
www.thehistorypress.co.uk

British Library Cataloguing in Publication Data.
A catalogue record for this book is available from the British Library.

ISBN 978 0 7524 6403 9

Typesetting and origination by The History Press
Printed in Great Britain

Contents

Acknowledgements

I should like to thank the following people for their assistance in compiling this book:

John Pearce for the original idea and for the generous loan of his files, from which much of the information used in this book was obtained. Others who helped me with information and recollections of those early days include Chris van den Arund, Mark Smith and Hein Burger and my many colleagues on the West Somerset Railway, who when they learnt about my efforts to write this book gave me so much help in the form of personal memories and records they had kept.

May I also take this opportunity to thank my wife Pat, for all the many hours that she spent editing the text and correcting my many errors, and for being so understanding when the programme of house decorating went back once again, and also Colin Howard for all his assistance. Finally to my son Philip who helped me sort out the many glitches that occurred because of my limited skills with the computer.

This book is intended as a tribute to all those people whose initial efforts were responsible for the restarting of the line, many of whom are still working on the railway, together with those whose names no longer appear on the roster sheets, either because of their advancing years or sadly because they are now only with us in memory. I thank you all!

Foreword

The West Somerset Railway runs through the Quantock Hills, down the valley of the River Doniford with views of the Brendon Hills in the distance, along the cliff tops at Doniford, through the picturesque towns of Williton and Watchet, then turns inland to Washford before returning to run along the beach at Blue Anchor, over Kerr Moor, and finally across Dunster Marshes to arrive on the seafront at Minehead. What many visitors who travel on the railway today do not realise is that without the tremendous efforts of a few dedicated people they would not have been able to enjoy their trip.

In this book I have described the events that led to the formation of the new West Somerset Railway and the struggles experienced in the early years of the company's existence. Many people who were involved with the formation of the new company went on to hold positions of responsibility in the new enterprise and their names together with others who became directors or held other managerial posts are mentioned frequently in the following pages. This is only proper because, without their vision, the West Somerset Railway as we know it today would not exist. However, please remember as you read this book, the tremendous debt we owe to the numerous unnamed members of the staff and volunteers who gave such unstinting help to the railway during the difficult years covered in this book. Lack of space prevents me from mentioning many of these stalwarts, some of whom are still working on the railway today.

Enjoy your read.

John Parsons.

1

A Brief History of the Minehead Branch Line

The original West Somerset Railway was created because of the need to remove coal and stone from the port of Watchet. Ships that had carried iron ore and slate from Watchet to ports in South Wales brought the coal and stone back across the Bristol Channel as ballast. The perilous state of the roads in West Somerset meant that, for a large part of each year, goods could only be carried away from the Watchet area by horse or donkey; carts often sunk up to their axles on the tracks that crossed the area.

The first railway route to be surveyed left the main Bristol to Exeter line at Bridgwater and would have been routed through Nether Stowey and Kilve to Williton, and from there to Watchet. This route would have involved heavy earthworks and much tunnelling, and would have been expensive to build and operate. The second survey to be carried out was to be undertaken by Mr I.K. Brunel, although in reality most of the work was done by his assistant Mr F.W. Bretherton, who proposed that the branch line should leave the main Bristol to Exeter railway line at a point two miles west of Taunton, known originally as Watchet Junction (later Norton Fitzwarren Junction), travel up the valley of a tributary of the river Tone, across the threshold of the Quantock Hills in the area of Crowcombe and then down the valley of the river Doniford to Williton, and from there to Watchet.

It was agreed that this would be the easiest route to construct and the cheapest to operate, and as soon as the necessary bill had passed through Parliament, construction work on the line began in the Crowcombe area in 1860. Work on the line proceeded rapidly, with few problems, and after the necessary Board of Trade Inspection was opened to both passenger and goods traffic in 1862. Built to the Broad Gauge, it was single track throughout, with a passing loop at Williton, and operated from the opening of the line by the Bristol and Exeter Railway. Stations were built at Bishops Lydeard, Crowcombe Heathfield (later renamed Crowcombe), Stogumber, Williton and Watchet.

The location of the stations owed more to the possible source of goods traffic and the avoidance of any unnecessary costs by the railway, rather than the convenience of any intended passengers. In the late 1860s the Luttrell family, who owned Dunster Castle and a great deal of the land in the Minehead area, became increasingly concerned at the growing prosperity of Watchet at the expense of Minehead and they decided that Minehead should be connected to the railway system. Many people felt at the time that this decision was taken because of the growing prosperity of the Wyndham family, owners of the recently extended and improved Watchet Harbour, who the Luttrells disliked intensely because of a family feud going back as far as the Civil War. Others thought that perhaps the Luttrell family were trying to exploit the dispute between the ironmasters who owned the Mineral Railway and the Wyndham family, caused by the increased harbour dues imposed by the harbour trust to recover the substantial – and totally unexpected – costs incurred in repairing the harbour after the damage caused in the great storm of 1860. If this was the reason they were to be disappointed because the dispute over the increased harbour fees was settled long before the line was opened to Minehead.

Had the Luttrell family not experienced delays both in getting the necessary bill through Parliament and many other problems which included disputes and numerous legal actions with a number of landlords whose properties the proposed line crossed, the ironmasters might have been persuaded to divert their ships to Minehead to load instead of Watchet. Further delays were caused when the navvies building the line were prevented from storming the Clerk of the Works' office to present their point of view (they had not been paid) when they were held at bay by the Clerk wielding a loaded pistol. The arrival of the Militia and the reading of the Riot Act ensured that the quarrel between the Wyndhams and the Mineral Railway was resolved before construction of the Minehead Railway was started. Some people believe that this is the reason that the line did not run closer to the Williton to Minehead road after leaving Washford, when it could have served the villages of Bilbrook and Carhampton. The numerous delays may also explain why the station at Minehead is situated at its present location and was not extended down to the harbour. Although the Minehead Railway section of the line was much the easiest section to build, it was not opened until 1874.

Like the West Somerset Railway, the Minehead Railway was built to the Broad Gauge, was single track throughout and was operated by the Bristol and Exeter Railway from its opening. Stations were built at Washford, Bradley Gate (later renamed Blue Anchor), Dunster and Minehead.

In 1876 the Bristol and Exeter Railway was absorbed by the Great Western Railway and in 1882 the GWR decided to convert the whole of the branch line to the Standard Gauge. One Sunday morning, after weeks of preparation, seven groups, each containing seventy labourers in each gang, set about the task of the conversion and that same afternoon the first standard gauge engine arrived at Minehead Station. Restricted services started the following day and normal services resumed on the Tuesday.

Towards the end of the nineteenth century it became obvious to many that improvements were urgently needed along the branch line, partly because of the increase in industrial activities in West Somerset, for example pit props from Dunster, shirt manufacturing factories at Bishops Lydeard and Watchet, flour mills and harbour at Watchet, paper mills and cattle markets at Washford and the stone crushing plant at Crowcombe, together with the increases in the population of Minehead and the surrounding area. The arrival of the railway had also heralded a period of growing prosperity for the farming industry which was still the biggest employer in the district. Although sidings and goods sheds had been built at a number of stations along the branch, the fact the branch was single-track throughout, with the exception of the passing loop at Williton, created numerous operating problems. Although they were aware of the problems the management of the GWR could do little to improve the situation, because of the many financial problems that the GWR was facing at that time, not the least of which was the conversion of the remainder of the system to the standard gauge, which was finally completed in 1892.

The rapidly improving financial situation of the GWR in the first decade of the twentieth century meant that many projects that had been under consideration for a number of years could at last be carried out. Major work carried out at this time included the building of the Berkshire & Hampshire line to give a more direct route to the West Country avoiding Bristol, and the new GWR direct line to Birmingham.

Of even greater importance to those living in the area served by the Minehead branch was the decision to build passing loops and second platforms at Bishops Lydeard, Crowcombe Heathfield and Blue Anchor in 1904. The provision of a second platform at Minehead the following year eased the problems caused by the increasing number of people who were finding the town an attractive holiday resort. The improvements went some way towards easing the problems that had by now become desperate because of the inflow of materials (bricks, timber slates etc.) arriving by rail to build the new houses and also the arrival of goods that the newly built shops were stocking to furnish the new homes. The establishment of other industries, for example gas works and, later, electricity generating stations, together with the by-products generated by these services, which included coke, benzene and tar, resulted in a further increase in traffic on the branch line.

It was about this time that the railways also became involved with the carriage of materials not previously on offer, for example petroleum products together with other items needed for the increasing number of vehicles with internal combustion engines. The increasing population also demanded the ever-widening range of consumer products that were becoming available, ranging from food stuffs to cookers, mangles and other household goods. These items were often produced in factories situated in close proximity to the railways, who were only too happy to carry and in some cases distribute their goods in GWR-owned lorries painted in the 'house colours' of the company whose goods the railway was distributing.

Passenger services also needed to be improved, not only to cope with the increasing number of holidaymakers but also the growing number of local residents. The outbreak of the First World War did not result in a huge increase in traffic on the branch, apart from volunteers for the new army and later enlisted men reporting for duty at distant locations, and a rapidly decreasing number of trained servicemen returning home on embarkation leave before they left to take part in battles on the Western Front, at sea or at other locations in the Middle East. As the war progressed increasing numbers of soldiers were trained on the former Sandhill Park Estate near Bishops Lydeard, before it became a prisoner of war camp for German officers.

The Grouping Act of 1923 meant that at last the West Somerset Railway and the Minehead Railway were absorbed by the Great Western Railway (the only railway to retain its original title under the Act). As they had retained their shares in the Minehead Railway this meant the Luttrell family finally had a seat on the board of the Great Western Railway and it is believed that they used this influence to persuade the GWR to action the many improvements that were carried out on the branch in 1934.

A loop was built at Kentsford to avoid the need to run troop trains to Blue Anchor after the troops – who at first were TA reservists and later regular soldiers (and in the 1960s members of the RAF Regiment) – had disembarked at Watchet to march to the camp at Doniford. The camp was built to billet the thousands of men who were to be trained as Ack Ack or Anti Aircraft Gunners at the gunnery site established nearby at Helwell Bay. The loop also had the advantage of breaking up the long section of single line between Blue Anchor and Williton and allowed a rather more frequent service of trains during the peak summer period.

An additional passing loop was also put at Leigh Woods, again to increase the frequency of the trains along the branch by breaking up the long single-line section between Williton and Crowcombe during the periods of heavy holiday traffic. Further efforts were made to increase the number of trains that the branch could handle by doubling the sections of the branch line at Norton Fitzwarren and Bishops Lydeard, and Dunster to Minehead. Platforms were also extended at Blue Anchor, Crowcombe and Dunster. At Minehead the platform was extended to a quarter of a mile long to accommodate 14-coach trains from Paddington, South Wales, Birmingham (Snow Hill) and even Merseyside (Birkenhead). Unfortunately the GWR did not take the opportunity to upgrade the branch line to take main line engines of the Castle or Hall classes which brought these trains to Taunton, and this resulted in delays whilst the larger engines were uncoupled from the train and either one large prairie tank or two small prairie tanks substituted to bring the long train forward to Minehead. To avoid delays to other trains heading for the West Country this substitution was often carried out on the relief road at the rear of Taunton Station, a line only used by goods trains on weekdays.

The outbreak of the Second World War in 1939 affected the branch line to a much greater extent than in the First World War. The gunnery range at Helwell Bay received larger numbers of trainee gunners than before the war and this in turn meant more anti-aircraft guns on the site, which required more ammunition than ever before. A number of American tanks were brought along the branch line to Minehead so that their crews could be trained on Exmoor in preparation for D-Day. Together with the large number of troops in the tented camp near Crowcombe Station, these disappeared overnight just before the event itself.

After the invasion had started large numbers of wounded Americans were treated in Sandhill Park House which the American forces had commandeered as a base hospital in 1943. Many of the wounded were brought from the ships which returned them to this country in 'Ambulance Trains'; they were then collected by ambulances from either Taunton or Bishops Lydeard stations. Throughout this period the harbour at Watchet was taking considerable amounts of traffic from and also generating large volumes of traffic for the branch line.

After the war ended in 1945, the continuing shortage of petrol (still rationed) meant that the majority of materials available, including foodstuffs, were rationed. Servicemen returning home after demobilisation and others returning to the district from war work elsewhere ensured that mid-week services on the branch were well patronised, but at weekends the branch, like the entire railway system, struggled to cope with the large numbers of people who were determined to have their first holiday for six years or more, and where else was there to go other than the seaside? Minehead like many other British resorts enjoyed probably the busiest decade in its history from 1945: continuous employment for many years had awarded some people more money than at any time before in their lives and because austerity was still the way of life, there was very little else for people to spend their money on.

It was a long time after the railways had been nationalised in 1948 before goods such as new cars were released for the home market and rationing of food and clothing finally ceased. It was then that people, fed up with the long delays they had experienced in taking their holidays by rail, decided to buy cars to transport themselves and their families in future, only to experience even longer delays on the Exeter bypass on Saturdays in the summer months. In the 1960s the advent of package holidays to continental resorts, rebuilt after the war, resulted in an even greater decline in the number of people visiting seaside resorts in this country, and Minehead was no exception.

2

The First Rumours of Closure...

Is This The End of The Branch Line?

With the building of the Butlins campsite at Minehead came an increase in the number of passengers using the branch line, and because the branch line remained open when other routes to the outside world from West Somerset were closed during the hard winter of 1963, many people believed that the branch would escape the 'Beeching cuts' of the 1960s.

To many railwaymen, and others who used the branch line regularly, it was obvious that BR was intent on closing the line. After steam services ceased and diesel railcars were introduced no real attempt was made to bring in economies that could possibly have ensured that the line remained economically viable. Any attempt to benefit from the reduced costs that occurred because of the introduction of DMUs and the reduction in staffing levels at the intermediate stations along the branch were more than offset by the reduced income generated on the branch because of BR's attempts to prevent passengers travelling on the line. This was achieved by reducing the branch to what BR called 'Basic Railway Status'. The passing loops at Kentsford, Leigh Woods and Crowcombe were removed together with all the ancillary equipment, leaving Williton as the only passing place between Blue Anchor and Bishops Lydeard, thus ensuring that fewer trains could use the branch line. Furthermore, by ensuring that the trains from the branch line arrived at Taunton minutes after many main line connections had left, it ensured that even fewer passengers would use the service.

Other 'improvements' carried out on the branch included removing the footbridge and reducing the length of the loop at Williton, reducing the double-track section between Dunster and Minehead to two single tracks, so that if a train needed to get from the Bay to the main platform at Minehead it had to travel via Dunster. Futhermore the removal of all the sidings at Minehead including the run round loop meant that locomotive-hauled trains from the main line could no longer use the branch line.

The decision to 'zonalise' all the goods traffic on the branch to Taunton meant the end of traffic from the harbour at Watchet to the nearby paper mill, stone traffic from Crowcombe and cattle traffic from the markets at Minehead and Washford, together with the other goods traffic that had always been the mainstay of the line. The prompt removal of all the sidings and other equipment at these and other intermediate stations meant that closure of the line to Minehead was inevitable. Nonetheless, it was still a shock to many residents when, after months of rumours, the first official notice of the closure of the line appeared in the Friday 23 August 1968 edition of the *Evening Post*, which read:

B.R. THREAT TO CLOSE WEST RESORT LINE

BRway's board announced today that unless objections are received, the Minehead to Taunton branch line will be closed from January 6th next year.

The closure would affect scores of young people who travel to and from daily [sic] to their studies at the Taunton Technical College and other educational centres, also thousands of week-end travellers to and from the Butlins Holiday camp at Minehead.

At the time Mr Tony Crosby, Area Manager for Butlins, said, 'We can prove with facts and figures that our use of the line is on the increase, rather than the decrease, and we would have thought that it was in the interests of BR to keep the line open.' He then added, 'We will join in any protest to be made against closure.' A formal holding objection was also lodged by Minehead Urban District Council, who said they were prepared to collaborate in the preparation of a case against closure with the Somerset County Council. The SCC had also undertaken the co-ordination of objections and present a consolidated case to the Area Travel Users Consultative Council, on proposals affecting lines and stations wholly within the county. Another report in the *Evening Post* on 28 August 1968 not only outlined the scenic beauty of the line, it also made out a strong case for the line remaining open, before giving an interesting insight into how neglected the line had become during the 1960s compared with many people's memories of the pristine appearance of the line remembered up to the 1950s. Under the following headline the writer stated:

UNHAPPY ENDING FOR THE FAIRY TALE LINE
Minehead Link to be Axed

A few years ago Taunton was able to boast of its rail connections, as the County Town they felt that they had something special. There were four branch lines serving the Town, as well as the main line. The branch lines were the Taunton–Chard, Taunton–Yeovil, Taunton–Barnstaple, and Taunton–Minehead.

Now there only remains the Taunton–Minehead line and this is threatened by the latest shock announcement by BR. The Western Region now state that they propose to discontinue all passenger services between Minehead and Taunton with effect from January 6th 1969 'if no objections were lodged to the proposal'.

That objections will be lodged there is very little doubt. Minehead Urban Council is lodging a 'holding objection' because they feel hardship will be caused. Somerset County Council will probably register a formal objection. This means there will most probably be a public enquiry into the threatened closure when the case of hardship versus railway economics will be heard, and the Minister left to give his decision.

This picture book line with its views of fairy tale thatched cottages, Dunster Castle and the sea is some 24 miles long. There are eight stopping places – Bishops Lydeard, Crowcombe, Stogumber, Williton, Watchet, Washford, Blue Anchor, and Dunster. The line passes through some of the most delightful country between the Quantock Hills and the Brendon Hills. During thirteen weeks of the year in the summer, it is a much used line on Saturdays. Last Saturday one train alone, the 10.35 from Taunton, carried 270 passengers and there are a number of trains each day up and down the line.

Not only do Taunton people and those along the route use the line, but passengers come from as far afield as the North of England and other areas. Many come during the summer months to Butlins holiday camp, but these are by no means all. For many years the line has been the main link with Minehead for long distance rail passengers who enjoy Minehead. Some have been travelling year after year and they say the line is a great attraction.

The once well kept stations and halts are not what they used to be however, weeds now grow in the stonework of the stations, hemlock and willow herb thrive on the embankments, and some of the waiting room windows are boarded up.

Many people travelling to Minehead on Saturday last heard of the threatened closure for the first time. 'We have chosen to use rail transport in preference to road, but it looks as though we are being forced onto the road' they said. Mr and Mrs Alfred Carter, of Rochester Drive, Westcliffe on Seas, travelling on Saturday for a holiday at Minehead with their four daughters, said they preferred rail, and would regret the closure of the line, these views were echoed by local residents like Miss Violet Maud Keitch of West Monkton Taunton who said 'I visit people at Watchet frequently. I prefer train', and Mrs Mabel Bowerman of Staplehay Taunton, travelling to Blue Anchor, said 'I prefer train; it's so direct and comfortable'.

A retired railwayman Mr W.C. Watts of Priory Avenue, Taunton going to his caravan at Blue Anchor also extolled the comforts of travelling by rail. At Watchet looking at the now thriving port, Mr Watts recalled that it was only four years ago when all freight traffic on the line was stopped, and they had since pulled up, all lines to the harbour. Now that the Watchet port boom had come along the people could well use rail for transport. At one time the railway carried 500 tons (of goods traffic) a day from the harbour at Watchet, he said.

Mr Edgar Higgs, assistant area superintendent BR, admitted that on thirteen Saturdays during the summer the service was quite busy. On Saturdays they ran a train from London to Minehead, the 8.50 from Paddington which was fairly well filled, largely with Butlins people. There were also two through trains from Minehead to Paddington, at 10.40 and 13.00 which were also heavily loaded.

This was however only during the summer season. There was also the usual local timetable all the year round. In the summer some passengers came from many parts of the country. It's a sad story generally however. 'While we are busier on thirteen Saturdays in the summer this does not fulfil the economics for the remainder of the year' he said.

From the comments of the official in the last paragraph of the above article, it was obvious that no matter how good a case could be made for the line to remain open, BR were determined that it should be closed. Long after the line had closed a former Western

Region manager at the time told the writer 'we did not wish to close the branch, but we were told that we had to make further economies; because we could not make any other economies elsewhere we had no alternative'. He also went on to say that the revenue figures quoted to justify the closure of the line only included the moneys collected on the branch line, it did not include a portion of the fares paid by many of those holidaymakers referred to in the above article who boarded Minehead-bound trains at stations (including Taunton) away from the branch. Had the branch received a proportion of the total fare which should have been allocated for journeys over it, the figures would have told a very different story.

Long before the last train ran, a rather nostalgic article appeared in the *Somerset County Gazette* on 23 August 1968 under the byline of Peter Hesp's 'Somerset Notebook'. It was headed: 'Is This Really the End of the Line?' In the article he described not only the way of life that had existed on the branch line for many years in recent memory, but also showed that the railwaymen's attitude to the job had not altered even though many of them faced a very uncertain future. The article also mentions a 'character' who continued to work on the line for many years after it had been reopened by the preservationists.

Peter Hesp wrote:

I don't know whether Mr J. Bonham-Carter has ever stretched his legs along the platform of Williton railway station, or spent a pleasant half hour chatting with country railwaymen, at any other of the pearls of places which hang on the thread of permanent way between Taunton and Minehead, but if he has he must have heaved a sad, nostalgic sigh when he put his signature to a public notice the other day.

That public notice, which appears on another page of this newspaper, is from the BR ways board, of which he is general manager and what it says is that the Taunton to Minehead branch line will close down on 6th January if nobody has any objections. If there are any objections it will take a little longer.

What a miserable job Mr Bonham-Carter must have! 'Heigho' he says, shaking his head over the memory of bygone branch lines bordered with nasturtium and booking offices that might have been dreamt up by Robert Searle. He puts his signature to the death warrant of yet another railway track and he can't like it a bit. But this is a question of economy don't you see...

Half forgotten

When I first went for a sort of preliminary look at the Williton Station this week a gang of lengthmen were busy adjusting new ballast under the track. Ralph Manning, who has been there almost a quarter of a century, popped his head out of the sliding window of his signal box to give me his usual cheery welcome. It all looked healthy enough but, just the same, there was a sort of museum air about the place.

The waiting rooms had an empty, unused look, although they were kept spic and span. The ticket office was locked and shuttered. The gas lamps over the now forlorn footbridge, and deserted platform, belonged to an age that is already half forgotten. For over a hundred years people in these parts have lived with the local railway. Their daily tasks have been punctuated by the cheerful hoot of the steam train echoing among the hills. The same sound, piercing bravely through a stormy night provided food for fireside conversation as cottagers have looked at their clocks and discussed the sort of weather which could have delayed the last train. For us, the permanent way is just that; something as permanent as stones on Dunkery or worts on Staple Plain. We can't believe it's really going to disappear. As I climb the steep flight of stairs to the signal box, I wonder what in the world Parson Poole would have said if he could have foreseen this day. As Vicar of St Decuman's he presided over the public dinner which was held at Watchet in April, 1862, to mark the opening of the line from Taunton to the little port.

We know too, that with the passing of the railways will come the end of that remarkable race apart, the railwaymen. 'There aren't any railwaymen coming on these nowadays, not of the kind I knew as a boy,' Mr Manning told me as he polished the bright steel handles of his signal levers. When he joined the railway, starting in 1923 as a lad-porter at Norton Fitzwarren, his father was signalmen at Taunton Station, one of his brothers was a locomotive driver, another a railway clerk, a third a signalman, and two of his brother-in -laws worked on the railway. Being a railwayman wasn't just a job, nor even a career, it was a way of life. Young men were keen to take up the calling and proud to spend the whole of their lives in the service.

The great days of their immaculately polished and beautifully painted steam locomotives have gone, but he memory lingers on in the signalbox at Williton (and no doubt in all the others on the branch line). Ralph Manning and Harry Horn, who has just received his gold watch for 45 years service, still keep the brasswork gleaming, polish the floor, and shine up the handles on the big levers, painted red, yellow, blue, black and white, to such a degree that they will never touch them with their bare hands. They use a special BR tea towel so that no perspiration will mar the burnished metal with rust.

Between them they take it in turn to man Williton Station, where only a few years ago there was a stationmaster, porter, two signalmen, and a railway lorry driver. Each in turn does all the cleaning, sees to any parcels, answer the telephone, deals with inquiries, lights the gas lamps in the station and trims the oil lamps in the sigmals – and of course attends to their 21 levers, the block telegraph and other paraphernalia the mysteries of which are only to be fathomed by the dwindling brotherhood of signalmen.

And in between times, I dare say, they brew up a lovely cup of signalmens tea and stare out of the big, sliding windows of the box across the empty metals, over the roof of the forsaken station to where the farmland reach up to the fir woods, which climb the western Quantocks, dark and high against the sky.

They also remember the last days of a way of life which seemed as if it would go on for ever.

Harry Horn continued to work on the line at Stogumber, after the branch line reopened, as stationmaster at Stogumber until he was over ninety years old.

After several emotive pleas in the local press (of which the above article is just one) and representations from both the county council and Minehead Town Council, and questions to the then Minister of Transport Mr Fred Mulley by the newly elected MP for the Bridgwater constituency (which included Minehead) Tom King, BR finally appeared to relent and said that they were prepared to keep the line open if the local authorities were prepared to pay BR an annual subsidy of £140,000.

It appeared that the county council was not opposed in principle to paying a subsidy to keep the line open but queried why BR was demanding what they considered to be such an excessive amount of subsidy. With hindsight it is obvious that BR were making such a such a demand because they realised that the county council could not justify such an outlay, and when the subsidy was not forthcoming BR could claim that it was the refusal of the local authorities to co-operate that lead to the closure of the branch line and therefore they could be absolved from any blame.

The failure of the parties concerned to reach an agreement meant that a public inquiry was inevitable. Despite strong representations from the local authorities and numerous pleas from local residents claiming that many individuals and communities in the area would suffer real hardship with the closure of the line, the inability of the county council to pay the subsidy required meant that the members of the tribunal had no alternative but to accede to the request by BR to closure of the branch line.

One stipulation that was made by the tribunal was that the line was not to be closed until a suitable alternative bus service was operating. The failure of the Western National Bus company to implement this condition within a reasonable timescale meant that the closure of the line was delayed, but eventually the authorities were satisfied with the standard of the bus service (even if many of the residents were not) and it was announced that the last train would run on Saturday 2 January 1971.

3

The Last Train

The news that the last train would run on the Minehead branch on 2 January 1971 appeared in all the local newspapers including the *Somerset County Gazette* and the *West Somerset Free Press*, but many of the local people were surprised to find news of the closure of their branch line had made the national newspapers. Articles appeared in the *Daily Mirror* and the *People*, whilst the *Daily Express* reported on the final passenger train to travel on the branch. The final trip itself was a complete sell-out, with 200 passengers filling the service from Taunton to Minehead. The line, which had been open since 1874, was described as 'uneconomic', and was due to be replaced by a bus service:

Saturday 2 January was a cold wet and miserable day and the failure of the earlier 9.20 a.m. train, resulting in the passengers being forced to complete their journey by bus, was not a good omen for the rest of the day. Many people arrived to travel on the line on that last day, some of whom had covered considerable distances to witness the event. Dr Lionel Pimm had set out from his home in Ipswich at 5 a.m. in order to film the journey. 'I used to live in Minehead as a boy of three,' he told the *Western Daily Press* reporter. 'I have come back every year since then and have been filming the line since 1961.'

When other branch lines had closed they ran a last train; the Minehead branch – which never believed in half measures – succeeded in running three (or was it two?) last trains on that day. I have worked on the branch line for many years as a volunteer and numerous people have informed me that their husbands, fathers, brothers (in-laws as well), uncles and sons were drivers or guards on the last train. I assumed that the driver or the guard must have had a lot of relatives, but this information may go some way to clearing up this mystery.

The first of the 'last' trains was organised by the Taunton Branch of the Great Western Society and was advertised as the last daylight train to Minehead; it was due to depart from Taunton at 3.30 p.m. and return to Taunton at 5.20 p.m. The fare for this memorable trip was £1 for adults and 15s (75p) for children.

For the record this 3-coach DMU was driven by Mr Ken Cridland of Taunton who at that time had been working trains on the various branch lines around Taunton for twenty-eight years. The guard on this trip was Mr Walter Thyer, also of Taunton, who had been a guard on the Minehead branch for ten years. The area manager, Mr James Ross, travelled in the cab of the DMU, presumably to keep an eye on the proceedings.

LAST TRAIN

Saturday, 2nd January, 1971

MINEHEAD · TAUNTON · MINEHEAD

Depart 7.30 p.m.   Approx. arrival 10.5 p.m.

TICKETS £1 Inclusive of:
(LIMITED NUMBER)

**SHERRY RECEPTION 6.45 p.m.
AT THE BEACH HOTEL**

COMMEMORATIVE BOOKLET

SOUVENIR TICKET

PLEASE APPLY: PASSMORE'S, THE PARADE, MINEHEAD

SPONSORED BY MINEHEAD AND DISTRICT ROUND TABLE
ALL PROFITS TO LOCAL CHARITIES

COX, PRINTERS, WILLITON AND MINEHEAD

Pictures appeared in the *Western Daily News*, the *Express* and *Echo* of Mr Harry Lee, who was to become the mechanical engineer of the West Somerset Railway for a time during the early years of the line's history, fixing the society's plaque to the front of the train. On arrival at Williton a piece of local history was enacted when young Edward Martin exercised his family's right to sell fruit to passengers travelling through Williton, a concession that his forbears had obtained from the Great Western Railway many years before.

When the train arrived at Minehead it was coupled to the next service train standing in the platform for the return journey to Taunton. As the train crew came off duty they were interviewed by the local press. The driver Ken Cridland stated, 'It is easier driving diesels, but you are on your own,' going on to say, 'and there is not the same comradeship as on the steam trains.' When the guard Walter Thyer was asked for his observations he 'admitted feeling a bit of nostalgia about it'. He went on to say, 'There's a different trend now, not so much romance, you don't get the same feelings.'

It is worth contrasting the feelings of the train crew who were facing an uncertain future in the railway industry, but who still enjoyed their work, albeit with some reservations, with the remarks made by the area manager, Mr James Ross, whose future was presumably secure, who informed the waiting reporters that 'riding the last train was just another job' and continued 'I've been through it all before'. If this attitude was prevalent throughout the BR management team at this time it is not surprising that the railways were in such trouble.

<u>Summary of Minutes of Inaugural</u>

<u>General Meeting held on Friday May 7th, 1971</u>

<u>at the Black Horse Hotel, Bridge Street, Taunton.</u>

<u>The Meeting</u> was convened by an informal Steering Committee with the approval of the Directors of the incipient West Somerset Railway Co. Present.Mr. J.S. Pearce (in the chair), Messrs. Brabner, Cornelius, Jones, and Lee (the Steering Committee); Mr. B.H. Jackson; Messrs Shaw and Fear (on behalf of the West Somerset Railway Co. Ltd) and approximately 30 other persons.

1. Mr. Pearce opened the meeting and introduced Mr. G. Byam Shaw.

2. Mr. Shaw outlined the functions which it was hoped the Association would fulfill, especially participation in the operation of the West Somerset Railway, the success of the scheme for the acquisition of the line being highly probable. He welcomed Mr. B.H. Jackson to Taunton and was glad that the two parallel schemes (West Somerset Railway Association and Minehead Railway Preservation Society) were being brought together. Mr. Jackson then spoke of the importance of the Association being rapidly developed into a national body, and of membership of the Association of Railway Preservation Societies.

3. Nomination forms for the election of officers having been distributed, and the procedure for election agreed, the following Officers and Committee Members were elected: Secretary, D.R. Jones; Treasurer, S.P. Bowditch; Publicity Officer, B.H. Jackson; Committee Members, H.R. Lee, Dr. A. Bakker, R.F. Norris, and K. Davidge. Mr. Pearce, who did not wish to stand on the new Committee, agreed to remain in the Chair and conduct the remainder of the Meeting.

4. The Subscriptions recommended by the Steering Committee (£2.00 adult, Junior, student and O.A.P. £1.50) were adopted, and the appointment of the Somerset and Wilts. Trustee Savings Bank as Bankers, was approved.

5. The appointment of Mr. R.W. Barnes, A.A.C.C.A., A.T.I.I., of Barnes, Turl and Co., Bridgwater, as Auditor, was approved.

6. The Constitution and Rules of the Association, as drafted by the Steering Committee, were explained from the Chair. The Committee were authorised by the Meeting to codify these into a form suitable for registration as a Company Limited by Guarantee, and to establish rules based on those of the A.R.P.S. for volunteer working parties. From the floor, Mr. Parker stressed the importance of proper recognition by the Company of the work of the Association.

7. In response to a question from Mr. Steel, Mr Byam Shaw explained more fully the organisation and structure of the West Somerset (Private) Railway Company.

8. The meeting was temporarily adjourned at 9.30 p.m. and resumed at 9.50 p.m. when Mr. Bowditch occupied the chair and answered questions from the floor. It was made clear that the elected Committee regarded themselves as responsible for promotion of membership, and progress towards incorporation, parallel with the progress of the Company, and would call a fresh General Meeting when these tasks had reached an advanced state. Immediate progress would be reported to a meeting to be held on Wednesday May 19th when it was hoped some membership literature would be made available.

9. The Chairman closed the meeting at 10.15 p.m. and 17 subscriptions were received from prospective members.

The second of the 'last' trains was organised by Minehead and District Round Table and the price of their tickets was also £1, but their tickets included a sherry reception at the Beach Hotel opposite Minehead Station at 6.45 p.m., before boarding the 7.30 p.m. train for the last round trip from Minehead to Taunton. For their pound the members of the Round Table also received a commemorative booklet and a souvenir ticket. Before the party left the hotel the chairman of the Minehead Urban District Council made a speech in which he recalled memories of the old line and added, 'I only hope that the track will not be taken up until we are satisfied that an adequate bus service has been provided.' As it was a condition imposed by the Tribunal that the line should not be closed until the bus service was satisfactory, I find the chairman's remarks rather puzzling.

After the large crowd that had gathered outside the hotel and sung 'the sad song of the last train', written by local schoolteachers David Beach and John Holroyd, accompanied by the Minehead Band, the Round Tablers carried a magnum of champagne on board the train (to be raffled for charity), whilst other members of the party tied a plaque bearing a black wreath to the last coach. Watched by a crowd of 500 people, the train left with Driver Ernie Dingle at the controls, accompanied by a burst of fireworks.

Some people felt that the Round Table chairman, Mr Peter Kirkham, incurred the wrath of many of those who had fought to keep the line open due to a number of light-hearted and flippant remarks throughout the evening. His subsequent reply that 'it was no use blaming the undertaker for the death of the patient' did little to improve matters. On the arrival of the train at Taunton the travellers were subjected to another speech, this time given by the Mayor of Taunton, Cllr St John Carew-Fisher.

The 'third' and official last round trip from Taunton, the 9.10 p.m. departure, was delayed so that the 3-car DMU set that had been used on the Round Tablers' excursion could be attached. The train finally left at 9.40 p.m.

Although the crowds on the earlier trip had been fairly subdued (it appears that they had all been busy filming and recording the last trip for posterity), the same could not be said for this journey. The departure from Taunton was tumultuous, with horns blowing and a noise that would have done justice to a battery of artillery! And so the trip continued with much singing and the bidding of farewells, the people who lived alongside the line coming out to see the end of the 'Minehead Tiddler' (report *County Gazette*).

At every station along the line people got off the train to greet or say farewell to friends and relatives on the platform, and at Watchet a potentially serious accident was only avoided when someone pulled the communication cord, after the train started to pull out of the station with the train doors still open and people trying to scramble back on board the moving train. It took 35 minutes to reset the butterfly valves on the train (to enable the driver to release the brakes) and because of this, and the delays that had occurred at other stations along the line, the train was 90 minutes late arriving at Minehead. This meant that the last train from Minehead did not leave until 11.40 p.m., with the remaining passengers now in a rather subdued mood. The atmosphere on the last up train was more like mourners at a funeral, in contrast to the high jinks on the down train. As the train passed Crowcombe Mrs Marjorie Brown closed the level crossing gates for the last time – another hardworking member of the railway staff whose job had come to an end after nine years spent at this rather lonely spot.

And so what many people thought was the last train to run on the Minehead branch arrived back at Taunton at 12.40 a.m. on Sunday 3 January 1971.

4

Trains to Run Again on the Minehead Branch?

One of the first indications that trains might continue to operate along the branch line from Taunton to Minehead, after the supposed last train on 2 January 1971, was a report in the *Evening Post* in December 1970 which revealed that Mr Tim Burton of the Exmoor Society had received a letter stating that Somerset County Council was considering a feasibility study on the use of the line as a private railway. Mr Burton added, 'We would be wholeheartedly behind such a scheme.'

Mr Eric Grimes, Somerset County Council press officer, confirmed that the planning department was making enquiries about the possibility of the line being taken over to be run privately. He also went on to say, 'Several lines formerly operated by BR were now being operated by private societies. There was the Dart Valley Line in the west, and the Bluebell Line in Sussex and a number of other lines.'

One of the passengers travelling on the 'last train', Mr Douglas Fear, was also heard to remark that he was 'interested in exploring the possibility of forming a company to keep at least part of the line open'. Later he is reported to have said that, 'If only a section of the line could be retained, say from Bishops Lydeard to Williton, and run privately by steam, I am sure it would prove to be a great attraction to many people.'

Little time was wasted before some positive action was taken: a public meeting was held in Taunton and it was decided that a working party should be set up to study the feasibility of operating the line as a private railway.

In April the report of the working party was published, which I reproduce in full below.

Introduction

The line was completed by the West Somerset Railway in 1862, terminating at Watchet and was not extended to Minehead until 1874. On opening it was leased to the Bristol & Exeter Railway and is the last of four branch lines to be closed which diverged from Taunton.

The branch is 24.75 miles long and has eight intermediate stations. For some 2.5 miles from Taunton it runs adjacent to the West of England main line to Norton Fitzwarren where it takes a north westerly turn and passes between the Quantock and Brendon hills to meet the Bristol Channel at Watchet.

From this brief description, it will be seen that the line enjoys many advantages. One terminal is at Taunton, the County town, with its main line station and extensive business and shopping facilities. The other is Minehead on the edge of Exmoor, a progressive and popular holiday district. Between these two points lies an expanse of some of the best country in Somerset.

The last service trains ran over the branch on Saturday January 2nd 1971. The number of passengers carried on this day was considerable. During the preceding week the number had risen progressively to the climax on Saturday. In addition to the normal service there were a number of special trains crowded with enthusiasts.

The process of closure followed what has become known as 'standard pattern', the exercise covering a period of two years. The customary appeals, petitions and representations were made and in due course the usual sympathetic replies were received; nevertheless the line was closed.

Public feeling was responsible for a well attended meeting organised by Somerset County Council which took place in the Shire Hall, Taunton, on Friday 5th February 1971, under the chairmanship of Mr J.R. Vincent, Chairman of the county council's Planning Committee, to consider problems arising out of the closure of the line, and to provide a forum for suggestions concerning its possible future.

The meeting was told that the county council understood that BR were willing to consider feasible suggestions that might be forthcoming, for the operation of the line under private enterprise. Furthermore, BR had indicated that access to Taunton Station by an independent operating company, involving the use of the North West Bay on platform 3 was not impossible.

The county council would not consider operating the line themselves, but they were willing to co-operate, wherever appropriate, to facilitate consideration of proposals that might be put forward for the reopening of the line on a commercial basis. The county council required some parts of the line for highway improvements but if a feasible scheme for the reopening of the line were put forward they would be willing to consider alternative routes which would not interfere with the working of the railway.

The meeting decided that every effort should be made to re-instate the rail service along the whole length of the line and that a working party should be formed to undertake a feasibility study, with a view to the line being reopened as a private venture.

The information contained herein, is the result of the survey carried out. The basic responsibility of the working party was to decide whether or not the line was viable. This they have done and this report suggests that a company be formed with a Memorandum adequate to operate the Railway in accordance with the scheme suggested, on the assumption that sufficient financial backing can be obtained.

In a letter to the Transport Users Consultative Committee conveying his decision to close the branch line, the Minister admitted that the volume of traffic conveyed to Minehead during the holiday season could not be handled by road transport and because of this some hardship might be anticipated.

There is also a progressive increase shown in the volume of commuter traffic to Taunton and there is every reason to believe that this increase would continue in the future if the line was reopened. People who travelled to Taunton each day by train agree that the alternative bus service provided is not so satisfactory, mainly because the scheduled time of travelling is greater than by train. Furthermore it is aggravated by traffic congestion entering and leaving the town which can, and on most occasions does, amount to twenty minutes delay in each direction. This is a condition that is likely to worsen rather than improve.

The number of complaints that have come to hand during our enquiries, both of inconvenience and hardship due to the absence of the railway service are too numerous to mention in this report, but there is strong case in support of the continuation of the line as a public service.

Method of Operation

The obvious question is, if it is possible to operate the branch economically, why could not BR do it? The brief answer is twofold.

Firstly, BR, we believe, treat branch lines in all respects as part of the national network, bearing their share of all overhead expenses. Furthermore a private business would be able to operate more economically and provide a service to suit the needs of the locality that it serves.

The volume of passenger traffic carried on the line has been quite considerable when compared with some other routes. Records show that an average of 4,850 people used the trains each week, throughout the year. As would be expected on a holiday route, the number fluctuated considerably according to the season. In summer as many as 5000 people a day used the Railway, and there were also considerable numbers who transferred from long distance trains at Taunton at weekends. Our examination of income and expenditure reveals that a commercial service of a few trains a day, at a time to suit local needs would, together with economies in capital and running costs, very substantially reduce the loss reported by BR prior to closure. The trains provided for this service, would have to be diesel multiple units as used by BR prior to closure of the line. The trains would be operated by full time professional staff of ex-railwaymen.

Secondly, an operating company could introduce the use of steam locomotives during the summer period for occasional use on scheduled trains and for some excursion traffic. There could also be a steam-hauled passenger train between Minehead and Watchet two or three times a day as a special holiday attraction.

Facilities could be made available on lease, to railway preservation societies for their activities, including the opening of a steam base at one of the stations, where sufficient space was available. Accommodation of this sort is, of course, scarce and should be a valuable possession. Furthermore, there are, on the branch, two sections of track amounting to a total length of five miles which have been redundant for some time due to the withdrawal of double line working. This would enable any Society train movements to take place without interruption to service trains – a great asset not only to the railway, but to the district as a whole, because of the number of visitors that would be attracted to an area which is in close proximity to the Quantock Hills Area of Outstanding Natural Beauty, and the Exmoor National Park.

There are at present about twelve privately owned railway companies in the British Isles, all of which are enjoying a fair measure of success, The Dart Valley Railway Co. in South Devon has been particularly successful, returns show that a quarter of a million passengers are carried every season.

Practically all these are in rural districts where a journey by road has to be made to reach them, but this would not be the case in this instance and we think would be a considerable advantage especially at Minehead, where the railway station is on the sea front.

Practical Considerations

During the process of our investigations, we had discussions with the Divisional Manager of BR, and with the Railway Inspectorate Section of the Department of the Environment. In both instances the interviews were most cordial and helpful. At this stage, there would appear to be no insurmountable obstacles in obtaining a Light Railway Order operating the proposals outlined earlier.

If the project is to proceed further, access from Norton Fitzwarren to Taunton Station is vital. We discussed this matter in detail with the Divisional Manager and while feeling that the Railway board would agree to a private operator using a bay of Taunton Station, he would have to ascertain the Railway boards attitude towards the running of trains by an independent operator on the section of track between Norton Fitzwarren and Taunton – because this section was immediately adjacent to BRs main line. It is very likely that special operating conditions would be involved, especially in respect of the level crossing at Silk Mills under the control of BR. We are expecting the board's decision in the very near future.

A provisional survey of the track, bridges and general engineering works has been carried out, and on the whole the condition would appear to be sound. It must of course be borne in mind that the line was in use until only three months ago, at which time it would have been maintained above a minimum standard.

On the advice of the Watchet Urban District Council, we inspected a site near Watchet, where the cliff had subsided near the railway boundary. Even without the benefit of professional advice, it would appear that a certain amount of work would be required at this point, possibly within the next two years. Nevertheless, we felt that this would not be a major item of expense.

Our enquiries revealed that there will be no difficulty in obtaining a diesel multiple unit and a diesel locomotive. It would be possible to obtain on lease two steam locomotives in working order, to enable a start to be made should circumstances permit.

It is likely that BR will lift the permanent way within the next two months or so unless an undertaking is entered into. It is necessary therefore to emphasise the extreme urgency of the situation.

Capital Structure

Whilst we have felt that in detail of sources of capital would take us beyond our brief, we have made some preliminary enquiries because they have some bearing on the financial estimates which follow (set out in the appendix hereto).

Before a company is formed, its promoters need an assurance that part at least of the ultimate capital needed would be forthcoming quickly. We think that it would be difficult at this time to attract equity capital on a sufficient scale to finance the whole project. A general invitation for the public to subscribe would involve the creation of a public rather than a private company at a far greater cost in time and in money. As regards to Bank borrowing, it is the opinion in merchant banking circles that money for a project of this type would have to be guaranteed by a substantial independent body. These points have to be considered against the certainty that BR would want a considerable deposit before they would enter into negotiations for sale. On the other hand, a company in existence and assured of possession could use the line itself as security for a loan issue. If the project is proceeded with, we therefore suggest the following steps:

1   Formation of a company with a relatively small authorised capital (say £5,000) which would be sought from local interests willing to subscribe this amount.
2   The company to obtain overdraft facilities from a local bank, up to a further £100,000, to open negotiations.
3   The company to issue loan stock, secured on the assets, for the balance of the capital required, to which subscription would be invited in small units from interested bodies and individuals.

Summary and Conclusions

1   Reopening of the line would be dependent on BR's willingness to sell or lease it. It is likely that they would be willing to sell, but might well refuse to lease.
2   The scheme of operation depends on BR allowing an operating company's trains to run into Taunton Station. There are technical difficulties about this, which BR have promised to consider, but we see no reason why a suitable working arrangement could not be made.
3   If the line is reopened it should be run by a commercial company whose principle objective would be the operation of a limited regular scheduled service all the year round using diesel locomotion.
4   It is unlikely that such a scheduled service in isolation, would constitute a paying proposition. However, a company with the facilities of the line at its disposal could, for a marginal additional capital and operating cost, run a summer excursion service using steam locomotives.
5   The proved attraction of steam trains and the success enjoyed by other private railways running steam trains. indicate that such a service could be very remunerative. Activities

allied to steam excursions, such as sale of publications, special outings, catering etc., could bring in useful additional revenue.

6   An arrangement between a commercial operating company and a volunteer Association formed in parallel with the company could offer advantages to both, by giving railway enthusiasts facilities to pursue their hobby and the company a pool of labour.

7   Run on a mixed/commercial attraction basis the line would be likely to show a profit on its earnings without outside support.

8   If the line is to reopen, and as soon as the question of access to Taunton is settled, a company should be formed to operate it.

9   The requirement for capital would be quite large and a secured loan offer would offer the best method of raising it. Initially, however, it would be necessary for a substantial sum to be available, probably by guaranteed Bank overdraft, before negotiations for purchase to go forward.

Appendix

Financial Estimates

BR claimed that the annual deficit for operating the branch was £400,000. The estimates that follow certainly point to a loss on a commercial line run in isolation but not of this magnitude. We do not know the breakdown of the BR figure (although the manner in which is calculated is described) and hence we cannot make a reconciliation with our projections. It may be relevant that:

1   BR's service, as noted above, was operated at quite a high frequency (15 trains per day).

2   Staff, largely because of the higher service frequency, was larger than a private operating company would need.

3   The method of allocation of overhead charges is not known, but presumably the branch would have borne its share of general expenses – management, advertising etc., – which would have been heavy.

4   It is possible that certain overhead items, such as station maintenance, were allocated on a 'Blanket' rather than on an actual basis.

5   The line was signalled to a higher standard than would be necessary under the scheme of operation described in the report. The figures for costs and revenue in the tabulation which follows are necessarily approximate. They have been checked by a member of the working party who has practical experience of rail operation and also confirmed, where appropriate with a member of the Dart Valley's Management team. But it remains the case that they are for the most part broad estimates which we have biased deliberately towards an unfavourable rather than a favourable result.

The expected purchase price is particularly critical; the nearest indication BR were prepared to give at this stage was that it was unlikely to be less than £100,000 or more than £200,000 (the lower figure being apparently based on minimum estimated break-up value). We have therefore used the higher figure for calculation.

The figure for estimated gross commercial passenger receipts depends on:

1   Fare structure
2   Number of journeys annually
3   Average length of journey

We have assumed a fare structure based on an end to end ordinary return fare at BR's latest published figure at 85p plus 10%, day return at two thirds ordinary return (BR 55p) 25% of journeys at half fares and 50% day returns 50% period.

The number of journeys is based on BR's Daily Station User analysis of 1968, reduced by 30% to allow decline in traffic and lower service frequency.

The average journey length used (6 stations) is the winter/summer average minimum journey which is consistent with the 1968 analysis.

The derived forecast of receipts checks reasonably with BR's gross passenger receipts for 1969, allowing for the fact that the last figure given to us did not include through passengers.

Shorter notes on other figures used are included in the tabulations in the following pages.

Capital Requirement

Capital Works at Taunton	£2,000	fencing and crossing control
Diesel Multiple Unit	£1,500	BR Surplus
5 coaches @ £300	£1,500	BR Surplus
Diesel locomotive	£5,000	BR Surplus
Movement of coaches	£400	
Tools & jacks	£700	
Stock of spares	£1,000	
Fuel point and tank	£400	
Inspection pit	£300	
Maintenance shed	£800	
Re-instatement of telegraph and signal system	£5,000	
Legal costs	£3,000	
Purchase of line & buildings	£200,000	
Total	**£221,600**	

Commercial Service – Operating Cost

Staff 12 @ £27 overall average P.W.	£1,700	
4 train, 3 track maintenance, 1 Fitter, 4 control crossings, Signals		
Payment for volunteers supplementing above	£500	
Rolling stock depreciation	£800	Written off in 10 years

Repair and paint	£1,200	8 vehicles @ £150 p.a.
Mechanical Maintenance	£1,000	D.M.U. and diesel loco
Fuel, 4 double trips daily	£1,300	@ 2mpg between DMU and Diesel
Line and fence maintenance materials	£3,500	@ £150/mile
Reserve for bridge maintenance	£5,000	
Telephone rental	£250	between main stations
Insurances, public liability, employers fire, consequential loss	£1,000	
Office and stationery	£300	
Ticket and printing	£300	
Rates	£500	
Building and maintenance materials	£400	
Buildings depreciation @ 5%	£1,750	
Heating and lighting	£600	
Publicity	£500	
Audit and accounts	£250	
	————	
	£36,150	
Loan capital service charge	£17,600	£220,000 @ 8%
Total	**£53,750**	
Estimated gross annual passenger receipts	£45,000	
Estimated net annual deficit commercial service only £8,750		

Steam Excursion Service – Cost

(a) Additional Capital Cost

Assuming that, initially at least, locomotives for the service would be leased, not purchased, the additional capital commitment would consist of extra coaches 6 @ £300, or £1,800 (no extra charge for movement if they travel with coaches allocated to commercial service) and facilities for coaling, watering, and running maintenance £1,500.

(b) Additional Operating Cost

Lease of two locomotives, 18 weeks per annum	£2,500	
Locomotive movement to branch	£500	
Coaches depreciation	£180	Written off in 10 years
Repair and paint	£900	(6 vehicles @ £150 p.a.)
Fuel and lubricants, 16 excursions per week, 18 weeks	£230	(at 5p per mile)
Water	£100	
Staff train crew 2 @ £27 per week 18 weeks	£970	

Payment for volunteers and duties other than footplate   £500
Publicity   £2,000

                                                         _____

Total   **£7,800**

(c) Additional Receipts

Assuming 16 excursions per week, 18 weeks per year, 4 coaches at 75% capacity, adult fare 50p, average fare 42.5p, estimated profits are £29,500.

(d) Overall Return, Commercial and Steam Services

Net steam excursion surplus
Receipts   £29,500
                                      Less costs £7,880
say   £21,500
Less commercial service deficit   £8,750

                                      _____

Overall surplus   **£12,750**

From which management salaries and return on equity to be found.

This report was compiled by Douglas Fear (Chairman), and George W. Byam Shaw MA ACWA and grateful thanks are conveyed to the other members of the working party who assisted:

> Mr R. W. Barnes, AACA ATII
> Mr H. R. Lee, Mechanical Advisor
> Mr S. G. Taylor, Dip. Art (Poly) ARIBA
> Chairman, Taunton Group
> Great Western Society Ltd

Thanks are also due to the Somerset County Council and their Clerk and other officers involved, and also to BRways (Western Region) and their Divisional Manager, for their co-operation and assistance.

In May after all the parties involved, had accepted the working party's report, the West Somerset Railway Co. Ltd was formed.

At the same time the volunteer group that was to assist the company was in the process of being organised and they held their inaugural meeting, which some 200 people attended, at the Black Horse Hotel in Taunton. The society was put on a workman-like basis with the appointment of officers and the fixing of subscriptions for membership of the Society (£2 for adults; £1.50 for OAPs and children). Before the meeting closed at 10.15 p.m., a number of subscriptions had been received and it was arranged that the next meeting of the society would be held on 19 May.

However business-like the two groups may have been individually, neither of them appeared to be very good at communicating their aims – not least to each other – and on 2 April 1971 an article appeared in one of the local newspapers under the heading: 'Lines Crossed in Rescue Schemes for Axed Railway'.

The article stated that conflicting announcements had been made by the Minehead Railway Preservation Group, which appeared to be operating independently of both the West Somerset Railway and the Taunton-based Railway Association, to newspapers in the same week. Mr Chris Dyer was quoted as saying, 'It was all a misunderstanding; I have made it clear that we would not want to cross swords with anyone. We want to co-operate in any way that we can.' The Minehead Railway preservation group was subsequently disbanded.

At the end of March Mr Fear had addressed a private meeting in Williton (before the report of the working party was published), at which representatives of Minehead, Williton and Watchet district councils were present, and they had discussed the possibilities of reopening the branch line on a commercial basis. He informed the meeting that, although the financial study was not yet complete, preliminary estimates indicated that to operate the line solely to provide a commercial service would not be a paying proposition; nevertheless there was a way it could be done. After questioning he went on to say, 'If the facilities of the line could be used for steam excursions or similar holiday attractions in the summer months, the project might be viable.'

After pointing out the success that the Dart Valley Line was enjoying at that time he informed the meeting that he thought £50,000 would be required to start the trains running again. He added that the working party believed that the success of the project, assuming that agreement could be reached with BR, depended very much on public support. The working party were also investigating ways in which the money could be raised and if all went well he felt that the line could be open in the summer of next year (1973). Furthermore the possibility of the sale or lease of the 23 miles of line with buildings and the use of facilities at Taunton had already been raised and he stated that BR had been most helpful and had promised to give their views as soon as possible.

Further encouraging news came from Mr Chris Dyer at Minehead who stated that since the news broke about the formation of the West Somerset Railway his telephone had never stopped ringing and he had received letters from well-wishers all over the country, together with offers of financial help, but he pointed out that hundreds of thousands of pounds would be required to reopen the line. As Mr Fear had commented during the same week that only £50,000 was required it appeared that the interested parties were still not singing from the same hymn sheet.

The optimism felt by many local people regarding reopening of the line was maintained by numerous reports, one of which appeared in the *Evening Post* in October 1972 which confidently claimed that the line would be open in five months. It went on to say that negotiations with BR were in their final stages and that the contracts would be signed very shortly.

Some fifteen months later, in the 14 December 1973 edition of the same newspaper, there were claims that trains were not likely to be operating over the line until late summer of 1974. This information was based on a statement from Mr Fear when he addressed a meeting of railway enthusiasts in Minehead. Mr Fear had in the meantime entered into a series of extremely complex negotiations with BR, to determine the terms on which BR would dispose of the land in their possession together with the track representing the line between Norton Fitzwarren and Minehead, in order to see if there was any way in which the line could be opened as a private railway.

When the discussions were at an advanced stage, Somerset County Council suddenly became interested and decided to purchase the trackbed from the BR board for the sum of £245,000, with a view to leasing the line to the West Somerset Railway for operation. Also included in the deal was the offer of a loan to the fledgling company of £50,000 to help them establish a commuter line between Minehead and Taunton. At first this decision appeared to ease the fundraising needs of the new company and ensure that rail services would reopen in the near future. If anything this gesture was to put back the opening of the line for many months. There was an immediate storm of protest by irate ratepayers who questioned whether the county council had the authority to use ratepayers' money in this way!

Although the Council spokesmen informed the protesters that they were getting a 'good deal' for their money, because of the valuable land they had acquired not only on the trackbed but also the land and buildings around Minehead and the other stations along the line; however, the debate continued with increasing bitterness.

Some local people thought at the time that the county council had taken this action to prevent the directors of the new railway 'from asset stripping' the company's assets, although there is no evidence to suggest that they ever had any intention of doing so. Once the purchase had been completed it was then necessary for the legal formalities to be completed for the transfer by BR to the county council and the issuance of a Light Railway Order. Railway law is an extremely complex matter and anyone who has read the enormous detail of the final Order, which specifies all the rights to every level crossing, footpath rights of way and so on, will appreciate how complicated these negotiations must have been, and the directors of the West Somerset Railway probably breathed a huge sigh of relief that the county council had stepped in and taken over the responsibility for this work.

As soon as the negotiations were complete and formal notice given that the county council was applying for the transfer of the Light Railway Order there were a large number of formal objections and notice was given that a public inquiry would be held to listen to these views. The date set for the public inquiry was 21 January 1973.

Although the bus company had known of the date of the inquiry since the previous February, an objection to the transfer of the Light Railway Order was only lodged days before the proceedings were due to start. The barrister representing the railway, Mr Charles Fay, asked for an adjournment of the hearing because they were uncertain of the reasons for the bus company's objections. The county council, which was in support of the Railway's application, at first agreed that the start of the inquiry should be delayed but after a long discussion it was agreed to hear evidence unrelated to financial matters before adjourning.

In their submission a spokesman for the bus company stated that they had just heard the railway was to receive a subsidy for operating a commuter service between Minehead and Taunton. He went on to say that there was no objection to the line opening as a steam railway tourist attraction but regular services would adversely affect the bus route between Minehead and Taunton. Later he added, 'Our service operates without a subsidy and includes additional journeys put in by order of the Ministry of Transport when BR withdrew their service.' Unfortunately no one at the time thought to ask this official why nobody had objected to BR operating a subsidised commuter service.

There was considerable speculation about the late moves of the bus company and the activities of the three private objectors – the only objectors at that point. Subsequently one of these, Birmingham businessman Mr Guy Somerset, who owned a weekend cottage at Bilbrook, admitted that he had tipped off the bus company. At first Mr Somerset claimed that the bus service was adequate (a view not shared by many other people), but when questioned he admitted that he drove down to his cottage at the weekend by car and that he also used his car for his journeys around the area.

Another objector, Captain Tom Miller, a retired Indian Army Officer of Bishops Lydeard, denied that he had any contact with Western National. Just how much this gentleman's word could be trusted was thrown into some doubt when Mr Ian Campbell, the general manager for Western National, later admitted that Captain Miller had written to the company about the anti-railway group.

Captain Miller had said earlier that he objected to a private company, subsidised by him, running the line at a loss, 'especially when it is operated by a crowd of amateur enthusiasts who may not know what they are doing'. When questioned, Captain Miller admitted that he had bought a house adjoining the line after it had been closed on the understanding that there was no possibility that the railway would be reopened. When he heard of the moves to reopen the line he formed DRAG, the Disused Railways Action Group, and claimed to have 200 members in his movement, of whom just 20 per cent lived in the immediate area. After further questioning he went on to say that he would not have the same objections if the line were operated by BR, the inference being that he did not mind professionals running the line, who appeared not to know what they were doing.

Other submissions were received from the National Union of Railwaymen, whose members operated the buses – the Western National Bus Co. was created from the bus services formerly operated by the Great Western Railway. They were concerned that the revived service would lead to the closure of the bus station at Minehead and the redundancy of twenty of their members. Had these same members of the National Union of Railwaymen shown the same concern for their fellow union members working on the branch line, perhaps the line would have remained open.

Mr Whitcutt for the county council submitted that a pleasure line from Minehead to Williton would be successful, but that a commuter service from Minehead would operate at a loss; however, this could be offset by a county council loan of £60,000 and a £10,000 operating subsidy for two years. He went on to say that the county council would be acquiring the line from BR for £245,000, but they intended to retain the land around Minehead Station. Mr Fear for the railway announced that the railway now had a paid-up share capital of £10,000 and an authorised share capital of £25,000. After hearing from Major Anthony Griffiths, a former Army railway expert, he considered that the whole line was in a sound condition and that no major repairs to bridges were likely to be incurred over the next five years, and the permanent way and buildings were also sound.

Other 'expert' witnesses called included Mr M. Draper, who was at that time the general manager of the Severn Valley Railway. He claimed that it was not a practical idea to attempt to run a 20-mile-long preserved railway. What was not established was where the point came between the practical 16-mile Severn Valley and the impracticable 20-mile West Somerset Railway. Another expert witness was Mr David Shepherd who agreed with Mr Draper, although what was not known – or admitted – at the time was that this gentleman was in the throes of purchasing a section of line at Cranmore, not many miles away. This was later opened as the East Somerset Railway; was he worried about the possible competition?

Supporting evidence was given by a number of local residents and Mr Fay handed to the inspector a large number of letters. After receiving 177 letters from individuals, eighty from councils, and 120 from other organisations, and listening to the bus company's case, presented by Mr D.R. Wilding, in which he stated that if the proposed rail service resulted in the bus company operating uneconomic services, they would either have to withdraw their services or apply to the county council for a subsidy, the inspector, Mr J.L. Palmer adjourned the inquiry until 2 April.

5

In the Meantime

During the period that the inquiry was adjourned the volunteers continued to tackle the many tasks that needed to be undertaken before trains could start to run over the branch line again. One group of young people undertook a sponsored track walk in strong winds and heavy rain and raised £100. In anticipation of the successful outcome of the inquiry others started to clear the heavy vegetation that had started to grow on the trackside and on the trackbed in places. No work other than general tidying up could be undertaken until the Light Railway Order had been transferred.

Whilst these activities were going on, members of the two groups, together with the management team, started work on two projects that would become extremely urgent if and when the inquiry agreed to the transfer of the Light Railway Order, and by entering into preliminary discussions at this time it was hoped that the opening date could possibly be brought forward.

The first objective of the management during this period was to continue with their efforts to raise the capital necessary to ensure – hopefully – that the new line would be successful, and the second task was to endeavour to determine what terms BR would insist upon, together with the probable cost, if the branch line was to be successful in its attempts to reach Taunton.

At the same time members of the two groups were visiting Barry scrapyard to determine whether locomotives that would prove useful were still available in Dai Woodham's yard and what their cost might be. Having identified three potentially suitable locomotives, they asked for 'reserved' notices to be put on them and returned home to set about the task of raising the sum of money required for the deposit on the three engines. They had already realised that it would be a long and costly project to restore these engines to full working order, and that their most immediate need was for locomotives and rolling stock that could be made operational, with the limited funds that were available, before services restarted on the line. Just how successful they were in meeting these objectives will be described in the later chapters. Had the application been refused then all of these efforts would have been wasted.

6

The Battle Continues

When the public inquiry reopened on 2 April 1974 Mr John Whitcutt representing the county council stated that when the Light Railway Order was approved, the county council would seek authority to lend the West Somerset Railway £80,000 as working capital at 10 per cent interest. He went on to say that the financial terms approved by the outgoing council had been endorsed by the new council, with the proviso that there would be no further financial support for the company.

Mr Robert Busby, the company's consultant engineer, later informed the inquiry that, with the help of a team of sixty volunteers working every weekend, the section of the line between Minehead and Williton could be opened within six months and the Williton to Norton Fitzwarren section in a further six months. He went on to confirm that there would be a paid staff of nineteen people with an additional locomotive driver in the summer months. He stated that all members of the staff would be BR-trained. When questioned, he added that most of the work on the line would be repairs rather than reinstatement and most of this work could be done by volunteers under professional supervision. Asked about the fears of noise and smoke voiced by Mr Somerset, Mr Busby observed that two small shunting engines would be very different from the large steam engines one remembered from years gone by.

Outlining his objections, Mr Somerset was critical of the 'hidden subsidies' and suggested that the county council would be borrowing dear and lending cheap. He went on to claim that BR was selling at less than the scrap value of the metal and he doubted whether this was good policy for the taxpayers in general. Finally he said that in his opinion the money spent on these subsidies could be better applied to improve the bus services to remote villages rather than using the money to duplicate an existing route.

These views were supported by Captain Millar, but their case against the reopening of the branch line was weakened when Captain Millar admitted, under questioning, that instead of the 200 supporters of his DRAG movement, as previously claimed, he had in fact only obtained ten signatures to support his objections and that the majority of those signatures were from people who lived outside the area.

In reply to the fears expressed by Mr Somerset, Mr Whitcutt explained that if the Light Railway Order were granted, the county council proposed to lease the line to the West

Somerset Railway Co. at a peppercorn rent for the first year and then at a fixed annual rental of £14,000 per year thereafter. He went on to say that the payment of an annual subsidy would mean that the company would pay only £4,000 per year, including £1,400 to cover coast erosion contingencies which would be the responsibility of the county council.

After listening to both Mr Whitcutt and Mr Busby, it appeared that Mr Somerset's attitude towards the line was changing. He confessed that if he had been conversant with all the arguments to be put forward at the resumed meeting, he might not have bothered to attend. Afterwards he added, 'I am now changing my mind about this project because obviously a pair of redundant shunting engines from the Austin Motor Co. are not going to make the same noise or smoke as the Royal Scot. If I could be reassured about these aspects I think I would probably withdraw my objection. After all with 175,000 passengers [the wildly optimistic forecast of the numbers of passengers who would be using the line] on the one hand and a modest amount of noise, smoke and pollution on the other, one can obviously see where the balance lies.'

In an attempt to allay Mr Somerset's fears Mr Busby explained that main line trains only produced a lot of smoke and noise because they were pulling heavy loads. But on this line, he added, trains would have light loads, would not take long to get going and would coast along quite happily with the minimum of noise. The smoke and noise intrusion in this case would be quite unlike the railways we used to know.

A great boost to the morale of the volunteers came when Mr Guy Wilding, the spokesman for the Western National Bus Co., confirmed to the inquiry that although the company was still concerned that the rail company would be receiving a subsidy, and the bus company would not, they would be withdrawing their objections to the proposals, following discussion with the directors of the West Somerset Railway. Mr Fear, for the West Somerset Railway, added that the bus company were withdrawing their objection because it had been agreed that both parties would be working together with the greatest co-operation, following agreement that the fares on the railway would be set 10 per cent higher than the corresponding bus fares (88p Taunton–Minehead).

Finally, the news that Mr Somerset had withdrawn his objection, together with pledges of support from a number of local councils and organisations, and with a petition, organised by Mr Merrick, containing 1,540 signatures from local residents supporting the opening of the branch, meant that the volunteers were reasonably optimistic that they had won their case.

After listening to the final summaries from the interested parties, the chairman announced that he was closing the inquiry and would be submitting his findings to the Secretary of State.

7

More Problems

When the public inquiry restarted the directors of the West Somerset Railway thought that they had agreed terms two years earlier with BR for access to Taunton Station and for the use of a platform there. It was on the basis of these discussions that many of the figures used at the inquiry were based. This new-found optimism soon turned to gloom, however.

Mr Fear informed the *West Somerset Free Press* that originally BR had agreed the charges for the use of a 2-mile section of track and a platform would be £6,000 per annum. Following the adjournment, the directors of the WSR were now being informed that the cost of these services had now risen to £11,350 per annum. Furthermore, a one-off charge of £1,500 was required for the installation of additional signals at Norton Fitzwarren.

Mr Fear went on to contrast the attitude of the Western Region of BR with their colleagues in Yorkshire who were charging the Keighley & Worth Valley Railway (another private preserved railway) the sum of £350 per year to rent a quarter of a mile of track, a bay platform, toilet facilities and the use of a footbridge. Based on these charges the costs to the West Somerset Railway should be £3,000 per year.

It appeared that the Keighley & Worth Valley had been extremely lucky in their dealings with BR; the independent professional economists contacted by the WSR directors stated that in their opinion a charge of between £5,000 and £6,000 was a fair price to charge for the use of a 2-mile section of track. Mr Fear concluded by stating that obviously the railway could not afford these charges because they would take up the entire subsidy that had been negotiated with Somerset County Council for the operation of commuter services.

When the Western Region of BR refused to consider any reduction to their proposed charges the directors wrote to both Mr Tom King, the MP for the Bridgwater constituency that included Minehead, and also to Mr Richard Marsh, the chairman of BR. In their reply to Mr King BR claimed that the increased charges reflected the additional maintenance costs for the increased track and additional facilities that the West Somerset Railway had requested at Taunton Station.

On hearing these remarks, Mr Fear could not agree. He said, 'We have asked for no additional facilities at Taunton Station and our plans for six trains a day into Taunton have not been altered. We have said now that some steam trains will run into Taunton, but this should make no difference to the signalling equipment required.' Much of this equipment was already in place, he claimed. After further correspondence it was obvious that BR was unlikely to radically alter its position and a meeting was requested between the directors of the WSR, Mr King and members of the BR board.

At the meeting it was pointed out to the BR board that the facilities in question were not in current use and it seemed absurd to charge an inflated price to a prospective customer for assets that otherwise had no revenue earning capacity, but which, if used as desired, would provide a remunerative feeder service to their own services. It was also pointed out that their stance appeared to be at variance with the Government's policy at the time, which deplored a nationalised industry's attempts to inflate its charges in a way that penalised the public, as would be the case with users of the WSR service.

In a rather heated discussion it was pointed out that it was not good commercial practice to expect a customer to pay an owner to put equipment in good working order that he wished to hire and, having done so, for the owner to then double the charge for the use of the equipment. The directors went on to state that they could not imagine that a commercial firm, whose business it was to hire out its assets for use, could run this way for one moment; and they suggested that the public had a right to expect no worse treatment from BR than any commercial company.

After considering the strong representations that had been made BR announced that they were revising their charges. The new charges would only be £10,370 per year, a figure that still swallowed up the subsidy offered by the county council to operate a commuter service, and the council had already stated that no further funds would forthcoming. As a spokesman for the WSR pointed out at the time, BR had not reduced their charges at all, they had simply reduced the expensive modifications that they had proposed to carry out at Taunton Station and these savings accounted for the whole of the reduction.

There is a well-known saying that trouble always comes in threes and that was certainly the case for the WSR at this time. The first indication the public received that locomotives and rolling stock for use on the WSR had been successfully obtained came when BR announced that the charges for storing these items – in BR sidings around Taunton – in readiness for the opening of the line would be increased from £2 per unit per week to £1 per unit per day. If this news was bad, worse was to come with an announcement by the National Union of Railwaymen that West Somerset Railway trains would never reach Taunton. As outlined earlier the NUR had set out its case before the inquiry, but it appeared that the union had little conviction in their arguments carrying any weight.

Without waiting for the outcome of the inquiry, the West Somerset NUR secretary, Mr Clive Barclay, repeated his assertion that 'If regular commuter services are run on the railways, they will shut down the bus station at Minehead. That would mean a loss of fifty jobs, with our members standing little chance of finding other work.' He added, 'The decision to 'black' trains beyond Bishops Lydeard is not a local one. It was taken by the NUR national executive in London and is not reversible.' Why they had not shown these concerns when BR was running a commuter service, together with their lack of action to safeguard the jobs of their members who were made redundant after the BR trains ceased to run on the branch line, again went unchallenged.

It seemed that BR, unable to operate the branch line as a viable enterprise itself, was determined to ensure that no one else would be given the opportunity to do so. When the costs of running services into Taunton were raised by another £50,000 – because of BR's insistence on a separate entrance to the WSR platform at the station costing £25,000 and track alterations at Silk Mills level crossing costing a further £25,000 – the directors of the WSR realised that whatever the officials of BR were saying in public about their support for the West Somerset Railway, behind the scenes they were doing everything possible to prevent the WSR trains from reaching Taunton.

The announcement by BR slightly after the period covered in this chapter (March 1979) that the set of points controlling access to the branch line from the main line were 'time expired' and would only be replaced if the WSR were to pay out a further £18,000 to replace them dictated that any further attempts to extend the line to run into Taunton were abandoned. The mounting costs incurred due to the imminent opening of the line to Bishops Lydeard meant there was no way that the struggling company would be able to meet this new demand.

The board now realised that the only way that they were going to link up with Taunton Station was by means of a bus link. The drivers working for the Western National Bus company had already informed their management that they were not prepared to operate the bus link service between Bishops Lydeard and Taunton Station. Such was the arrogance of the unions at this time that it was quite common for the management to be informed by the union members what work they would, or would not, be prepared to do.

The general public, largely unaware of the problems that were being encountered behind the scenes, had their expectations of an early reopening of the line raised by a constant stream of optimistic headlines in the local press. The headline in the *West Somerset Free Press* on 1 April 1974 (please note the date) read 'It's Almost Full Steam Ahead for the Railway' and claimed that the branch line would be reopened during the summer of that year. Later, the same newspaper informed its readers, 'October Opening Discussed for Railway', whilst in 1975 the *West Somerset Free Press* (again) and the *Somerset County Gazette* were forecasting that the line would open in March 1976.

It would appear that the frequent enquiries from the members of the public were sorely trying the patience of the many volunteers on the line, because on 7 December 1973 the following letter appeared in the *West Somerset Free Press*:

Sir – Mr V. Merrick is correct I feel, when he says that the majority of people in West Somerset are behind the re-opening of the Taunton–Minehead line except for the few sceptics who have put up objections. This line could now be well on the way to an early re-opening. As it is, these short sighted objections have bogged down this scheme, in the hope that a public inquiry will find against the railway.

If petrol rationing is introduced as now seems likely, West Somerset could be badly hit, especially the tourist trade, so I wonder if those people who objected to the SCC using public money on the line will eventually realise what a wise move it will be? For the price of a not really needed road improvement scheme at Dunster, the people of West Somerset will get a railway and the Tourist trade a much needed boost. So let us hope that the Environment Inspector dismisses these objectors so that the line can reopen soon. Signed S. Martin

The same Steve Martin is now the operations superintendent on the WSR.

WEST SOMERSET RAILWAY ASSOCIATION

TAUNTON / MINEHEAD RAILWAY

MEETING
TUESDAY 26th FEBRUARY 1974
AT THE
COUNTY HOTEL
SOMERSET SUITE
TAUNTON
7.45 p.m.

TO OUTLINE THE AIMS AND FUNCTIONS OF THE WEST SOMERSET RAILWAY ASSOCIATION, THE OFFICIAL SUPPORT BODY TO THE WEST SOMERSET RAILWAY COMPANY.

GUEST SPEAKER MR. A. S. W. GRIFFITHS MANAGER W.S.R.C.

SLIDES AND FILMS   **ADMISSION FREE**

Membership Secretary:

The notice that was to be responsible for the restart of the West Somerset Railway.

8

The Steady Progress Continues

During the period that the volunteers and the board of directors were awaiting the decision of the inquiry, the majority of those involved remained convinced that the Light Railway Order would be transferred to the new company, a degree of optimism that was all the more remarkable in view of the many setbacks they encountered.

As stated in an earlier chapter, people were involved in a great variety of tasks which they hoped would enable the line to be opened quickly once the go ahead was obtained. Some volunteers, whose work behind the scenes went unrecorded for some time, were those who had been set the task of obtaining suitable locomotives and rolling stock for the new railway. One person in this group was Harry Lee, who had fixed the plaque to the last daylight train on 2 January 1971 and who had become the first locomotive superintendent on the new line. The group used many – sometimes devious – methods to persuade owners to send their locomotives to work on the new railway and when these failed they would (if sufficient funds were available) resort to paying them to locate their engines on the new line.

Some of the locomotives that arrived on the line in those early days were, in hindsight, likely to be of little use. One of the locomotives which had been on display at Butlins for many years, and was part of Sir Billy Butlin's collection, was a former Southern Railway 'Terrier' Class 0-6-0 tank locomotive (No. 32678), signed on a loan agreement from Butlins. Other locomotives which were to prove equally unsuitable were a 7.5-ton 0-4-0 diesel locomotive with chain drive that for many years had shunted milk tanks at the Unigate Dairy at Chard and an 0-4-0 'fireless' locomotive originally located at Huntley and Palmers biscuit works at Reading. Harry was also a member of the consortium of members of the preservation group who acquired 1163 'Whitehead', an 0-4-0 saddle tank built by the Peckett Co. for use on the line.

However, it was their success in persuading firstly the Diesel and Electric Group, owners of Class 35 (Hymeks) diesel locomotives numbers 7017 and later 7018, together with Class 14 locomotive number D 9526, to locate their base at Williton in exchange for the opportunity to operate their engines on the new line when it opened and in persuading the Somerset & Dorset Trust, who were being forced off the site that they had been using at Radstock, to relocate their operations at Washford Station on the Minehead branch line, that were to prove to be so beneficial to the new line in the years that followed.

The Somerset & Dorset Railway Trust were the owners of 7F locomotive 53808 (or S&D No.88), an engine which although initially designed as a heavy goods engine had been used successfully to haul heavy passenger trains over the steep gradients on the Somerset & Dorset Line. Once the engine was located at Washford, protracted negotiations were started between the S&D Trust and the WSR, which eventually led to an agreement being signed in which the WSR stated that it would complete the restoration of No.53808 back to full working order in exchange for a ten-year exclusive hire agreement to run on the WSR.

These arrangements ensured that the new line would have sufficient locomotive power to haul its trains in the future, but the pressing need was for motive power that would be available in time for the reopening of the branch line. To meet this need two industrial saddle tanks built by Bagnall for shunting duties were acquired from the Austin car plant at Longbridge. Although not ideal for passenger train services, it was thought that although they required minor attention they could be put into working order before the opening day.

Shortly afterwards the Dart Valley Line announced that they had a small ex-Great Western pannier tank No.6412 that was surplus to their immediate requirements. When it was discovered that not only did this locomotive have a current boiler certificate but was also in good working order the West Somerset Railway Association was persuaded to purchase it for use on the WSR. Shortly after the purchase was completed the engine was driven, under its own steam, as a light engine movement from Buckfastleigh on the DVR to Totnes and from there along the main line to Taunton by Dave Rouse, who continued to work on the WSR for many years until he retired from the railway in 2001 on the grounds of ill health.

Pannier tank No.6412 went on to become not only the first engine to steam on the line once the Light Railway Order was transferred but it also became the first engine to earn revenue for the company before the line opened because of its starring role in the children's television film *The Flockton Flyer*. The purchase of two 2-car diesel railcars (Class 103 built by Park Royal), in preparation for the commuter service that there was still hopes of running, ensured that the management were well prepared for the start of services on the line, once the go ahead was given.

About this time Harry Lee, who had made a number of trips to Dai Woodham's scrapyard at Barry in South Wales, found three small prairie tanks available that were likely to be 'snapped up' by other preserved railways if they were left for much longer. The 45XX, 4575 and 55XX Class tank locomotives had frequently appeared on the Minehead Branch in GWR and BR days as well as most of the other branch lines throughout the West Country; indeed one of the locos available, No.5542, had been shedded at Taunton when Harry was there and had worked on the Minehead Branch in the 1930s and 1940s. After much discussion, it was realised that although the restoration of these engines would be a long-term project (just how long nobody realised at the time), if the association did not purchase them it would miss an opportunity that was not likely to reoccur. A deposit was paid to secure the locomotives and eventually – after the full price of £14,000 including the transit costs was paid – the engines were brought to the branch line. The subsequent purchase of two Mark 1 passenger coaches and later a further two 2-coach DMU sets, one

Bagnall saddle tank *Victor*.

of which was a Class 101 Metro Cammell set and the other a Class 105 Gloucester CW unit, completed the preliminary shopping list.

One locomotive that travelled the other way – going from the branch line to the main line and then on to Swindon works for restoration – was No.6229 *Duchess of Hamilton*, a member of the Duchess Class of locomotives built for the LMS railway. This locomotive had been on static display at Butlins and when the camp no longer required it they offered it to the National Railway Musuem. If the WSR had shown an interest it is possible that the engine would have come to the branch instead. No interest was shown due to a feeling that a large locomotive of this type would be of no benefit to the line. Some years later, in 1989, another large engine, 9F No.92220 *Evening Star*, was responsible for turning around the company's fortunes in a spectacular manner. Could the *Duchess of Hamilton* have achieved similar results earlier? Who knows.

9

Good News At Last

At last, on 12 November 1975, came the announcement the volunteers had been waiting for: the Minister for the Environment, Mr Anthony Crosland, had accepted the recommendation of his inspector that the Light Railway Order should be transferred. Once the legalities had been resolved the eager volunteers wasted no time in removing the wooden shutters that had been covering the windows of Minehead Station since its closure. As soon as others had gained entry to the buildings they set about the task of clearing four years' accumulation of dust and dirt and preparing the premises for decoration. A volunteer permanent-way gang was organised by Harold Blackmore, who had served as a track worker on BR for thirty years, which set about the task of the spot replacement of the necessary sleepers and the oiling of fishplates on the section of track between Minehead and Blue Anchor.

A grant of £49,000 from the Government's Manpower Service Commission, to enable the company to take on fifty young men on short-term employment to clear the track bed, was also a considerable help. Shortly after this group had started work the readers of the *West Somerset Free Press* were informed in a report from Mr Fear that these people were clearing 2 miles of track each week. So impressed were the directors that they arranged a special ceremony to which the chairman of the South West Committee of the Job Creation Scheme, Professor Robert Leaper, was invited, together with local dignitaries and the local press. On 15 February 1976, the day of the ceremony, the professor unfortunately had influenza but the celebrations carried on in his absence.

Another surprise gesture in view of the continuing threat by the NUR to black all work for the WSR was the decision of certain BR staff to shunt the various items of WSR stock located at sidings in the Taunton area onto the branch line. These movements together with the arrival of pannier tank 6412 took place over the very same set of points that BR were later to claim were 'life expired' but, thankfully for the WSR, were still available for use at this time. Once 6412 arrived the various items of stock could be shunted to locations along the branch line where volunteers could start work on preparing them for the opening of the line.

The new-found mood of optimism was shattered within a fortnight, however, when a report in the *Somerset County Gazette* stated that volunteers belonging to the West Somerset

Railway Association had found, in spite of the large sums of money that they had raised to assist the numerous projects that the WSR had in hand, together with the vast amount of unpaid work they had carried out, that they had not been offered representation on the board of the new company. The association was even more upset at the proposals of the new board to appoint two new local directors, Mr Piers Makin, a Williton solicitor, and Mr Pat Hypher, a retired civil servant who also lived in Williton, neither of whom had at that time been involved with the railway. The association also expressed concern at the board's decision to appoint a general manager, which they felt the company could not afford at this point in time. Concern was also expressed that the company had failed to start operating a steam service in the autumn as envisaged.

Mr R.J.L. Rolt, the editor of the association newsletter, proclaimed, 'In spite of the company claiming that we are both working toward the same ends, they appear to be pursuing a them and us attitude.' He added that, 'In the Association's constitution which was drafted by the company, it clearly states that Chairman of the Association was to be a Director on the board of the WSR,' a stipulation that it appears the board now wished to ignore.

When he learnt of the opinions expressed in the newsletter Mr Fear is reported to have said, 'They are entitled to a representative on the board, not a director, and he can attend board meetings but he cannot vote.' He then added, 'The Association's members had every justification for being extremely disappointed over the progress in reopening the line. They have worked very hard over the past three years, and it is difficult for them to realise that, in effect, the company was only born a fortnight ago with the signing of the lease.' If these comments were intended to try to placate the volunteers, it would appear that they had exactly the opposite effect. The only good to come out of these exchanges was an invitation by Mr Fear for the members of the association's management committee to attend a full board meeting to be held on 24 November 1975, in an attempt to clear the air. This appeared to have been a positive step as the following week's edition of the *Somerset County Gazette* claimed that railway enthusiasts, who had been somewhat upset over the refusal of the WSR to give them a seat on the board of directors, had obtained an agreement from the company that at its next annual meeting – to be held at the end of December – it would consider offering a seat to a member of the West Somerset Railway Association. Mr Douglas Fear is reported to have said, 'The Association appreciated that the appointment of one of their committee members as a director must, by law, be in the hands of the shareholders. Nevertheless the directors of the company recognise the benefit of such an appointment, and will discuss it at the annual meeting.'

After this meeting a statement was made that it had been agreed that a joint liaison committee would be set up to improve communications and consultations between the two bodies. The statement continued, 'Both the company and the Association have every reason to believe that, with the new arrangements for close co-operation now in place, the development and success of the company is assured.'

This attempt at reconciliation was wasted, however, because a few days later the board made the following announcement: 'The West Somerset Railway Co. have appointed an ex-BR man to be their new general manager.' Mr David Butcher, the statement claimed, started his career on BR by serving for eight years on the footplate, before transferring to the clerical grades. He was involved in railway traffic management and was then a yard manager at Peterborough prior to becoming area manager for BR at Westbury. After leaving BR five years previously he had worked in the private sector and had gained experience in private commerce. During that period Mr Butcher stated that he had also been a volunteer with the East Somerset Railway and that he had been working on the footplate as a driver for that concern. Mr Butcher also claimed that he wanted to run the Taunton–Minehead line 'as a railway and not for entertainment purposes, and that the whole thing was to be a total operation'. Just how successful the first general manager was to be the reader will be able to judge in the next chapters.

As the concerns of the association had apparently been completely ignored it was no surprise when the following article appeared in the 2 January 1976 edition of the *West Somerset Free Press* under the heading 'Railway Volunteers Have Raised £50,000'. Reference to the West Somerset Railway's lack of funds and to confusion regarding the appointment of a professional railwayman to head the organisation are contained in the year-end bulletin of the voluntary supporters' group, the WSR Association.

The bulletin mentioned how the railway company engaged a project manager as long ago as 1972 and then found it could not afford the salary. A £10,000 bank loan was made available to cover the project manager's salary but lacking alternative funds the company felt it was unwise to start up, states the bulletin.

Bagnall saddle tank *Vulcan*.

Surprise

The Railway Supporters' Association found it all the more surprising in view of these circumstances that a general manager had been engaged in the form of Mr D. Butcher.

Their report goes on to say that their assets stand at £50,000. The statement concluded that no one could accuse the association of not putting its money where its mouth was, the report then went on to appeal to the railway company to show equal strength.

After a public spat of this type it was obvious that some form of reconciliation was essential if the railway was to progress. Shortly after the above letter appeared Mr Rolt claimed that a frank exchange of views on deteriorating relations between the WSR and the association was conveyed to the local press in a deliberately 'low key' format. He declared that another member of the association had deliberately 'leaked' unofficial reports to the press and that these had not been toned down to suit either the association's or the WSR's requirements. In an attempt to avoid these problems the association had appointed a press officer who in future would handle all communications with the press. When this new press officer for the West Somerset Railway Association, Mr Iain Miles, was contacted by a reporter from the *West Somerset Free Press* to confirm reports that the association had withdrawn all volunteer working parties because of the refusal of the board to discuss with the association plans for the reopening of the line he denied that there were any such problems.

Financial problems continued to occupy the minds of the directors and when Mr John Whittaker for the SCC announced that the legal formalities between the county council and the railway had been completed and that the first instalment of the loan, amounting to £1,000, had already been paid to the WSR, the impression was created that at last progress was being made.

At the same time a completely different picture was being painted by Mr Fear. He announced that there had been a 'hitch' with the £60,000 loan agreed with the county council to cover initial running expenses to rehabilitate the Taunton–Minehead commuter rail service. He went on to say that a firm of consulting economists had informed the board that the minimum sum required to cover initial expenses was £60,000. That estimate, he claimed, had been given eighteen months previously and now the county council felt that, due to inflation, another £30,000 could be required to do the same work. To make sure that the schemes were completed the county council were now insisting that they would only release the money for specific projects when they were completed, and that they would require the WSR to match their (the county council's) funds pound for pound.

As an indication of the commitment of the WSR Mr Fear stated that the railway had already raised £14,000. He went on to say that the railway aimed to augment the council loan by a further £30,000, which it hoped to raise by means of a public share issue in the new year. In spite of these problems the hopes of both the volunteers and the general public were raised when the first non fare-paying inspection train carrying representatives of the new line, together with their guests, ran from Bishops Lydeard to Minehead on 21 December 1975.

The train, hauled by the Bagnall saddle tank locomotive *Victor*, consisted of a 10-ton covered wagon and a brake van. It appeared that the first official run must have been one of the worst-kept secrets in Somerset because thousands of enthusiasts cheered the train all the way from Bishops Lydeard Station to Minehead. Two hours later, having been delayed by the need to stop at Williton to replenish *Victor's* water tank from a mobile road tanker, the train pulled into Minehead with what was described as a triumphal hoot on her whistle. On arrival at Minehead the directors, together with their guests who included Mr Tom King, the local MP, Cllr Mrs Christine Gibbons of the West Somerset District Council, Mr P. Hypher, Mr B. Makey, Mr G. Byam-Shae, the BR Press relations Officer, Mr P. Flint (BR) and three members of the Association (unnamed), alighted the train.

Mr Fear announced that the trip had been a great success, whilst the driver of the train, Mr Harry Lee, was left to explain that the consumption of 1,800 gallons of water by *Victor* on the trip was not unusual for a saddle tank of this type! Following this announcements were made in the local press both by the WSR and the association that the line would definitely open from Minehead as far as Blue Anchor in March 1976 and that further sections would be opened subsequently, with the aim of having a service operating to Taunton by the end of 1977. To achieve this aim Mr D. Butcher was arranging for working parties to descend on the line to carry out rehabilitation work under his guidance at weekends.

The very necessary task of trying to raise sufficient funds for the line to start operating continued. The public share issue of £30,000 had been increased to £60,000, and the association was also trying to raise funds, not only by increasing the number of its members, but also by organising a grand draw. They were also raising money for a stock fund, to enable the purchase of more locomotives and carriages. The price of tickets was 5p each, with a first prize of £20 to be drawn on 4 June. We must assume that this draw was successful because it went on to become an annual event, although by the year 2003 the price of the ticket had risen to 25p and the first prize had gone up to £1,000.

Finally came the announcement that everyone had been waiting for: the line would officially reopen between Minehead and Blue Anchor on Sunday 28 March 1976. If the volunteers and staff had been under pressure before; it was nothing to what was to happen now.

During the period prior to the reopening, volunteers often had to work late into the night and sometimes all through it, to ensure that the two locomotives (*Victor* and 6412) would be ready for the opening day, and after the line had opened ensure that they were available to operate service trains the following morning. Unfortunately, in spite of all the volunteers' efforts, they were not always successful. The final obstacle to the reopening of the line was cleared on Tuesday 23 March when Major Peter Olver for the Railway Inspectorate cleared the line for the use of passenger trains.

As the line was about to reopen, the directors of the WSR announced that a total of £65,000 had been raised on the share issue; a far higher sum than they had expected.

10

Steam Trains Return to Minehead

In an attempt to ensure that everyone, including some 2,000 children who were arriving at Butlins that weekend – and not just railway enthusiasts – was aware that the railway was to reopen on 28 March, notices appeared in the local newspapers, leaflets were handed out to the passing public and large posters displayed at Minehead Station.

When the opening day arrived the weather certainly did not encourage the crowds – the skies were overcast with rain threatened and a bitterly cold wind was blowing (in Minehead!). In spite of this, hundreds of enthusiasts turned up long before 10 a.m. for the opening ceremony that was to be performed by Lord Montague of Beaulieu. Ahead of time, the shivering but cheerful groups along the platform, along with children clutching Union Jack flags, turned their heads as one when the cry went up 'There she is!'

Slowly backing down the track towards the six waiting carriages, *Victor* looked immaculate. Her maroon paintwork was highly polished and bedecked with bunting. As the locomotive gently coupled up to the train the crowds surged forward for a better view, cameras clicked and the Watchet Royal British Legion Band struck up with a spirited rendition of *Ain't she sweet*.

Once the band had finished, the assembled dignitaries started their speeches. Lord Montague stated that 'tenacity and enthusiasm had created the railway, which was now a reality'. Mr Douglas Fear, who had done so much to ensure that the line had reached this stage, stated that the railway had a tremendous future, but warned that it would need the continued support of the local population if it was to succeed. After outlining the history of the line since closure, he then went on to urge the assembled crowds to participate in the new share issue.

Further good wishes came from Mr Leslie Axon, chairman of the West Somerset District Council who was resplendent in his gleaming chain of office, but the biggest cheer of the morning went to a slight silver-haired man who most accurately sensed the mood of the crowd when, just before sitting down, he announced to the crowd, 'You did not come here to listen to speeches; like me you came here to see the train draw out.' That gentleman was Professor Robert Leaper, chairman of the Government-backed job creation programme which had pumped £50,000 into the work of clearing the track, and who had been unable to attend the ceremony outlined in the previous chapter.

After the applause had died down Lord Montague stood up, donned the tall top hat that seemed to go with his blue blazer and yellow striped tie, strode up the platform, waving acknowledgements to the crowd surging over and under the rope barriers. When he reached the spot on the platform where the engine was standing, he placed his foot on the buffer beam of the locomotive and, after waiting for the television crew who were present to catch up, he led the crowd in three rousing cheers before waiving a green flag for the first train to depart at 10 a.m. – first ensuring that he had removed his foot from the buffer beam.

After acknowledging the right away with two blasts on the whistle, the footplate crew started the train on its way to Blue Anchor, accompanied by the strains of the Watchet band playing *Viva España*. The train crew consisted of Harry Lee as driver and David Rouse as fireman, both of whom have already been mentioned in this text. Don Spencer was the guard on the train and this was a nostalgic moment for him because he had been one of the BR staff at Minehead. Although Don has long since retired from the railway he often travels on the line as a passenger, to ensure that it is still being run in the correct and approved manner.

On this first trip, 250 people, all of whom had paid a special fare of £3.00 each for the privilege of travelling on the first train (the fares for the remainder of the day were just 50p), drank a champagne toast from paper cups. The festivities were recorded by the film and television crews that travelled on the train and many of the revellers, it is believed, were embarrassed when they saw themselves on the various television news and feature programmes during the following week.

After the first round trip was completed a further 2,000 passengers were carried on the opening day, the last train not returning to Minehead until 7 p.m. because the company had to run three more round trips than planned in order to cope with the crowds. On the opening day a total of 1,000 platform tickets were also sold at 5p each and it was claimed that 5,000 people watched the proceedings from the various vantage points alongside the line. Later it was announced by the company that a further 5,000 passengers had travelled on the line in the eight days following the opening day ceremonies and the newly opened line continued to attract welcome publicity when pictures appeared in the local press showing Mr Chris van den Arund, who was at that time the West Somerset Railway company secretary (now station master at Williton), presenting a rather surprised passenger, Mrs Eileen Wheeler, with a bouquet of flowers, a bottle of sherry and a free ten-journey ticket as she stepped from the train. She was the 10,000th passenger to travel on the newly opened line. For the record, in 2003, the West Somerset Railway announced that they had just carried their three millionth passenger.

On 1 April (shame about the date), HTV, the local television company, broadcast a programme called *The Day the Train Came Steaming Back*, which dealt with the reopening of the line and the effect it was likely to have on the local community. The commentator was Richard Cottrell, who at that time was also the presenter of the daily evening local news programme *Report West*.

Shortly afterwards, on 23 August 1976, the next section of the line between Blue Anchor and Williton was reopened to the public. Although the initial passenger figures were promising the WSR continued to try to encourage more passengers to travel on the trains, and towards the end of the year they announced that they would be operating a Santa Special train. Unlike the Santa Special trains that are now operated every year, the original service was operated with the co-operation of Floyds, a department store in Minehead, and the whole event was sponsored by the local rotary club. Father Christmas was due to arrive by Santa's special steam train at Minehead Station at 10.40 a.m. There he would be met by the 'Christmas Fairy' and they would proceed to Floyds department store, via The Avenue, with an escort of some of their animals, who would be collecting money for a mentally handicapped children's fund. The special service for Santa was also scheduled to operate daily from the following Monday until the next Saturday.

Sadly, in spite of initiatives of this kind, the WSR was to announce that it had made an operating loss of £42,216 for the first six months that the line was open. As soon as these trading figures were announced at the board meeting the directors passed a resolution of no confidence in the managing director, Mr Douglas Fear, and demanded his resignation. When Mr Fear refused to resign he was dismissed by the directors. Both resolutions were passed unanimously and the board appointed Mr G. Belton as the new managing director.

11

Storm Clouds Gather

In November 1976 Mr Fear issued this statement following his dismissal:

An enormous amount has been said and written about the affairs of the company I founded nearly six years ago – The West Somerset Railway, and much of it has been biased.

It has been said that the company made a trading loss of £77,000, and that the main reason for this loss was the incompetence of the board, which allegedly made inaccurate forecasts and did not control expenses. What did we actually forecast for the year to the end of July 1976, and what did we actually spend?. On revenue, expenses, salaries and day to day costs were £43,000 against a forecast of £42,000 after depreciation, not such a bad shot.

However for reasons of financial prudence, the board decided that all expenditure on renovation of the line (amounting to approximately £15,000) must be written off, and not capitalised. Also that provisions for future maintenance must be made, including those 'one off' items against the trading results, together with a provision for A.G.M. expenses. This increased the final declared expenses to nearly £71,000, and the loss by £27,500. These figures are all there to be seen in the audited accounts and the company's books, and show a loss of £18,500 (after taking out 'one off' figures).

Mr Fear continued: 'This is not much to shout about, but it is a great deal better than £46,000 or the misquoted £77,000 which includes the previous year's expenses, and Share Issue costs.' Under the heading 'Capital' he explained:

First Capital Expenditure. Although at £31,000, including £15,000 for renovation, was below the forecast for the year, the programme of work was also behind schedule. Back in June, the board instructed the General Manager and the technical staff, that money must be saved, but by the end of July it was estimated that the overspend on completing the renovation to Taunton would be not less than £22,000, of which £8,000 arose from an increase in BR's capital charge. This was potentially a very serious drain on cash.

Income was short of the target of £42,000 partially because of retail profits from the shop and restaurant that were particularly dismal. The board took advice from Mr G. Belton (who has subsequently been elected to a directorship) and implemented as many of his proposals as were practical during the remainder of the season in an effort to bring in extra income, but there was still another hole in the cash budget.

In July the board were advised that no further loan advances would be made by Somerset County Council. That combined with the N.U.R. non co-operation statement, disposed of any possibility of reaching Taunton for many months ahead. The board at once advised the General Manager of the financial implications of these decisions, and that any delay in reducing current costs, including staff costs, would make it impossible to maintain a winter service. There just would not be the cash for it. Unhappily the logic of this argument was not accepted (by the General Manager) and instead of constructive corrective action, a long and expensive political squabble ensued.

Under the heading 'Personalities' the statement continued:

Reference has been made on a number of occasions to a 'clash of personalities' being a prominent element in the saga, but this I do not accept. The old board was deeply concerned regarding the inability of the General Manager and staff to accept its instructions, and it was because of this serious and insoluble situation, that there were resignations from the board.

I have no wish to whitewash the old board, but we were not such morons as people make out. The moves – first to reduce the number of staff in the winter, then to close the line completely during the winter months were the only sane courses open to us.

I venture to hope that the lessons will not be lost on whoever has responsibility for the company next year. I am sure that Mr Belton's accession will fill a need in the promotion field, and look forward to hearing his comments on anticipated business for 1977/8.

The newly formed West Somerset Railway Independent Review Body recently circularised shareholders nominating the present directors. The case made against the old board was incompetence, primarily arising out of its decision to close the railway for the winter and to reduce the staff to a minimum. It is interesting to note that this is precisely what the new board has done. Will it be successful in saving the business and preserving the railway? I am hopeful that it will, but, nevertheless drastic economies would have to be enforced. The staff levels for next season will have to be reduced, and fewer trains run etc.

In the final part of his statement, under the heading 'Guidance', he concluded:

I do not think that the present board is so well equipped to deal with the situation as their predecessors. The new directors are all part time, no full time members, and few of them live locally

Any company has to recognise a duty to employees, shareholders and its customers, plus in the case of the West Somerset Railway, the volunteer association, but if the claims of any of those groups are such as to put the whole of the business in jeopardy, then they must be resisted to the end by any governing body. If the situation was not recognised for what it is – that the company has yet to establish itself, and must submit to firm guidance to turn a difficult start, into a secure future – then no succession of boardroom changes, committees, publicity campaigns and meetings will save it. I am absolutely certain of this.

It was extremely unfortunate that Mr Fear's involvement with the railway should end like this. It was only later that the general public learnt that Mr Fear had worked for the railway for the first four years without pay, in what was to become virtually a full-time job. Although he had been in receipt of a salary since April 1976, when he had been offered a five-year contract, he had only accepted half the salary due to him because of the difficult financial situation that the company was in. He had been involved in gathering support for the idea of a preserved railway, the paperwork involved in the Light Railway Order, the public inquiry and the raising of £200,000 in public share subscriptions.

If the board thought that they had heard the last of Mr Fear they were very much mistaken; their offer of a 'golden handshake' of £1,500 was angrily rejected and Mr Fear promptly lodged a claim against the company for unfair dismissal, seeking a sum of £23,400 in compensation, which included £1,000 in out-of-pocket expenses and £2,000 in unpaid salary.

Mr Gerry Belton, when he learnt of this development, announced: 'The board held a twelve-hour meeting, and Mr Fear had been removed by the unanimous vote of the board.' He then added that a letter was sent by hand to Mr Fear's home giving him the opportunity to resign and accept an *ex gratia* payment. He then stated, 'Mr Fear has decided that he is not going to play it that way.' Mr Belton declined to comment on the sum that had been offered to Mr Fear but claimed that it took four hours for the board to decide on the amount to be paid. He also claimed that the figure offered was, in the opinion of the board, based not only on fairness but what the company could afford. At the same time, Mr Belton announced two new appointments to the board – Mr Christopher Dowrick (still a director, and also stationmaster at Dunster Station), a bank manager from Crediton who became financial director, and Mr Richard Stevens, a chartered surveyor who was appointed to watch the legal aspects of properties and insurance. Both of these gentlemen had been committee members of the review body. The first task facing the new board was to close the line for the winter months and make a number of the staff redundant: the very policy they had criticised the original board for suggesting.

The next embarrassment for the new board concerned the 'Ghost Train', or as it was known in some circles, 'Debauchery Special'. An announcement by an Environment Department spokesman censured the railway for running the train at night, without lights over unmanned crossings, and along track not authorised for passenger use. The spokesman announced that the railway had been given a stern warning and had since apologised. This was the first hint that the press had received of this story and they wasted no time in seeking more information. When they approached Mr Fear to see if he could throw any light on the story, he informed them, 'I had heard rumours of a party taking place in Dunster, but this was rather more than that. It was a ride to Crowcombe and back, with debauchery en route.' He claimed, 'The joy ride included a halt for a party at Dunster Station, which ended in the early hours of the following morning and cost (the company) £3 per mile.' The party was arranged to celebrate the twenty-first birthday of the line's operating superintendent, Mr Nick Jones. Among the eighty guests at the party was the company's general manager, Mr David Butcher. The directors claimed that they were unaware of the event until after it had taken place.

West Somerset Railway
TRAINS TO WORK IN WATCHET

Mondays to Saturdays

MINEHEAD dep 7.20 a.m.
WATCHET arr 7.48 a.m.

Going home:

WATCHET   dep 5.05 p.m., 6.40 p.m.
MINEHEAD arr 5.35 p.m., 7.10 p.m.

10 Journey Ticket: £3.50

Valid over any number of weeks.
Can be used for 10 single journeys
or 5 return journeys.

Cheap Day Return: 80p

Minehead Stn. (Tel: 4996)   PB1/76

West Somerset Railway
TRAINS to WORK in MINEHEAD

Mondays to Saturdays

WILLITON   dep 7.58 a.m.
WATCHET   dep 8.04 a.m.
WASHFORD   dep 8.11 a.m.
BLUE ANCHOR dep 8.20 a.m.
MINEHEAD   arr 8.33 a.m.

Going home:

MINEHEAD   dep 5.55 p.m.
BLUE ANCHOR arr 6.10 p.m.
WASHFORD   arr 6.17 p.m.
WATCHET   arr 6.25 p.m.
WILLITON   arr 6.30 p.m.

10 Journey Tickets save you
money. Use them over any period
in either direction.

See list of Cheap Fares.

West Somerset Railway
AFTERNOON SHOPPING

Daily

WILLITON dep 1.55	MINEHEAD dep 4.20	
WATCHET dep 2.00	DUNSTER dep 4.25	
WASHFORD dep 2.08	B. ANCHOR dep 4.35	
B.ANCHOR dep 2.18	WASHFORD dep 4.42	
DUNSTER dep 2.24	WATCHET dep 4.50	
MINEHEAD arr 2.30	WILLITON arr 4.55	

5.55 p.m. train from Minehead
     for late shopping.

Cheap Day Returns to and from Minehead

WILLITON 85p   Child 50p
WATCHET 80p   Child 45p
WASHFORD 65p   Child 40p
B.ANCHOR 50p   Child 30p

Journey Tickets to/from Minehead

WILLITON £3.75 ⎫ Valid for any number
WATCHET £3.50 ⎪ of weeks. Can be used
WASHFORD £2.75 ⎬ for 10 Single or 5
B.ANCHOR £2.25 ⎭ Return Journeys.

West Somerset Railway
SHOPPING in MINEHEAD

Tuesday, Friday and Saturday

WILLITON dep 9.55 a.m.
WATCHET   dep 10.00 a.m.
WASHFORD dep 10.08 a.m.
B. ANCHOR dep 10.18 a.m.
DUNSTER   dep 10.24 a.m.
MINEHEAD arr 10.30 a.m.

MINEHEAD dep 12.30 and 4.20 ⎫
DUNSTER   arr 12.35 and 4.25 ⎪
B. ANCHOR arr 12.45 and 4.35 ⎬ Both
WASHFORD arr 12.52 and 4.42 ⎪ daily
WATCHET   arr 1.00 and 4.50 ⎪
WILLITON arr 1.05 and 4.55 ⎭

No Charge for Prams or Push-Chairs
Plenty of room for large parcels
OUR STAFF ARE THERE TO HELP YOU

SENIOR CITIZENS AT CHEAP RATES

12

1977: A Fresh Start

Before the new season started there were more changes in the boardroom and to the management team. It was announced that Mr David Butcher had resigned on the grounds of ill health and had been replaced by Major Tony Griffiths, who had been the company's project manager from 1972 to 1974. It was also announced that Mr Richard Stevens had taken over as company chairman from Mr Gerry Belton who had become publicity director.

Due to the disappointing passenger figures after the first few weeks of the 1976 season, the WSR was determined to improve in 1977 by organising a number of special events. To mark the opening of their 1977 summer season a steam special was operated, on Sunday 3 April, running from Minehead to Williton and back to Minehead, stopping only at Watchet. The advertisement read: 'Many seats already sold – book now or turn up early to avoid disappointment'. The return fare for this train, which left Minehead at 3 p.m. and returned at 4.42 p.m., was 85p (children and OAPs 45p), the same fares that had been set for the previous year.

Another event that took place shortly afterwards, on Sunday 8 May, was a lifeboat steam special. The return fare for this event was £1 and there were no concessions. Again the train went from Minehead to Williton, only stopping at Watchet. On this occasion the train left at 2.30 p.m. and returned at 3.55 p.m. Just how much the Minehead Lifeboat Institution benefited from this event is not known, but it appears to have been successful because this was the first of many efforts by the railway to raise funds for the lifeboats. The same fundraising event in 2003 featured the Grimethorpe Colliery Brass Band which played to a full house at the Regal Theatre in Minehead. The proceeds from this event benefited not only the Minehead Lifeboat but also the Regal Theatre, as well as the Friends of Minehead Station. Santa Specials were also run later in the year.

The fame of the new railway seemed to be spreading. Roland Karmer, aged three years old, and living in the town of Rietgatt on the German/Dutch border, fell in love with the railway when he saw picturesque shots of it in the television serial film *The Flockton Flyer*, which had been showing on the continent. Not knowing whether the line actually existed or not, the boy's father wrote to the 'Flockton Flyer, England', to enquire if such a line existed. When they received a reply stating that the *Flockton Flyer* was in being and was operating on the West Somerset Railway, the entire family came to this country to see the line for themselves. After they had travelled from Minehead to Williton and returned, Mr Karmer said, 'It's wonderful, every bit as beautiful as the film.' The WSR ensured that this newsworthy item reached the local press and some publicity issued by the WSR shortly afterwards carried the legend 'Minehead is Flockton'.

Another initiative which was proposed in 1977, which unfortunately surfaced rather too late to have a dramatic effect on the passenger figures for that current year, was to offer to the public weekend package holidays in conjunction with the Beach Hotel at Minehead (which at that time was owned by Trust House Forte). The Friday to Sunday afternoon breaks, which cost approximately £24, included full board, tours of Minehead Station, travel on the WSR and a film show about the WSR at the hotel in the evening. The manager of the hotel, Mr Ian Hughes-Rixham, said, 'I think there is a good market. It will be the whole town that will benefit from the extra trade.' He then stated that the first weekend had been planned for the end of November and a further six events were to follow. If demand was greater than anticipated arrangements had been made for further parties to be accommodated at the Luttrell Arms Hotel in Dunster.

In an attempt to boost the passenger figures still further, two special trains were to be run from Minehead beyond the existing terminus of the line at Williton, to Bishops Lydeard. These two special trains were to run on Saturday 22 October and were to be named the 'The Tauntonian' and the 'West Somerset Express'.

The Tauntonian was due to leave Minehead Station at 10.00 a.m., calling only at Williton and Crowcombe, and was due to arrive at Bishops Lydeard at 11.10 a.m., where a coach connection waited to take passengers to Taunton Station and town centre. On the return trip the coaches left the town centre and, after picking up passengers at Taunton Station, arrived at Bishops Lydeard Station in time for passengers to catch the 4.30 p.m. train departure, arriving back at Minehead at 5.30 p.m. The bus that was to take passengers into Taunton from 'The Tauntonian' had already collected passengers from the town for the 'West Somerset Express', which left Bishops Lydeard Station at 11.30 a.m., and after calling at Crowcombe ran non-stop to Minehead. The return trip left Minehead at 2.30 p.m. and ran non-stop to Crowcombe and then to Bishops Lydeard, where another bus connection was available for passengers to reach Taunton. Both trains were hauled by the *Flockton Flyer* pannier tank No.6412.

To encourage as many people as possible to travel, a special 'budget' fare was agreed of £2.90 (£2.50 for children) for either train, the price including a reserved seat and a guide. The bus link, which, incidentally, was provided by Berry's Coaches of Taunton, was free to holders of train tickets. Once the WSR trains started to run to Bishops Lydeard on a regular basis, the same company – Berry's – continued to operate the linking bus service to Taunton until long after the period covered by this book.

After this service was announced, the company received numerous enquiries asking when it was going to be operated on a regular basis. Mr Chris van den Arund, who had become the company's administrative director initially for a period of three months which became three years, informed the *West Somerset Free Press* reporter who contacted him, 'that special train into Bishops Lydeard cannot be developed into regular services until level crossings between Stogumber and Crowcombe have been made safe'. He continued, 'We have been given permission to run these two steam specials on October 22nd, and another diesel excursion for shoppers in early December, but we cannot run regular services into Bishops Lydeard until the level crossings at Roebuck Gate, and Leigh Woods are protected by flashing lights.' Finally he warned that this would take a long time to materialise, depending on available finance and labour.

The appointment of Mr van den Arund arose because of the resignation of Mr Gerry Belton, who had only recently been appointed the director responsible for publicity. Speaking to reporters after announcing his resignation, Mr Belton stated, 'I feel that in the last six months I have completed the work I set out to do', unfortunately this work was never clearly defined. The other changes that occurred at this time concerned Major Tony Griffiths, who earlier in the year had been appointed general manager, now becoming personal assistant to the new chairman, Mr Richard Stevens.

In September the other Bagnall saddle tank locomotive, *Vulcan*, entered service without any formal ceremony, just in time to ease the pressure on the locomotive department, which, up till then, had been trying to operate a daily service with only one serviceable engine (6412). This problem had been caused because *Victor* was undergoing boiler repairs in the former goods shed that had become the locomotive shed. Unfortunately, the respite was to be rather brief because shortly afterwards the Pannier tank was again required for filming commitments. This was for another series of *Flockton Flyer* duties, a source of income the company could not afford to turn down, no matter how many problems it caused elsewhere.

Because of the company's inability to operate services during the previous winter many people were somewhat surprised when Mr van den Arund announced that, although the winter timetable had not been published, it was expected that the company would operate a winter service. Included in the new timetable would be a limited number of steam services which would be used for winter break holidays with the co-operation of Trust House Forte.

Mr van den Arund continued, 'Regular commuter services operated by diesel railcars would link Blue Anchor, Washford, Watchet and Williton and a further section of line should be open by Christmas. We intend to improve on last year's winter service by running every day except Sundays.' When asked if he felt that the company's results had improved sufficiently to carry out such an ambitious winter programme he said that the season so far had been not bad, but not as good as had been hoped. Questioned further, he went on to say that the company expected to make a small loss that year, the reason for this, he claimed, was that there had not been as great a response to the steam trains as expected, but the loadings on the diesel service from Minehead to Watchet had been much higher than anticipated. The diesel services had been used by local people and visitors alike. The *Flockton Flyer* had also had a very positive impact on the figures, he added.

The whole area experienced a downturn in visitor figures during the year under review, so it would have been unrealistic to assume that the WSR would not be affected. Discussing the trading results for 1977 at the AGM held the following year, Mr Stevens announced that the company had made a loss of £16, 879 for the year compared with the deficit for the previous year of £42,216. He then went on to inform the shareholders that the company was now on a sounder footing for the future, and added that the turnaround had only been achieved by painful and difficult decisions, admitting that the loss was still too high but was much lower than the previous year.

It emerged that the improvement was largely due to staff cuts, the results of which had reduced the wages bill from £42,000 to £21,500 per annum. Income for the period (fifteen months) was boosted to £77,433, of which fares accounted for £49,376. A total of 65,000 passengers had travelled on the line, of whom 25,000 travelled in the diesel rail cars and 40,000 on the steam services.

A disturbing fact that was not commented upon at the meeting was that although the company ran 2,000 trains during this period, and established a first-class record for being punctual, these figures represented an average loading of just over thirty-seven passengers per train. With average loadings as low this it was not surprising that the line was unable to operate at a profit. The company would have benefited greatly if some research had been carried out to determine why these figures were so low. Were they running too many trains, for example, or were they running trains at the wrong times perhaps?

Mr Stevens then announced to the shareholders that the company was about to ask them for an extra £60,000, in the form of a new share issue, to put the company on target to break even in 1978. The money, he said, would enable the company to repay the whole of their debenture of £33,942 owed to the Somerset County Council. It would also enable crossing lights, costing £10,000, to be erected at the level crossings at Leigh Woods and Roebuck gate, as part of the planned reopening of the line to passenger traffic as far as Bishops Lydeard. Further money was needed for another locomotive costing £5,000 and tools and a turntable costing a further £11,000. He then claimed that the balance of over £47,000 (although where this figure came from I cannot understand) would primarily be used for the purchase of rolling stock. The long-term situation was not satisfactory at the moment, he claimed, based as it is only on the two 0-6-0 Bagnall saddle tanks. Finally, he stated, 'For the same sum that was to be used for repayment of the debenture we would be enabled to go right through as far as Bishops Lydeard with our own motive power. We are now running to a break-even budget, but would not expect to see a profit until trains can be run on the section of line between Williton and Bishops Lydeard.'

During the period of the meeting when the shareholders were invited to question members of the board, one of the shareholders suggested that the line should not be extended beyond Williton. Mr Stevens replied, 'If the length of the line was cut then the loss of revenue would be greater than the saving of costs achieved in 1977.' He also admitted that more volunteers and additional locomotive power would be needed when this section was opened.

13

1978: Cold Winds

The new year, 1978, did not start well for the WSR. At the January meeting of the finance sub-committee of the Somerset County Council, the chairman of the sub-committee, Cllr John Luff, persuaded members to recommend to the full council that the sub-committee considered the West Somerset Railway should not proceed with its plans to provide a commuter service between Minehead and Taunton. This was because they considered the idea to be no longer viable or practical. It was their opinion that the WSR should be persuaded to limit its operations to running 'pleasure' trains between Minehead and Watchet.

Their lack of confidence in the private company's expansion plans and financial forecasts was underlined by the sub-committee's refusal to extend the repayment period of a £33,942 loan beyond September. The same sub-committee also turned down a request by the WSR for the terms of their lease to be changed. The original agreement had been for a cost of living-linked rent increase after the first five years of operation and because of the high inflation rate caused by the fuel crisis of the early 1970s the WSR was worried that the annual rent could rise from the present rate of £6,000 to £28,000 by 1981.

In case the reader were to gain the impression that Cllr John Luff was in the anti-rail lobby I feel that I should point out that he was the county council member for the Shepton Mallet area, which included Cranmore, the headquarters of the East Somerset Railway, and I have been unable to find any evidence that he had in any way spoken against the activities of that railway.

The attitude of the sub-committee was welcomed by Mr Clive Barclay, the branch secretary of the local busmen's branch of the NUR, who said, 'We are relieved at the county council's attitude; wisdom has at last prevailed.' He continued, 'I would have thought that the railway company would have been relieved at having a huge financial millstone removed from around their neck by the county's attitude. Competition from the railway would have hit Western National's revenue which is already in the doldrums.' After reiterating his concerns for the jobs of his forty-two members at the Minehead Depot, he explained that the Minehead–Taunton bus route was the mainstay of the bus company's services and, therefore, his members' future depended on the retention of this service. He concluded by saying that the NUR had no particular axe to grind with the WSR except over the proposed commuter services: 'We feel a bit sorry for the railway company. I think they have been used as a target for the council's venom.'

At the annual general meeting of the West Somerset Railway, held on 28 January, after the accounts for the previous year – as detailed in the previous chapter – had been outlined to and accepted by the shareholders, Mr Richard Stevens bitterly accused the county council finance sub-committee of acting in bad faith by breaking the confidentiality agreement of a private meeting between the company and the sub-committee. He then went on to accuse the officials of trying to put the railway out of business. He continued, 'They [the county council] do not want an honest return on their capital, but instead they appeared to be looking for the type of super profits that even the property speculators of 1972 could not achieve.'

Replying to the suggestion that the company should operate as a 'funline' to Watchet the chairman stated that all the financial forecasts the company had made were based on the assumption that the line would operate to Taunton and that should remain the long-term aim of the company. He observed that there could not be many people who would query whether the money was in the bank nine months before payment was due. Mr Stevens explained that until now the company had enjoyed cordial relations with county council officials, adding that opposition to the railway appeared to be coming only from council officials blaming Cllr Luff for the problems that had arisen. 'If contributions continue to come in as present, we will be able to pay the county council,' he stressed, 'but it does not go down well to be informed by the councillors that apart from our cash reserves, all we have is a load of scrap.'

The finance director, Mr Chris Dowrick, also criticised the local councillors when he said: 'They appear to be completely out of touch with the company's operations; when we met the councillors they were not even aware that we were operating a winter service.'

Some good news did come out at the meeting because it was announced that Minehead Station had been saved from the bulldozers. The decision of the board to apply for listed-building status for the station had lead to the county council dropping its plans to knock down the original buildings and 'redevelop' the site. Mr Stevens added that the company would now be able to landscape the site, with the exception of a small area that the council wished to retain on a temporary basis as a car park.

It was at this meeting that Mr Stevens disclosed that the company was considering selling some of its locomotive stock as part of a stock rationalisation programme. He said, 'We are finding out who would like to buy some of our restored engines. We feel we have more engines than are needed on a long term basis. We cannot afford to keep capital tied up in some locomotives, because it is essential to keep the basic business of the railway working.' He did, however, give assurances that *Victor*, *Vulcan* and the prairie tanks would be retained. The number of engines sold, he added, would depend on the response to their enquiries, but it was hoped that several thousand pounds could be raised.

Before the conclusion of the meeting he paid tribute to the WSRA and, after admitting that relations in the past had been rather strained between the two bodies, he thanked those volunteers who were busy clearing the section of the track between Bishops Lydeard and Crowcombe at the association's own expense. Because of this the company hoped it would be able to operate trains on this section of the track on fifteen Sundays that year, starting in May. Finally, in passing, he referred to the possibility of freight traffic being moved from Watchet Docks by rail, which he claimed could be very profitable for the WSR. The remarks about freight services came as a surprise to many people but arose because of the concerns of Watchet at the large number of heavy lorries travelling to and from the docks through the narrow streets of the town. The problem had arisen after the rail sidings were removed from the dockside and the recent mini boom in traffic at the harbour had made matters much worse.

When the town council approached the WSR on the subject, the railway stated that they would be prepared to consider laying track on the section of land between the railway and Harbour Road (now used as a lorry park) but added that this offer was dependent on the outcome of discussions with other parties. Some discussions must have taken place with other bodies on the feasibility of the project because Mr Stevens admitted on 3 February that BR had given favourable consideration to the proposals and had indicated that if there were sufficient interest BR would consider paying half of the estimated cost of £25,000 to link the branch to the main line.

The reaction of the NUR was predictable. It reiterated that all the railway's efforts would be 'blacked', even though the movement of freight traffic would not affect their members driving buses and once the traffic reached the main line it would provide their fellow members with work.

What was not foreseen was the attitude of Mr Douglas Reid, the managing director of Willie Shipping Group, operators of the services within the harbour. In a blunt message to the railway he said, 'Forget it, it is not a viable proposition. They do not stand a prayer of handling the type of trade we have at Watchet at the moment.' He then added, 'I am surprised that the railway company's shareholders allow themselves to be told that they can expect this type of traffic through the harbour, without asking if the shipping company backs it. One of the reasons we took no financial or other interest in the railway was because we thought it was not on.'

'We are always prepared to sit down and talk to someone if we think they have got a scheme that will work to the benefit of everyone, but we do not think rail freight will work. It will be far too expensive; road transport is the answer.' After pointing out that Willie, the owners and operators of the docks operation, also owned S&M Streets, the road haulage company, he outlined further reasons why he considered that the proposals were not feasible. 'They [the railway company] say only mini liners carrying 2,000 tons would be able to offer cheap enough rates to interest customers. But Watchet is not geared to this kind of business; our cargo is made up of scores of small companies who ship 100 or 200 tons once a month.'

In conclusion, he stated, 'Using the railway would mean goods being manhandled four to five times, sending it by road involved only loading it onto a lorry at the dockside, for direct delivery to the customer's doorstep.' He also stressed that the railway would need a conveyor belt system to get the cargo from the ships to the railway wagons, which he estimated would cost £20,000 to £30,000 to install, 'and that is before you have to start paying the wages of the men who are to operate it'.

When he heard of Mr Reid's remarks, the chairman of the WSR board replied, 'The company did not make statements without being able to substantiate them. Initial talks had been held at management level with Watchet Marine who belong to Willies, and we got the response we were looking for – that the shippers did not have a closed mind over the possibility of transporting goods by rail.' Adding that Wansborough Paper Mill had also said that they were interested in rail services, if they could be offered at a competitive price, he went on to say, 'Our first objective is to open more lines on which to run passenger trains. Freighting is only a possibility for the future, we have got draft plans for the loading and unloading of goods at the harbour, and these do not involve a conveyor belt.' He concluded by saying that he did not consider the technical difficulties to be insuperable, adding that they were sufficiently encouraged to think that it might make sense.

During the week commencing 12 February 1978 the weather had been bitterly cold; for most of the time the temperature had been hovering around freezing and occasional flurries of snow fell, which in spite of the bitterly cold easterly wind, normally melted by about midday if the sun was out. Because these conditions had lasted all week, by Saturday 19 February most of the local people had decided that – no immediate improvement in the weather being likely – all they could do was try to go about their normal tasks as best they could.

On Friday 18 February, eight volunteers set out from various parts of the country to drive to Washford, their aim being to spend the night in the sleeping coach that had been provided by the Somerset & Dorset Railway Trust, so that they could get started early the following morning dismantling locomotive No. 53808 for its complete overhaul. Having worked as long as possible during the daylight hours available at that time of year, it was then their intention to return to their respective homes on the Saturday night.

As planned they were up bright and early and set about their task, protected from the elements only by a tarpaulin that had been attached to a steel frame covering the engine. Cursing when their knuckles were skinned when spanners slipped on icy nuts that had only been persuaded to turn after liberal applications of WD 40, or removing nuts that refused to turn even after a dousing, they then had to use club hammers and cold chisels, at the same time trying to avoid shivering in case they missed the chisel and hit their thumbs. During the afternoon it started to snow and before long they realised that they were in the middle of a raging blizzard, with the snow drifting and piling up. Soon it was clear that their stay at Washford was going to be slightly longer than they had expected.

When the last DMU materialised out of the gloom that afternoon, on its way to Minehead, the guard, noticing the conditions on the nearby A39 where nothing was moving, observed that it might be necessary to run an extra train later that day. After the volunteers had retired to the station building and lit a fire to warm themselves and to try get dry, they heard the sound of the DMU making a valiant attempt to climb Washford bank. When they went out on to the platform they found that an extra train had been laid on so that people, who would otherwise have been stranded in Minehead, could get back to their homes in Washford, Watchet and Williton. The train not only managed to get through to Williton, but it also returned to Minehead later that night.

The volunteers were fortunate that not only did their sleeping coach have cooking facilities but they also had a reasonable stock of food between them. One of their number was an accomplished cook and, having decided to pool their food supplies, they realised that they were not going to starve. After they had eaten a warm meal they retired to bed. When they awoke next morning they found a completely changed world. Everything was under several feet of snow and where drifts had formed they were well above platform level. They could no longer discern where the WSR trackbed was; therefore the first task of the group was to dig their way from the coach to the station building. Having eaten their breakfast they decided that they would telephone the WSR to offer their assistance, when an attempt was made to reopen the line.

To ensure that when the WSR decided to attempt to run trains along the track they would not be delayed at Washford, the volunteers formed themselves into two gangs and set about the task of clearing the snow in the station area. When evening came, the two shovel gangs had cleared about half the site, working up and down the line from the level crossing, and clearing the snow down to rail level. The length of the site is 800ft and so our volunteers estimated that they had shovelled away approximately 13,000 cubic feet of snow and they had the aching muscles and blistered hands to prove it.

On the main road alongside the station a JCB slowly dug its way towards Minehead, to be followed shortly afterwards by a snow plough operating out of Williton. To add insult to injury the volunteers' cars, which were already buried, were covered in even more snow because of the efforts of the road clearance vehicles. Apart from a few tractors, the snow clearance vehicles and a few four-wheel-drive cars, nothing moved along the A39 all day and no trains managed to get through to Washford.

On the Monday morning the gangs continued to clear the snow with their shovels and early in the afternoon they had reached the over bridge in the cutting to the west of the station where the going was a little easier because the snow was not so deep. Because of the lack of traffic there was little sound and everything was still. Suddenly the gang paused when they heard the unmistakable sound of the whistle of *Vulcan* as it left Blue Anchor and the definite change in the note of the exhaust from the engine as it crossed Black Monkey bridge and started its climb up Washford bank. Shortly afterwards *Vulcan* came into sight, having battered it way through the drifts from Minehead. It succeeded in reaching Watchet that day, before returning to Minehead.

On the Tuesday, after they had been fortunate to augment their dwindling food supplies from the local shop, the volunteers continued with their task of snow clearance. That evening two members of the party decided that they had to try to return to their homes in the Bristol area, but less than two hours after their departure they returned to Washford; not only had they been unable to get through to either Bridgwater or Taunton but they had also been turned back by the police, who informed them that the roads were still blocked by snow drifts of between 18 and 20ft deep.

Because of the situation in the West Somerset area the BBC set up a temporary broadcasting station at Taunton (this was before the days of local radio, of course). This service was used to collect and disseminate information, and to put out emergency

Heavy snow in 1978 at Bishops Lydeard Station. (Stephen Edge)

messages. Later that afternoon a telephone call came through from the WSR at Minehead asking the 'gang of eight', as they had become known, to stand by with their shovels and if the works train that was about to leave arrived at Washford could they join it and assist those already on board in their efforts to get through to Williton.

For what seemed like ages *Vulcan* could be heard labouring up the 1/65 Washford bank, eventually pulling slowly into the station platform coupled to a DMU set. Pausing only for the team to climb aboard, and for the fireman to rebuild the fire (most of the fire having blasted out of the chimney in the attempt to climb the bank), once the boiler pressure had come round and the boiler was replenished, the train rapidly picked speed and charged through the lighter snow drifts. It almost reached Watchet, at which point deeper drifts necessitated a further increase in speed and almost continuous blasts on the horn of the DMU. About a quarter of a mile beyond Watchet the train came to a sudden halt, embedded in an impenetrable-seeming drift. In desperation the crew reversed the train to Watchet and charged the drift again, this time breaking through and continuing on to Williton.

On arrival at Williton it was decided that the attempt to get through to Bishops Lydeard should be left until the next day because all on board the train were exhausted. Due to the level of snow on the tracks and the low clearance of the DMU, it was also decided that it would be impossible for the DMU to get through to Bishops Lydeard without the assistance of a steam loco. The Washford shovel gang were dropped off at Washford when the train returned to Minehead.

The following morning the shovel gang rejoined the train at Washford which proceeded much more easily through Watchet and arrived at Williton without any major problems.

Beyond Williton all the works gang were of course venturing into the unknown, but after stopping at various isolated farms alongside the track to determine what help, if any, was needed, they arrived at Stogumber without too much trouble.

Crowcombe was reached after a certain amount of digging, but when the crew arrived there they could see deep drifts extending for some distance into the cutting beyond the station. *Vulcan* took a run at the drifts, but the resistance was too great and she was halted. When she retreated back to the station she left a beautiful impression of her front end in the compressed snow. The DMU was detached and the locomotive made another attempt to charge a way through the drift, which was again unsuccessful.

This meant that there was no alternative but for both gangs to start to shovel their way through the drifts, often waist-deep in the snow. When the crews reached the far end of the drift they clambered as far up the bank as far as they could, and watched in amazement as *Vulcan*, with regulator 'through the roof', forced its way through the remainder of the snow and promptly disappeared out of sight over the summit of the line, returning shortly afterwards to collect both the DMU and the shovel gangs, before proceeding on its way towards Bishops Lydeard. One more deep drift was encountered before their destination, but because the volunteers were again exhausted by their efforts it was left to *Vulcan* to repeatedly charge this large drift until the locomotive battered its way through and eventually made a triumphant entry into Bishops Lydeard Station.

News of the impending arrival of the train seemed to have travelled fast, because as soon as the train pulled up at the platform, two GPO vans drew up with 150 bags of accumulated mail for the Watchet and Minehead areas. As soon as the mail, together with some drugs urgently needed by a patient at Blue Anchor and some fodder for the livestock in isolated farms alongside the line, had been loaded, the train set off on its return journey.

The return trip was reasonably straightforward, because most of the track remained clear after the morning's efforts. After dropping off the fodder at various locations and unloading the mail for Watchet the entire crew were in high spirits when they considered all that they had achieved. As the train climbed Kentsford Bank the 'Washford shovellers' relished the thought that before long they would be having a well-earned cuppa, some hot food and they would soon be thawing and drying out in front of a blazing fire.

When they reached the top of the bank they suddenly realised that their dreams of refreshments and warm fires were still some way away, because the thaw had started and water was gushing across the track and pouring through the level crossing gate and across the road towards the houses on the opposite side of the road to the station. The residents were hastily putting sandbags in front of their doors in an attempt to stop their homes from being flooded; obviously this was not the first time they had faced this problem.

When the Washford crew alighted from the train they realised that they had a major problem on their hands. They found that the site drains were blocked with great lumps of ice and so they set about the task of clearing them. No sooner had they started on their task than they realised that the train they had recently alighted from was slowly reversing back towards them, with the footplate crew blowing the engines whistle furiously. The locomotive crew shouted to them that the track was blocked by a landslip in the cutting at the top of Washford

Bank and although the Minehead gang had started to clear the problem more help was needed. Four members of the Washford crew immediately climbed aboard the locomotive and set off to join the remainder of their colleagues who were clearing the landslip.

The depleted Washford crew continued with their efforts to clear the drains and after about an hour their efforts were rewarded when they found the drains were accepting the flood waters that were sweeping into them in great volume, making a roaring sound as they did so. To the relief of the owners of the houses opposite the station, the flood levels on the main road started to go down, enabling them to ease up a little in their efforts with the sandbags.

Having cleared the site drains the four volunteers made their way down the track to join the remainder of the gang trying to clear the landslip. The trouble had again been caused by blocked drains which in turn created another mill race, leading to the landslip. The volunteers worked late into the night to clear nearly a half mile of the track and unblock the drains on this stretch of line, to enable the train to get back to Minehead late that night.

Whilst the train had been struggling to return to Minehead the WSR had received a number of requests for help, to get people to hospital in Taunton, to bring patients back to the hospital in Minehead and enable those people trapped in Minehead to get away, if they needed to leave the area. Not only had the WSR obtained a special dispensation from the Ministry of Transport to operate a train carrying passengers over the section that had not yet been officially opened, they had also arranged for buses to bring people to and collect people from the special train that was to run on Thursday 24 February.

It appeared to our luckless volunteers that no sooner had their heads hit the pillow than they were woken with a message asking them if they could check the cutting in the area of the landslip, to ensure that another train could run through to Bishops Lydeard. Having carried the necessary clearance work our intrepid volunteers returned to the station at Washford to inform the WSR at Minehead that the cutting was clear for the train to come through. They were then asked if they would join the train on its arrival at Washford and assist the remainder of the crew to get the train through to Bishops Lydeard. *Vulcan* eventually arrived towing a TSO coach and a DMU trailer. Shortly after leaving Washford they saw the Washford and Doniford rivers in full spate, the latter spreading across the valley and flooding the roads with richly coloured, red-brown water, because of the large amounts of top soil in suspension in the floodwaters.

On arrival the bus was waiting to collect the passengers from the train, having delivered the passengers to travel to Minehead. These included patients from East Reach Hospital who were to be collected by ambulances from Minehead Station to take them on to either the local hospital or to their homes. This time the return trip to Minehead was uneventful, but both the passengers and the crew of the train were aware of the almost continual noise of Royal Navy helicopters flying overhead ferrying foodstuffs and fodder to remote farms and communities that still could not be reached by any other means. On arrival back at Washford the volunteers probably took the opportunity to catch up on some of their lost sleep.

The following morning (Friday), word came through that the A39 to Bridgwater had been opened and so it was with some relief that the volunteers packed their belongings into their cars and set off on the long drive home. As they drove away they no doubt reflected that they had taken part in an experience that, with luck, was not likely to happen again in their lifetime.

They may also have thought that if 53808 had been available, how much more easily she would have cleared the drifts, as she had done so often in the past when fitted with the small snow ploughs she used when she encountered similar problems in the Mendips. Articles praising the efforts of the staff and the volunteers in their efforts to connect Minehead with the outside world appeared in both the *Western Daily Press* and the *Somerset County Gazette*.

Readers will notice that I was rather vague about the arrangements concerning the bus service that met the trains that had fought their way through to Bishops Lydeard. The reason for this is because of a report that appeared in the *Western Daily Press* on 24 February, under the heading 'Drivers Train Truce', which read:

> Western National drivers temporarily settled their differences with the West Somerset Railway yesterday. A bus was laid on to meet the company's second train to battle through the snow and carry passengers the last five miles into Taunton.
>
> The drivers belong to the National Union of Railwaymen which has threatened to black the company's efforts to run trains into Taunton. It says the service would threaten the jobs of their members.
>
> Railway officials obtained special clearance from the Transport Ministry for the journey, part of which was over track so far unlicensed for passenger use.
>
> Nearly thirty people many of whom had been marooned in Minehead travelled to Taunton. Hospital patients who had been airlifted out of West Somerset were ferried back to Bishops Lydeard by ambulance for the return trip.

Although it does not say so, the report clearly implies that the WSR made some kind of special arrangement with the members of the NUR driving the Western National buses. A number of people I have spoken to who were with the WSR at this time, including Mr van den Arund himself, are adamant that no such deal was struck. I accept their word of course, but what puzzles is how this co-operation between the two parties came about, with the mutual distrust that prevailed at the time.

As the following report that appeared in the *Somerset County Gazette* on 17 March made clear this was not the end of the problems with snow for the railway. Under the heading 'Hidden Snow that Wouldn't Go Away' it stated:

> Incredibly, workmen were still clearing snow from the West Somerset Railway line this week – but it was snow that had laid insulated under a blanket of mud. During the recent arctic spell about 200 tons of sodden earth formed a landslide in a deep cutting east of Crowcombe Station blocking the line. Last weekend earth moving vehicles, and men with shovels moved tons of the obstruction, but on Monday they found at the bottom of the landslip a snowdrift four feet deep.

'The thick covering of earth must have insulated the snow. Our men dumped it (the snow) to one side and let it melt away, but the earth has to be carried a considerable way out of the cutting,' said railway company secretary Mr Chris van den Arund.

Heavy rain squalls brought the work to a stand still on Tuesday, although it was possible by then to get a works train through.

Mr van den Arund then added 'the company is not expecting any help from the line's owners, the Somerset County Council, in paying for the clearance job, which was estimated to have cost about £2,000, but we hope that something may come of a promise we had last week from Mr Tim Horam Parliamentary Under Secretary for Transport, who said that he would put our case to the emergency minister Mr Denis Howell.'

If the staff and volunteers thought that their efforts in the snow would improve their relations with the incumbents in County Hall they were about to be disappointed. When the report of the finance sub-committee came before the full council for discussion only one councillor argued strongly on behalf of the WSR. Councillor Eric Jackson Stevens, who represented the Glastonbury area, pleaded for the council to show more patience and understanding in their dealings with the West Somerset Railway Co. He went on to say that, in his opinion, restricting the railway's activities to the Minehead–Watchet section would sign the 'death warrant' of the company, adding that he supported the efforts of the railway to run a commuter service between Taunton and Minehead.

Cllr Jackson-Stevens then went on to ask the council to intervene in the dispute between the WSR and the NUR and try to persuade the union to drop its opposition to WSR proposals. Finally he stated, 'I want to see this railway line retained as a tourist attraction for Somerset, and I would like the Council to adopt a wider outlook, and to show a little more patience on their part.'

Other councillors pointed out that the repayment problem was due to the failure of the county council to honour their promise to loan the railway a total of £60,000, when they refused to forward any further payments after only £33,942 had been made available.

In reply Cllr Luff denied suggestions that he had got his knife into the company, and went on to say, 'The reason that we lent them this money was to get commuter trains into Taunton and at the moment this does not seem possible.' He added, 'I am not against the railway, but I am the custodian of the ratepayers' money and I have to ensure that the sum of £33,000 is paid back in September.'

Denying claims that the council were trying to put the railway out of business, Cllr Penelope Phillips, chairman of the policy committee who had also questioned the practicability of the commuter service, stated in reply, 'The council has charged us to ensure that its money was well invested and that this was an economic proposition. However we will take into consideration the comments that have been made.' It seemed rather odd that the council was so concerned with the economic viability of a <u>loan</u> repayment of £33,000, whilst at the same time they made no attempt to establish the economic viability of the annual subsidy of £300,000 they were paying to the bus services in the county at that time.

As will be seen below, the WSR ignored the council's suggestion that they should terminate their services at Watchet when they extended their service to Stogumber on 7 May.

Whilst these arguments raged, the railway was continuing its efforts to attract as many passengers to the line as possible. The first major attraction for the new season was the first Gala Day, which was held on 7 May. The events announced included: steam and diesel services between Minehead and Williton; Hymek 7017 and other stock on display; numerous exhibits such as models on show; railway art exhibition and so on.

Another event, one which was not announced until shortly before it happened, was the reopening of the line as far as Stogumber. Because of the lack of run-round facilities at Stogumber the service was operated by a shuttle service of railcars from Williton, although a through DMU service from Minehead operated occasionally. Other events included slide and film shows at Minehead and demonstrations of steam-powered lorries and other vintage vehicles.

The following week, on 17 June, plans were made for the first train to run from Paddington to Minehead in nine years, bringing MPs and other dignitaries to visit the line. Other excursions arranged during the year included 300 visitors who travelled by train to Taunton and then by bus to Williton and another group travelling from London to Barry and across the Bristol Channel to Watchet and then on by steam train to Minehead. This service was a joint venture with R.A. Campbell, who operated a number of steamer services in the Channel.

These ventures were so successful that it was hoped to arrange a number of similar events. An event that was not successful was the issue of combined rail and admission tickets to the Stogumber Fête from Minehead and other stations along the line. The tickets, which cost £1, also included a minibus service from the station to the fête. Only sixteen people used the service and it was not repeated.

Despite an increase of between 12.5 per cent and 20 per cent in the fares charged on the railway from 8 May, the number of passengers using the line continued to show a considerable increase on the figures for the previous year. Another feature that was repeated in this year was the draw organised by the association to once again to boost its stock fund, but this year the value of the first prize had been increased to £100.

Because of the combined effects of the bad weather, the economies made by the board and the increased number of passengers travelling on the line, the chairman, Mr Stevens, was able to announce at the end of July that the railway had made its first half-yearly operating profit of almost £2,000 for the period from 1 January to 30 June 1978. He continued, 'This is a wonderful performance, our profits are climbing, despite the bad weather and falling holiday trade. Our fame is spreading with coach loads of people visiting the railway from the Bristol, and Exeter areas, also a large number of German and Dutch tourists were visiting the line to see the *Flockton Flyer* which had been shown on television in those countries.'

He went on to say that the line was, at that point, taking £7,000 a month through the booking offices, compared with £4,500 in the same period the previous year. Also, the passenger figures had increased to 75,000 for the year to date compared with 50,000 for the whole of the previous year. Finally he added, 'What delights us most is that the best is still to come.' The height of the holiday season was still to come and the company was confident of doing even better. Later he stated that he hoped that these results would start to thaw the strained relationship between the WSR and the county council and that soon the two parties would start to move towards a better understanding.

Further good news came shortly afterwards, when it was announced that Mr Douglas Fear had settled his claim against the company out of court. The sum of £8,500 was accepted by Mr Fear because, as he informed the press, he had no wish to jeopardise the future of the company and it was for this reason that he had also agreed to accept payment of this sum to be spread over a period of three years.

Two weeks later an industrial court sitting at Exeter dismissed a claim by Major Anthony Griffiths against the railway for unfair dismissal. The former general manager of the company told the tribunal, 'When I joined the railway I was appalled at the way the railway appeared and the apparently total disregard of the basic safety rules.' After claiming that he ran into staff trouble when he tried to implement proper schedules for the locomotives, he continued, 'The technical knowledge of the staff was minimal against my long technical and professional background', and it was for this reason that he considered that he had been unfairly dismissed. After listening to the evidence given by the directors of the WSR the tribunal came to the conclusion that Major Griffiths had been truly redundant.

Now that these problems had been resolved the directors felt that they could now proceed with the launch of the next public share issue for £60,000. Before long Mr Stevens was able to announce that contributions were coming in at a rate of £1,000 a day, with contributions ranging from £1 from an old age pensioner in Williton to a donation of £500 from a shareholder in London who had heard of the railway's problems through the press.

When the financial results for 1978 were discussed at the AGM held on 24 March of the following year Mr Stevens was able to announce that for the first time the company was able to declare an annual profit of £500. Unfortunately 'exceptional items', for example the payment to Mr Fear, would swallow up this profit. Nevertheless, it was a considerable improvement on the previous year's figures which had shown a loss of £22,000. In the year under review, he stated, fare income was up by 42 per cent on the summer diesel service and by 74 per cent on the steam services. Of great significance to the line as a year-round service was the 30 per cent increase in the income on the line during the winter timetable period. These results were achieved because the number of passenger journeys undertaken on the line exceeded 150,000 for the first time.

Any hope that a thaw in relations with the county council might have materialised, referred to when the half-yearly results for the previous year were announced, were dashed when Mr Stevens launched a bitter attack on the attitude of the council officials. He claimed that the officials refused to take the line seriously, 'Instead of just dismissing us as a fun railway for the tourists the council must start taking us seriously as a public transport system.'

Referring to the draft report that the council had drawn up, as required by the new Transport Act, he stated that the council was required to consult with transport operators, district and parish councils, and the council was then charged with developing a co-ordinated and efficient transport system. Instead, he said they were merely reporting on the status quo, rather than making a constructive policy of improvements: 'Their draft plan is only half the truth, and misses out a lot of information, by almost ignoring the existence of the railway. This plan is an apology for the council's continued subsidies to the bus services of almost a third of a million pounds a year and of its declared intention of not granting anything for the railway.'

After emphasising that the railway was not seeking grant aid or subsidies, he claimed, 'that by deliberately trying to minimise the railways effects on the district, and by omitting details of the proposals that the railway had put forward, they were failing to inform the district and parish councils of the true position'.

It will, I hope, be clear to the reader that apart from the problems with the NUR and the county council, the railway thought that it could look forward to the next year, 1979, with a great deal of optimism.

1 Much of the information on the efforts of the volunteers in clearing the snow was based on an article written shortly after the events took place by Chris Schofield; the other members of the party were Gordon Baldham, Gordon Dyte, Richard Locke, Chris Longley, Adrian Noble, Nigel Smart and Dave Martin.

The first Gala Weekend at Bishops Lydeard, 1979.

14

1979: A Disappointing Year

As in previous years the WSR continued to search for new ideas that would increase the numbers of passengers using the line and provide much-needed income. In addition, they looked at successful events which had been held previously to determine if they could be improved upon.

One such idea was the 'boat trains', differentiating from the previous year by also allowing local people to participate. On 21 April a train left Minehead at 12.30 p.m. bound for Watchet where the passengers were to board the MV *Balmoral* for a return trip to Minehead. Members of the Lea Valley Railway Club had left Paddington at 7.40 a.m. on a train consisting of air-conditioned stock hauled by a Class 45/1 diesel loco. The train called at Reading and Bristol Parkway before arriving at Barry where they transferred to the *Balmoral* to travel across the Bristol Channel to Watchet, then continuing their journey by steam train to Minehead. After walking along the sea front to the harbour, they re-boarded the steamer for their return trip to London via Barry. This arrangement ensured that both the steamer company and the WSR avoided 'empty stock' movements.

The demand for tickets from local people for this excursion was so great that the train from Minehead consisted of nine coaches, of which the last two were a 2-car DMU set which gave much-needed 'banking' assistance to *Vulcan* in its efforts to climb Washford bank. As the train passed Butlins, the 250 passengers on board were able to see the *Balmoral* making her way from Barry towards Watchet. When the train arrived at Williton, after the passengers had alighted at Watchet, the 2-car DMU set was uncoupled from the remainder of the excursion train to enable the 2-car DMU to continue its journey to Stogumber. After running around the train, *Vulcan* returned to Watchet to collect the rail enthusiasts who had travelled from London. In the meantime, Mr David Clayton, the chairman of the West Somerset District Council, had given a speech welcoming the trippers to West Somerset.

Another innovative idea that was dealt a severe blow by the actions of members of the NUR and BR management was an excursion train that was planned to run from Paddington to Minehead on 17 June. The first blow came when BR demanded £43,000 for the new set of points needed to allow the train to proceed from the main line to the branch. When the WSR suggested that the excursion train should run to Taunton and the passengers should be transferred to buses for the link to Bishops Lydeard, the NUR's bus driver members promptly 'blacked' the service, forcing the Western National Bus Co. to withdraw the service it had planned to operate. An NUR spokesman in London was reported to have said, 'We will not allow any through services, either buses, or trains, into Taunton until we have discussed with Western National the effect they will have on the profitability of bus routes in the area. Our people are not in favour of private railways being run to the detriment of public services. The feeling is so strong that we have got to be receptive to our memberships views the Union has to represent their interests.' Mr Viv Taylor, who was the NUR Southwest divisional secretary, repeated almost verbatim the spokesman's words later, but added, 'The new bus shuttle is seen by us as a stopgap that we are not prepared to participate in.'

As the drivers concerned had inconvenienced many of their passengers only two weeks previously by calling a series of unofficial lightning strikes in pursuit of a dispute with their management, they received little sympathy from the general public. On learning that the county council would sympathetically consider any request by a private company to operate the service the railway set about the task of finding a private bus company to operate the link, once the WSR opened the line to Bishops Lydeard.

Another Gala Weekend was held this year, over 9–10 June, which coincided with the opening of the extension of the line to Bishops Lydeard. The omens for the weekend did not look good when on the Friday evening before the event *Victor* was failed at Minehead with blown boiler tubes. In spite of the frantic efforts of the fitters, all attempts to complete the repairs to the locomotive for the following day failed. Red faces were avoided when the Diesel and Electric Group were able to provide Hymek 7017 and a crew to drive it at short notice, which was used to work the diagram that had been prepared for the second steam loco.

When the first day of the Gala arrived, the platform was crowded with enthusiasts, holidaymakers and local parishioners to witness Mr Ulick Huntington, the chairman of the local parish council, send the first train from Bishops Lydeard on its way. The train, hauled by *Vulcan*, had 200 passengers on board on what was to prove an eventful journey. As the train climbed Crowcombe bank it encountered two farm dogs who, being unaccustomed to sharing the track bed with railway trains, refused to move in spite of repeated blasts on the locomotive whistle by the driver. The train was brought to a standstill and the fireman got down from the foot plate to persuade the dogs that it would be far better for their general well-being if they were to have their morning naps elsewhere in future. After this incident the train continued on its way to Minehead without further delays.

This incident, combined with the unexpected number of people visiting the line, resulted in most of the trains running between 30 and 45 minutes late for the remainder of the day. Afterwards, a rather embarrassed Richard Stevens apologised to the many visitors to the line whose journeys had been somewhat delayed when he said, 'Our poor time-keeping performance could not have come at a worse time. We had advertised nationally the new service, we have always been so proud of our time keeping record, not a solitary train has been late until last weekend.'

He explained that most of the delays had been caused by *Victor*'s bronchial troubles and added, 'He blew a few tubes on Friday night. After working late into the night, the fitters had replaced the faulty tubes, only for the locomotive to blow some more, early on Saturday morning.'

Few of the hundreds of enthusiasts who turned up seemed to mind; as Mr Peter Stokes from Birmingham explained, 'I didn't notice. It was such an experience to be able to travel such a distance by steam train.' The private bus operator who had provided the replacement bus service, after the NUR members refused to work the buses that the Western National Co. had made available, said that they were very happy with the arrangements because between thirty and forty passengers had boarded the bus for each trip.

Other events held on this day included displays of vintage vehicles and model railways, art and craft exhibitions and trade stands put up by local organisations at the various stations along the line. A special stamp issue was also on sale to mark the first train reaching Bishops Lydeard. Despite the problems encountered the event was considered to be a great success.

Once the Gala event was over, except for special events, steam trains only ran between Minehead and Williton, due to the lack of facilities to water the engines at Bishops Lydeard. It would have been impossible for the small tank engines then available to do a round trip from Minehead without replenishing their tanks. Even though there was, at this time, a water crane in operatation in the 'six foot' at the north end of Williton Station that could be used to replenish the tanks of steam engines travelling through to Bishops Lydeard, the margin was extremely fine and the crane was normally only used to replenish locos returning to Minehead, until larger engines became available for use on the line some years later. 2-car diesel multiple units provided the service between Williton and Bishops Lydeard, although later, when three sets of compatible 2-car units became available, sometimes 4- or 6-car trains were run when required.

For this reason, with the exception of the occasional through DMU service from Minehead, most passengers travelling through to Bishops Lydeard from Minehead or other stations west of Watchet had to change trains at Williton.

Another effort to attract passengers later in the year was the autumn open day which was held on Saturday 7 October to introduce passengers to the new winter timetable, which had started on the previous Monday, 2 October. A flat fare of 40p enabled passengers to travel to any station on any train. I have been unable to find any indication that this idea was a great success and as it was not repeated I can only conclude that the company must have incurred a substantial loss on this project.

One piece of equipment that caused many traffic problems on its journey to Minehead in April was the 50-ton locomotive turntable which the association had procured for £1,000 from Pwllheli in North Wales. Unfortunately, this has proved to be a rather long-term investment and the turntable was finally installed in 2009.

Another purchase that was to be of great benefit to the railway in the more immediate future was the private purchase, on behalf of the association, of four Pullman coaches, which arrived in the former passing loop at Crowcombe Heathfield – which at that time had become a siding – on 23 July. These coaches, which had only been built in 1960 by Metro Cammell, were declared surplus to requirements by BR. A group of volunteers immediately set about the task of converting these coaches to form the Quantock Pullman

Set (later to become the Quantock Belle Luxury Dining Train) which was planned to start operations the following year. Because the work had proceeded much faster than expected the association was able to announce that it would be able to run a series of special 'mince pie and sherry' trains over the Christmas period using two of the coaches on which the conversion work had been completed.

In spite of the continuing problems with the county council over the outcome of their transport survey, outlined in the previous chapter, the finance sub-committee did recommend to the full council that the inflation-proof clause contained in the lease and due to come into operation in the next year (1980) should be deleted, thereby ensuring that the rent would remain fixed at £17,500 per annum, at least for the foreseeable future.

At the very end of the year, on 21 December, came the first news that the WSR were considering opening another station. Mr van den Arund announced that the company was looking for concrete platform sections. He said, 'We are looking for a disused platform which must be at least 120ft long. Some are still probably lying around on BR rubbish dumps due to station closures, and we would like to get our hands on one.' The station, which when built was to be called Doniford Halt, was intended to serve the local community and also the nearby Freshfields Holiday Village.

A suitable platform was eventually located on the site of the former station at Montacute, on the by-then-closed Taunton–Yeovil branch line. Volunteers dismantled it and after arranging to transport the sections from the site it was re-installed on the Minehead branch. To add to the atmosphere of a Great Western halt, volunteers later arranged for the 'pagoda' hut at Cove Station, on the former Exe Valley Line, to be dismantled, removed and re-erected at this location.

In spite of all the efforts of the staff and the volunteers who had worked so hard on the railway during the year, their hopes that the railway had perhaps started to turn the corner, based on the encouraging results of the previous year, were dashed when the chairman announced to the shareholders at the WSR AGM, held early in the new year, that although passenger journeys had increased by 3,500 during the year ending 31 October 1979, resulting in an increase of 17 per cent in fare income, the company had made a trading loss of £20,000. The loss incurred was in part due to increased staff and fuel costs. The poor results were not helped by the number of passengers travelling in the summer months being below expectations.

More bad news followed when Mr Stevens announced that the company had been unable to repay the £17,000 loan from the county council when it was due. He then went on to appeal to the shareholders saying, 'Two years ago the support of the shareholders enabled the company to progress, and altogether they had contributed £40,000 to the £60,000 that was then sought. The company does now need the balance of £20,000.' He continued, 'The directors have taken up more shares, and are asking the public to do the same.' Claiming that £700 had already been raised so far that year in new applications, he stated that a further £5 from every shareholder would raise the £20,000 that was needed to achieve the increase in working capital required.

15

1980: The Struggle Continues

In spite of the gloomy news at the Annual General Meeting, both the association and the company continued in their efforts to attract more passengers to increase the income on the railway.

One new venture by the association was an attempt to maximise the income from the Pullman coaches by using one of them, on which the refurbishment work had been completed, as a restaurant facility at Bishops Lydeard Station. An announcement in July stated that the coach, which was located in the short siding leading to the goods shed (now the museum), could seat twenty-four people and was open on Sundays only. A waitress service would provide light refreshments, including sandwiches, cakes, teas and coffees, and also strawberries and cream. The buffet service was available both to passengers and visitors. In a 'Siphon G van', a former Great Western milk van next to the Pullman coach, the association started what has now become their thriving sales outlet, selling a rapidly expanding range of railway curios and memorabilia.

A later attempt to create a similar restaurant service at Minehead, when a second coach became available, was not so successful because of the lack of volunteers to operate the facility. Further on in the year, on 7 November, the Quantock Pullman started to operate dining car services from Bishops Lydeard to Minehead. The trains left Bishops Lydeard on both Saturdays and Sundays at 12.15 p.m. and arrived at Minehead at 1.40 p.m. A four-course luncheon was offered for the sum of £9.25 per person; all seats were reserved and had to be booked in advance. A typical menu on the down trip consisted of, among a choice of starters, asparagus soup, followed by roast chicken in honey sauce, roast potatoes and mixed vegetables. Apple pie and cream often appeared as one of the sweet selections on the menu, followed by cheese and biscuits, and coffee. At Christmas time turkey and plum pudding maintained the festive spirit. After a brief stroll along the sea front the diners returned to the train for the return journey, which left at 2.30 p.m., and by the time the train passed through Dunster they were tucking into crumpets, éclairs, gâteaux and afternoon tea. The refreshments served in the afternoon were not included in the price of £9.25.

This service was started by the association and therefore was staffed entirely by volunteers. A number of those people who worked on the first of these trains are still involved with the railway or the Quantock Belle service. One volunteer, who joined the Quantock Belle service in 1983, is Mark Smith, who became the managing director of the company.

When the service started it was on a trial basis, for a period of two months between 7 November and 3 January. Before the trial period was up the project was considered to be so successful that it was decided that it would continue to operate until further notice.

Another attraction to appear at Bishops Lydeard Station was the extensive model railway layout, called 'Tamerig', which had been exhibited nationally. It was housed in premises that the Taunton Model Railway Club had built themselves, between the former goods shed and the main station buildings on the down platform. The building was opened in November and held a special Christmas exhibition on 20 and 21 December, when Santa made a surprise visit with his bran tub. The rental from these premises provided a welcome source of income for the company.

In December the company again organised 'Santa Steam Specials', with trains operating from Bishops Lydeard at 12.15 p.m. and Minehead at 10.15 a.m. and 2.30 p.m. Those wishing to see Santa could also board the train at other stations along the line, simply by signalling the driver to stop! Tickets for this event cost £1 and included a round trip on a steam train, a visit to Santa's grotto and a gift from Santa himself.

To return to events that took place earlier in the year, another innovative idea to increase the number of passengers using the line – at the same time as increasing the fare income – was the decision to advertise 'Early Bird' workers' tickets. Passengers travelling on the 7.30 a.m. train from Minehead or the 8.10 a.m. train from Williton could travel at half price, and return by any service that day. Another promotional offer comprised 'day tripper' tickets. These tickets were available on Saturdays only and if one person paid the full adult fare of £2 from Minehead to Taunton, they could take three other people with them for just 50p each.

The first indication that all was not well in the new season was the announcement by Mr Richard Stevens, the chairman of the WSR, who said that, 'Tourism this year, particularly in July, was a nightmare and cost us thousands of pounds. The number of passengers carried was approximately 7 per cent down on steam trains, and 2 per cent down on diesel services.' The only consolation the railway could gain from these disappointing figures was that their downturn was not as great as that experienced by other tourist attractions in the area.

Of even greater concern to all those involved with the railway was his observation that, 'The county council have examined our books, and have agreed that unless something is done about the rent, we shall have a serious cash flow problem.' Shortly after this announcement came the news that Mr van den Arund, who had been the company's publicity officer, and who, with Mr Stevens, had met Mr Sid Weighell at Unity House in London in an attempt to resolve the problems with the unions, amongst his many other tasks, had been made redundant. Some of the seasonal staff would also not be replaced. Explaining that the railway had been unable to avoid the general financial recession affecting the whole country, he said, 'It is a miserable thing to do, but one can't keep people on because one has known them a number of years, if by doing so, it would put us in an intolerable financial position. Our revenue is about 25 per cent up on last year, and for this reason the board were remaining calm.' The board also announced the appointment of Mr Len Clark as general manager in March, but unfortunately he was forced to resign on health grounds three months later.

Later Mr Stevens was able to announce that after protracted negotiations with the county council they had agreed to waive the £7,000 rent due for the current half year ending on 31 October, and the whole of the rent of £17,500 due in the year 1980/81. The repayment of a loan instalment of £4,000 had also been postponed until October 1981.

A county council spokesman later said, 'The council had noted that the season had been a bad one for tourism, and it had regard to the company's cash flow problems for the winter.' He said the company had been informed that the council would not contemplate waiving the rent beyond October 1981 and it would then expect the company to meet its obligations in full.

Another event that aroused considerable interest amongst the public was the announcement that a series of trials were taking place on the line with a road/rail bus. This vehicle, which was based on a Bristol LH bus, used a principle developed from a vehicle tested on Sadler Ashby's test track at Droxford in Hampshire in 1973. The vehicle ran on its rubber tyres, but the front pair of wheels had been replaced by a bogie with four pneumatic-tyred wheels and two solid rubber guide wheels which were raised when running on the road. A similar pair of guide wheels were fitted to the rear of the vehicle.

The vehicle, which was produced by the Centre of Alternative Industrial and Technological Systems, initiated by the Lucas Aerospace Combine Shop Stewards Committee, ran on rails from Bishops Lydeard Station to Roebuck Lane level crossing, where it continued its travels along the road. Many local residents were convinced that this was a last attempt by the board of the WSR to ensure that passengers could travel from Minehead to Taunton, without the need for interchange facilities at Bishops Lydeard. They were also convinced that provided the bus was not driven by a member of the NUR it would work. Further trials were undertaken in Edinburgh shortly afterwards and on the WSR again the following year.

Whether news of this development reached Paddington is not known, but it seems strange that shortly afterwards it was announced that BR Western Region Management were holding talks with leaders of the NUR over the re-instatement of the link to the Minehead branch. It was claimed by BR that if the branch was to accept traffic to and from the WSR it would result in an additional income to BR of £250,000 from these services. After the talks had finished Mr Viv Taylor for the NUR dismissed these claims by BR, stating that the figure would be much lower. He continued, 'Our members are still opposed to the West Somerset Railway running its trains into Taunton Station. Our railway members are even more adamant about it than our bus members. Both groups fear that such a service would put their jobs at risk.' Just how a quarter of a million pounds worth of extra business could jeopardise his members' jobs he could not explain.

Mr Taylor continued, 'I am afraid we are in an impasse situation, and I don't see any way out of it in the immediate future. The company [the WSR] knows that running their trains in Taunton would not be in the interest of our members.' Far from being depressed when he heard the news, the chairman of the WSR, commented, 'The fact that BR and the unions are talking at all about the link up between the West Somerset Railway and Taunton is positive progress. Everybody would agree that this is a new move, there has been a meeting and this is the furthest anyone has gone in the last four years. The West Somerset Railway all along has taken the view that this is a matter between BR, and the NUR and it is not for the WSR to talk to the union. BR has at last appreciated the benefits of the link, and they are now trying to persuade their work people of the value of those benefits.'

In response to a long-standing open invitation from the directors of the WSR, it was announced that the NUR would be sending some of its officers on a fact-finding mission to the West Somerset Railway, early in the new year.

The previous year the Diesel & Electric Preservation Group had launched an appeal to raise funds to purchase a Class 14 *Teddybear* diesel locomotive. The engine, which had been built at Swindon Works in 1964, had been in service with BR for only five years before being sold to Blue Circle Cement at Westbury, who had announced in 1979 that this engine was now surplus to their requirements. Now came the news that their appeal had been successful. At the time it was not realised what a benefit the purchase of this locomotive by the Group would be to the WSR in the difficult times they were to experience shortly after it was delivered the following year.

Other news that was not so beneficial to the WSR was the announcement by Mr Michael Street, a director of S&M Street, the road haulage company which, as mentioned in an earlier chapter, was associated with the company operating in Watchet Docks, that 'Trying to preserve something as pleasant as the West Somerset Railway is all very well but can we afford it?'

This outburst was made at a meeting that had been called by the villagers of Kilve who were concerned about the number of heavy lorries using the A39 road through the village. The meeting, was also attended by representatives of other villages along the road, who were affected, as well as Mr K.R. Knight, who was secretary of the Road Haulage Association, and also Mr Street. In reply to the concerns raised at the meeting, Mr Street said that his drivers would prefer to use the A358 road if it were improved to a standard that made it preferable to the A39, even though it added 13 miles to the round trip. He continued 'but there are snags – mainly the three railway bridges, on the section of the road between Williton and Taunton, which were too low for lorries. The bridge at Combe Florey would be particularly expensive to alter, set as it is, at an awkward angle to the road. It would have to be widened as well as heightened,' he claimed.

Mr Brown of Stogursey who was also at the meeting pointed out that the bridges were owned by the county council, and for this reason the meeting decided to ask the Somerset County Council to carry out a feasibility study on improving the A358 road and raising the bridges. This suggestion encouraged those councillors who were not supporters of the WSR to redouble their efforts to persuade the railway to terminate their services at Williton (from Minehead), and this was one problem that the beleaguered board could have done without in the difficult months that were ahead.

Difficult as the problems facing the railway were, the rival bus services appeared to be having an even worse time. The Western National Bus Co. announced that it would be making cuts to a number of its services in the West Somerset area and that redundancies were possible. But it was the decision of the bus company to close the Minehead bus station, due to the heavy losses that the company were making, that resulted in fierce criticism of the bus operator from the West Somerset District Council. The chairman of the council, Mr Tony Holman, pointed out that, in contrast to claims made by some of the drivers of the bus company, the routes on which the most severe service cuts were being made were those that were not in competition with the WSR.

The chief executive of the council also expressed his disappointment that the bus company had refused to retain a part of the site for bus services, as the council had requested. It was also pointed out, both by members of the council and other parties in the town, that the closure would not only affect passengers using Western National services, but small local private companies who also used the site as a departure point for their excursion trips around the surrounding area. It was also pointed out that long-distance coaches bringing visitors to the area might consider withdrawing their services due to the absence of a coach station.

Despite all these appeals, the bus company announced that it had received several lucrative offers for the site and that the sale would be completed and the bus station closed in the autumn. As a result of this decision nine drivers were made redundant, one of whom, Mr John Tozer, had worked for the company for thirty-three years; other drivers had between twenty and thirty-two years of service.

This did not mark the end of the bus company's problems, because a few weeks later a member of the Watchet Town Council, Major Alex Gordon, told the council meeting held on 7 December that he thought, 'The Western National Bus Co. should be asked to stop all services so that a private company could give a useful service at a useful price.' He then went on to claim, 'Many old age pensioners do not use the service because they cannot afford to.' In spite of these problems, the attitude of the bus company drivers showed no signs of any change.

The association continued to hold its Summer Draw, the prize this year being £100, with the cost of a ticket 10p, but they now faced competition from the Somerset & Dorset Railway Trust who were also trying to raise funds to complete the overhaul of locomotive 53808. Their tickets were also 10p, but the first prize was only £70.

Few people who had been involved with the railway during the year were surprised when the chairman of the company announced that the WSR had made a further trading loss of £30,000 during the year ending 30 October 1980. This loss would, of course, have been much larger had it not been for the concessions given by the county council earlier in the year, on the rents that had been due for payment during this period.

16

1981: Can Things Get Any Worse?

Many people involved with the railway at the start of the new year were asking this question, but few believed that the answer would be in the affirmative.

The year started promisingly enough when the railway, in an attempt to exploit the problems that the rival bus company was experiencing, announced that it would be operating an 'improved' winter timetable from January, 'in response to public demand'. However, by the time the summer timetable was due to come into operation the company was in dire straits. They had only one serviceable steam locomotive, together with a single 2-car diesel railcar set, and a chronic shortage of rolling stock, which meant they had no hope of operating the timetable that had been published.

When the Annual General Meeting of the company was held in March to discuss the previous year's results, some of the shareholders were aware of the difficulties facing the railway and seemed determined to try to rectify the situation. As soon as the first item on the agenda, the adoption of the Annual Accounts, was announced it was evident that the directors were facing a number of rather hostile shareholders. After the accounts had been presented to the meeting and the members were asked for their observations, there was an immediate reaction. One member described the accounts as a 'hotch potch', whilst others found a number of faults in the way they were presented. After Mr Stevens had outlined the reasons for the methods of accounting, the accounts were eventually adopted.

This did not mark the end of the problems for the directors; when the meeting moved on to the 'Any Other Business' section of the agenda, Mr Alan Body of Watchet launched a bitter attack on the board by asking why 'the board had not diverted at least some of the income the railway had received in the past year to buy the replacement locos the railway needed'. He went on to claim that locomotives were available at bargain prices at that time. In reply Mr Hugh Perrett, a director, agreed that locomotives were available for as little as £500, but they carried no guarantee and their purchase could be fraught with problems.

Mr Body retorted, 'If these problems are not overcome, our railway will fail because we have an over-ambitious timetable, and no means of fulfilling it. It would have been better to buy the locos we need. If, as it appears, members of the board have not got the time to acquire the rolling stock we require, would it not be better for all of them to say so and

West Somerset Railway
MINEHEAD - WATCHET - TAUNTON
WINTER TIMETABLE

		MONDAYS			TUES, THURS, FRI				
Minehead	dep	07.30	16.40	18.10	07.30	09.30	12.40	16.40	18.10
Dunster	dep	R	R	R	R	R	R	R	R
Blue Anchor	dep	07.41	16.51	18.21	07.41	09.41	12.51	16.51	18.21
Washford	dep	07.48	16.58	18.28	07.48	09.48	12.58	16.58	18.28
Watchet	dep	07.55	17.05	18.35	07.55	09.55	13.05	17.05	18.35
Williton	arr	08.00	17.10	18.40	08.00	10.00	13.10	17.10	18.40

Williton	dep	08.10	17.31	18.45	08.10	10.05	14.10	17.31	18.45
Watchet	dep	08.16	17.37	18.51	08.16	10.11	14.16	17.37	18.51
Washford	dep	08.23	17.44	18.58	08.23	10.18	14.23	17.44	18.58
Blue Anchor	dep	08.30	17.51	19.05	08.30	10.25	14.30	17.51	19.05
Dunster	dep	R	R	R	R	R	R	R	R
Minehead	arr	08.41	18.02	19.16	08.41	10.36	14.41	18.02	19.16

		WEDNESDAYS					SATURDAYS				SUNDAYS	
											STEAM	STEAM
Minehead	dep	07.30	09.20	12.40	14.50	18.10	09.00	13.00	14.50	18.10	10.15	14.30
Dunster	dep	R	R	R	R	R	R	R	R	R	R	R
Blue Anchor	dep	07.41	09.31	12.51	15.01	18.21	09.11	13.11	15.01	18.21	R	R
Washford	dep	07.48	09.38	12.58	15.08	18.28	09.18	13.18	15.08	18.28	R	R
Watchet	dep	07.55	09.45	13.05	15.15	18.35	09.25	13.25	15.15	18.35	10R42	14R57
Williton	dep	08.00	09.51	13.10	15.21	18.40	09.31	13.30	15.21	18.40	10R55	15R10
Stogumber	dep		R		R		R		R		R	R
Crowcombe	dep		R		R		R		R		R	R
Bishop's Lydeard	arr		10.20		15.50		10.00		15.50		11.30	16.00
Taunton BR Station†	arr		(10.45)		(16.15)		(10.25)		(16.15)		(11.45)	(16.10)
Taunton Castle Way†	arr		(10.55)		(16.25)		(10.35)		(16.25)		(11.50)	(16.15)
LONDON Paddington	arr		(13.37)		(18.36)		(13.22)		(18.36)			
BRISTOL Temple Meads	arr		(12.06)		(17.06)		(12.06)		(17.06)			
BIRMINGHAM New St.	arr		(14.45)		(19.48)		(14.45)		(19.48)			
EXETER St. Davids	arr		(11.32)		(17.15)		(11.32)		(17.15)			

											STEAM	STEAM
LONDON Paddington	dep		(08.25)		(13.20)		(07.25)		(13.20)			
BIRMINGHAM New St.	dep		(08.15)		(13.15)			(13.15)				
BRISTOL Temple Meads	dep		(10.07)		(15.00)		(08.05)		(15.00)			
EXETER St Davids	dep		(09.24)		(15.56)		(08.37)		(15.56)			
Taunton Castle Way†	dep		(11.00)		(16.30)		(09.30)		(16.30)		(11.50)	(16.15)
Taunton BR Station †	dep		(11.10)		(16.40)		(09.40)		(16.40)		(11.55)	(16.20)
Bishop's Lydeard	dep		11.35		17.05		10.05		17.05		12·15	16.30
Crowcombe	dep		R		R		R		R		R	R
Stogumber	dep		R		R		R		R		R	R
Williton	dep	08.10	12.01	14.10	17.31	18.45	10.31	13.55	17.31	18.45	12·R50	17R05
Watchet	dep	08.16	12.07	14.16	17.37	18.51	10.37	14.01	17.37	18.51	13R03	17R18
Washford	dep	08.23	12.14	14.23	17.44	18.58	10.44	14.08	17.44	18.58	R	R
Blue Anchor	dep	08.30	12.21	14.30	17.51	19.05	10.51	14.15	17.51	19.05	R	R
Dunster	dep	R	R	R	R	R	R	R	R	R	R	R
Minehead	arr	08.41	12.32	14.41	18.02	19.16	11.02	14.26	18.02	19.16	13·45	17.45

R Request Stop. Please signal to driver if joining; please advise Guard in advance if alighting.

† Coach service connecting Bishop's Lydeard and Taunton - fares quoted include coach travel

No trains will run on 25th/26th December Amended services may be operated over New Year period

* The 'Quantock Pullman' includes Pullman Dining Cars with full meal service. For table reservations and further details, please ring Bishop's Lydeard (0823) 432076.

STEAM Normally Steam hauled (RUA fares not valid)

SUNDAY SERVICE - due to engineering work, the Sunday service will NOT operate on Oct 12th and 19th.

Tel: Minehead **4996**

11th October 1980 to 28th March 1981

resign.' If this was a proposal by Mr Body it failed to find a seconder, and the board avoided a potentially embarrassing situation.

In attempting to reply to the criticism, another director, Mr Chris Dowrick, stated, 'It had been a matter of getting the priorities right; paying off the deficit in the current account had taken precedence over the purchase of replacement equipment.' The closing comment from Mr Dowrick, that the 'true answer is to sell more tickets to passengers', brought forth an observation from the body of the hall: 'Where are these new passengers going to come from, and if we attract them what are we going to carry them in?'

Addressing the meeting Mr Stevens defended the company against the suggestions made earlier that they were operating a 'cock-eyed' timetable, claiming that no timetable would ever satisfy everyone. He continued, 'I agree that the financial situation is grave, it is ridiculous; we cannot go on trading at a loss like this.' After stating that the situation would have been even worse but for the concessions obtained from the county council (and dealt with in detail in the previous chapter), he continued, 'Now that suitable arrangements have been made with the county council, thanks to the consideration shown by both officers and councillors, we are enabled to look forward with a greater degree of confidence than in the past – although it is essential that this year we make a profit, because next year the rent will again become a major factor in our budget.'

Before ending his speech, the chairman once again made an appeal for the shareholders to purchase more shares. Explaining that the company was still suffering from a lack of adequate working capital and only when this problem had been overcome would the company be able to invest in new locomotives and spares, concrete sleepers, new rolling stock and the much-needed electric token working between Minehead and Blue Anchor. He concluded by informing the shareholders that he had one bright piece of news, which was that the West Somerset Railway had just won a nationwide competition for tourist attractions, sponsored by Osram the electric light manufacturers, adding – almost as an afterthought – that the prize of £1,000 would come in very useful.

After the poor start to the year, and the problems at the AGM, some good news was received. The railway was able to announce in early May that the 'early and late' trains that the railway provided were beginning to build a regular and steadily increasing clientele, after a 'shaky' start, and therefore the 'half-fare' offer on these trains would continue for the time being. Unfortunately, these hard-won customers were to disappear shortly afterwards because of the numerous disruptions to the service that were about to occur.

Another announcement that gave great encouragement to all those involved was made by the association when it declared that its Quantock Pullman services had carried over 600 diners between 26 October and 11 January last. For this reason it would continue on Sundays only throughout the summer and would continue to leave Bishops Lydeard at 12.15 p.m. except on 29 March, 5, 12 and 26 April and 10 May, when it would depart at 11.45 a.m. It appeared that the decision to operate the service on Sundays only was not due to lack of demand from the public, but probably due to the lack of volunteers, because at the end of the article it was pointed out that on each trip a minimum number of fourteen volunteers was needed to man the train in addition to the train crew, and this observation was then followed by an appeal for more volunteers.

However, this was the only good news items to emerge in the months following the AGM. This was the period in the company's history when many of the passengers who arrived to travel on the trains, together with staff and volunteers who came on duty to work in the line, could be excused for wondering whether the initials WSR stood for 'Will Something Run'. Frequently, there were no trains operating at all on some days when scheduled services were advertised; sometimes this situation might last for several days at a time.

The reasons given for the non-appearance of the trains were many and varied: often it was due to the failure of the motive power the previous day when in service and, in spite of the fitters working through the night, they had been unable to complete the necessary repairs in time for the steam engine or DMU to enter service the following day.

Sometimes the work could not be completed, not because of the time factor, but because the funds simply did not exist to obtain the materials or spare parts required, until there was a further share issue. For the same reasons some trains could not operate because there were no supplies of coal or diesel fuel and the suppliers were refusing to make further deliveries until their accounts had been settled. Even when both passengers and staff did arrive on the railway and discovered that services were operating, there was no guarantee that the day would be trouble free. Breakdowns were frequent, which meant that passengers often arrived at their destination long after the booked arrival times of their trains. Some of the volunteers who travelled long distances to work for a day on the railway often brought sleeping bags with them, because, like the staff, they had no idea when they 'booked on' duty when they would be 'signing off'.

In another incident a locomotive was derailed at Minehead Station one Thursday afternoon. The failure to re-rail the locomotive until the following Sunday caused a severe disruption to services and the situation was not helped when staff could give no indication, either to the public or the press when normal services would be resumed. Mr Don Spencer who was at that time the operating superintendent on the line stated that the staff had been instructed that no statements could be released to the press except by the chairman of the company. In response to enquiries from intending passengers, they were told that services would be resumed after the Railway Inspectorate had examined the track and had given approval for services to restart. Normal services did not resume until the following weekend.

The situation would have been far worse but for the assistance of the Diesel & Electric Group at Williton. Very shortly after the arrival of the Class 14 locomotive referred to in the previous chapter, members of the group fitted it with vacuum brake equipment so this locomotive could haul passenger trains. Their ability to respond to numerous calls for help, and their willingness to provide this locomotive and the Hymek with a driver, often at very short notice, saved the company from many more embarrassing incidents. Later in the year the company announced that they would not be operating any weekday trains during the winter months.

If these disruptions were bad, worse was to follow, and later in the year no scheduled trains operated for four weeks. No reason was given for the cessation of services but after services had been resumed, there were further interruptions to the services when, on one weekend, no services could be operated because the company had no staff to operate the trains.

I have been unable to ascertain the shareholders' reaction to Mr Stevens' appeals for them to purchase more shares, but the attitude of the various groups associated with the railway could not be faulted. One group acquired a number of goods wagons from the Port of Bristol Authority; all of these wagons were found to be in good condition and shortly after their arrival they were pressed into service on the works trains. At the same time another group were negotiating with BR for the purchase of another 2-car DMU set to assist the two Park Royal Units that had been in service since 1976.

In order to fund these projects, which it was hoped would bring almost immediate benefits to the railway, it was agreed that some longer-term projects would have to be sacrificed.

One way out of this problem appeared to be the sale of the three prairie tank engines the association had purchased earlier. Work had already started on No.4561 and because it was hoped that the restoration work would be completed in the not too distant future (it returned to steam in 1987), it was decided that this locomotive should be retained and the other two disposed of. Work on restoring the other two locos had not started and could not do so until the restoration of 4561 was completed, due to the lack of funds and facilities, together with a shortage of volunteers with the necessary skills to carry out the work.

The Dean Forest Railway purchased locomotive No.5521 and if you visit that line you will find that they have completed the restoration of this engine to a very high standard. The other locomotive (No.5542) was acquired by a group of volunteers who eventually removed the locomotive to covered accommodation at Washford, where they completed the long process of restoration. The work on this engine, which had often worked on the branch in GWR and BR days prior to the closure of the branch, was completed in 2002 and is once again operating on the Minehead Line, almost seventy years after her first appearance there.

Another innovation this year was the decision of Scarlett Coaches, a small private company based in Minehead, to operate a bus service to and from Lynmouth and Porlock to connect with the WSR train services at Minehead

Once again it was decided to operate the 'boat trains', but this year the format was completely changed. The train left Bishops Lydeard at 12.15 p.m. on Sunday 14 June, was steam-hauled and passengers joined the paddle steamer *Waverley* at Minehead. Although the trip was organised by P&A Campbell who operated a number of steamer ships in the Bristol Channel, the *Waverley* had been restored and was operated by a group of volunteers. Although P&A Campbell's services no longer operate, I am pleased to say that the *Waverley* continues to call at Minehead from time to time. The steamer left Minehead Harbour at 4.15 p.m. for an afternoon cruise along the Somerset coast to Porlock Bay, returning to Minehead Harbour at 5.50 p.m. After a leisurely stroll along the sea front, passengers were able to board their train for the return trip to Bishops Lydeard. The train left at 6.15 p.m. and arrived back at Bishops Lydeard at 7.20 p.m. Connecting bus services were also provided to and from Taunton. The all-inclusive fare for this excursion was £6.20 for adults and £3.10 for children.

In 1981, as at the present time, there were never enough volunteers to carry out the numerous tasks that needed to be undertaken along the line. I am sure that Harold Blackmore, who was then over seventy years old and responsible for the maintenance of the track and the track side, welcomed the help the boys of Pyrland Hall School gave when their master Mr John Reeves decided that cutting the grass and clearing the cess alongside the line on the West Somerset Railway was an excellent community service project for the boys. It should not be imagined that school lessons were neglected; it was reported that at least one slow worm returned to the school in a camera case and a number of badger setts in the railway banks were thoroughly investigated. For some reason the number of volunteers was always higher when it was known that the 'tuck' shop on Bishops Lydeard Station was open. On a more serious note, the company had every reason to be very grateful to these boys who did a tremendous job, often in foul weather conditions.

The need to rely on the two Bagnall locomotives which were both overdue for a major overhaul and the absence of any positive response to the earlier appeals to locomotive owners to lease their charges to the line and ease the company's motive power problems, meant it became essential that the pannier tank No.6412 was returned to steam with the minimum of delay. This locomotive was owned by the association who would normally have been responsible for the overhaul. The normal method of funding this work was from 'operating fees' paid by the company using the locomotive to the owners (the association) which were normally calculated on a flat rate, based on the number of miles the locomotive had run in service during the period between overhauls. Because no 'operating fees' had been paid by the company to the owners and the 'ticket' on the locomotive had expired, the company was obliged to pay for the repairs to the engine. The estimated cost of the repairs was be in the region of £10,000 and as there was not enough money in the bank to meet the expected bill, yet another appeal was launched by the company to their long suffering shareholders and supporters, to provide the funds needed to complete this work.

In June it was announced that Mr Richard Stevens had resigned as chairman of the company for personal reasons, although he would retain his seat on the board. In spite of the tremendous amount of work Mr Stevens had undertaken he had failed to become the first chairman to bring the railway into profit. Mr Derek Portman was appointed as chairman in his place.

Shortly after his appointment Mr Portman announced that all services would be suspended for a fortnight and there would be a number of redundancies. In future he declared there would be no weekday services and only a skeleton service at weekends during the winter months. With the exception of four posts, all other personnel employed on the railway would be made redundant and, in future, a staff of just four people would be expected to run the railway. Mr Doug Hill, the general manager, the operating superintendent Mr Peter Henshaw and the locomotive superintendent Mr Arthur Young were amongst the senior staff who were forced to leave.

This announcement caused considerable bitterness, especially amongst the staff who lost their jobs, because it was proposed that when the line reopened in fourteen days' time their work would be undertaken by volunteers. This ill-feeling lasted for some time before fences were mended between the two groups. Many of the shareholders were also unhappy, as was Mr Richard Stevens, who resigned his seat on the board in protest at the proposals, because, shortly before he resigned as chairman, he had given undertakings to many of the staff made redundant that their jobs would be safe.

Afterwards when he was speaking to the press Mr Stevens remained optimistic about the future prospects of the company but he continued, 'One's personal disappointment is not important, what matters is for the railway to keep going. I don't think for one moment that this is the end of the railway.' His statement continued, 'One wants the railway to prosper, and if they can find volunteers to run the line at less cost, then jolly good. I do not dispute the logic of their argument, but I balk at the sheer impracticality of it. I have been around far longer than many members of the board, and can assure them that if there had been an untapped pool of volunteers we would already have made full use of it.'

In an attempt to stem the growing criticism of his action from a number of sources, Mr Portman issued a statement from his home near Reading, stating that the action had not been taken by him alone, but was a decision of the whole board. Claiming that the decision had been forced on the board by financial pressures, he added, 'We are reshaping the railway, so we shall be depending more on voluntary labour.'

The only outside support for the beleaguered board came from Mr Stan Taylor, chairman of the Minehead and West Somerset Chamber of Commerce (which had recently organised peace talks to try and get the NUR to lift its ban), who said: 'If the people of West Somerset wish to have a railway they must support it, and must get the holidaymakers to do so.' His views were echoed in many quarters, as were those of the district council's chief executive officer Mr Henry Close, who stated, 'This railway is vital to the area particularly in view of the massive cuts in the bus service we have all had to endure recently.'

Just how limited this support was became obvious when Mr Portman announced that once again the company would be seeking another meeting with council officers to discuss the company's debt situation. Before any decision had been announced, that persistent critic of the West Somerset Railway, Cllr Luff, the chairman of the finance sub-committee, was quoted as saying, 'All we have done is put off the evil day. At some time they have got to put their house in order.' Whilst the outburst from Mr Luff was to be expected, what was more disturbing was the support he received from other members of the council. Mrs Sally Prettlejohn commented, 'There must be a lot of people who could say because of their cash flow problems that they could not pay their rates', whilst her colleague Mr Brian Bailey when addressing a council meeting was reported to have said, 'I don't think we can go on much longer like this. I don't see that there will be any upturn in business next year. I suppose we have to give it [the WSR] a chance, but I think we must look at things very hard next summer, and we may have to be the ones to deliver the financial blow.' It appeared that the only member of the council prepared to continue supporting the WSR was Cllr Matthew Waley-Cohen who claimed that many of the railway's problems had been caused by their failure to run services into Taunton, because of the intransigence of the rail unions.

During the four-week closure of the line the volunteer members of the association had been busy tackling a number of problems. Locomotives and rolling stock had been overhauled and a permanent-way gang had also undertaken routine maintenance work on the section of track between Minehead and Williton. Other volunteers working at Bishops Lydeard had built an extension to the former goods shed and they were now able to undertake restoration work, together with the repainting of the Pullman coaches, under cover. One of the first tasks undertaken in the 'new' premises was the conversion of one of their coaches to a buffet/bar car in which teas, coffees and snacks could be served.

Although the winter service had been severely trimmed, the advance bookings had been heavy for the Quantock Pullman dining service and this service continued to operate every Sunday throughout the winter months. Following the restoration of yet another dining coach, the association decided that, in view of the success of the Sunday service, they would lease out the train set to operate a similar service on Saturdays during the winter months. This service was to be jointly promoted by the West Somerset Railway and BR, under the 'Merrymaker' banner. Through bookings were available from London, Reading, Bristol, Bath, Cheltenham and Gloucester. The newly restored buffet/bar coach was attached to this train for those passengers who did not want a set meal to obtain refreshments.

It appeared that the appeal for £10,000 needed for the overhaul of the boiler of the *Flockton Flyer* had been successful, because in November it was announced that the overhauled boiler was expected back on the WSR very shortly. Claiming that the overhaul programme was ahead of schedule and that as the wheels were also due to be returned in the near future, it was confidently expected that locomotive No.6412 would be back in steam in time for next year's summer timetable.

Even the Santa Special steam trains could not escape the cuts in the number of service trains operating during the winter months and this year only one train operated, on 12 and 19 December. The fares this year for this event were £1.50 for adults and £1 for children and OAPs. Children with a ticket for these special trains were able to visit Santa in his grotto and they all received a gift from him. The trains departed from Bishops Lydeard at 12.15 p.m. and returned to Bishops Lydeard at 4.30 p.m. Special Christmas shopping trains also operated to both Taunton and Minehead. Typical fares to Taunton were £1.60 from Minehead, Dunster and Blue Anchor, and £1.30 from Washford, Watchet and Williton; reduced fares were available for children.

Because of the frequent interruptions to the scheduled services and the adverse publicity the railway had attracted, due to the erratic performance of those trains that did operate, it was obvious to everyone associated with the railway that it was going to incur another substantial operating loss in the 1981 season. When the chairman of the company announced at the AGM held early in 1982 that a trading loss of almost £24,310 had been incurred in the twelve months up to the end of October 1981, some people were relieved that the results were not as bad as they had expected. It was only when these figures were examined did it become obvious just how bad the results really had been.

The operating loss had been £30,000 but this had been off-set by a profit of £6,000 (on a turnover of £34,000), made by the retail outlet that had been established at Minehead Station. Had the county council not given the railway the rent concessions referred to earlier, the operating loss would have been in the region of £50,000. These results showed that the line had made an accumulated trading loss of over £187,690 since it was opened.

17

1982: Signs of Recovery

The start of 1982 saw only four full-time paid staff operating services, with the assistance of volunteers, through what was to be a bleak winter when Watchet Harbour was badly battered and damaged by storms, although fortunately the snow storms were not as severe as in 1978. When it was time to start the summer season it was not surprising that the staff found they had not had time to formulate innovative ideas.

To obtain some indication of the company's plans for the coming season, it is necessary to refer to the reports of the AGM which was held at the Hobby Horse Inn in Minehead on 13 March. The numbers of shareholders attending this meeting was far greater than on previous occasions – many of those attending were unable to find seats and some finished up sitting on tables, whilst others were forced to stand throughout the meeting. The numbers present meant that the start of the proceedings was delayed until they had settled. The inflated presence at the meeting was in part due to the increased number of shares that had been issued to a widening group of shareholders and also to the fact that for the first time a shareholders' train had been organised.

This train brought those shareholders who wished to travel by rail from a number of locations around the country to Taunton, and from there they travelled by the bus link to Bishops Lydeard where they boarded the special 'Pullman' train for Minehead. During the journey the assembled party from the press received an address from Mr Portman and a guide pointed out the places of interest that were to be seen along the line to the shareholders. The 'shareholders' train' soon became a regular feature on the line, but it was to be twenty years before the guided tours were offered to booked parties travelling on the WSR.

After the financial report for the previous year had been adopted and he had outlined the problems that had been experienced, the chairman of the company, Mr Derek Portman, gave a very optimistic report on the future prospects of the company. Repeating the observations he had made to members of the press earlier he said, 'The West Somerset Railway is far from dying; it will go into 1982 with the backing of a substantial cash injection, and the support of a large band of enthusiastic and capable volunteers.'

Since the recent regrouping of the board, he said, the company had been through a very difficult period. To all practical purposes it was bankrupt and by conventional standards should not have carried on, but, he continued, 'You are not dealing with a conventional situation and it would be wrong to judge by those standards.'

Claiming that in the last six weeks the board had put together a package that they felt would see the company through the crisis it was facing, he continued by saying the main reason for the renewed optimism was that the company had received cash or pledges of £45,000, which he felt should see the company through the winter period. He warned that in the coming year the cash flow would need to be more positive. Stating that trains which did not pay for themselves must not be run, he claimed that in the last six months half the trains that had operated had not paid for themselves. Reiterating that in future the railway would be more dependent on volunteer labour, he said, 'One of the most rewarding things is the recent resurgence of [volunteer] support we have received. Large numbers of volunteers have come forward; the total volunteer force has been greatly strengthened.'

In the question and answer session that followed his address to the meeting, Mr Portman went to great lengths to reassure an anxious shareholder that the use of volunteers did not mean that the railway was being run by amateurs or unskilled people. He pointed out that many of the volunteers were fully qualified BR personnel who were working on the line on their off-duty periods or at weekends, one of whom he said was the fireman on the engine that had brought the shareholders to the meeting. Emphasising that the WSR was not a 'fun railway', but must be run as a business, he admitted when questioned further that steam traction was more popular with the holidaymakers than the diesel trains and on some occasions holidaymakers had turned round and walked out of the station when they had learnt that their train was to be diesel-hauled instead of the steam service they had expected.

Further questions ranged from commuter services, which Mr Portman confirmed the company was still interested in operating if they were profitable, to the commercial prospects of goods traffic from Watchet Harbour and Wansborough Paper Mills (worth having a go for), the attitude of the unions (no change), and the Taunton link (still being discussed).

Later Mr Portman confirmed that the appeals for locomotive owners to base their engines on the line had not met with any success and for this reason every effort was being made to ensure that the *Flockton Flyer* was restored to working order at the earliest possible moment. As he admitted, this engine was more suitable for operating passenger trains than the Bagnalls; presumably some of the passengers had started to complain of the 'surging' motion, when travelling in a Bagnall-hauled train.

After Mr Portman had finished answering questions, he made a further appeal to the shareholders to purchase more shares, before concluding the meeting by stating 'A break even situation is not good enough in the coming year. Sufficient capital must be available to ensure that creditors are paid. Your board feels that a cessation of trading would be a severe blow to the railway preservation movement, as well as losing for all time a magnificent stretch of railway... Your board is comprised of directors with wide business experience, as well as considerable experience and involvement in railway preservation.' He continued, 'Considerable goodwill exists towards your company from local traders, other railway societies and holidaymakers.'

In a final effort to impress on the meeting just how serious the situation facing the company was he said, 'The company cannot expect to escape the realities of life that beset companies with less glamorous activities, the company must earn its corn.' After admitting that Mr John Whittaker, the chief executive of the county council, had informed him that if the next £17,500 instalment of the rent due in May was not paid on time there would be no further concessions, he concluded, 'If you feel that enough is enough, and if you, and other shareholders, decide not to make any further investment, we shall understand your response as your instruction to the directors to wind the company up.' At this moment the future of the company hung by a thread, and it must have been with some relief that the chairman was able to report shortly afterwards that the response to his appeal had been good and that money was coming in. At the same time he paid tribute to the excellent support received from the staff often working under the most difficult conditions, together with the outstanding help being given by the steadily increasing number of volunteers.

One piece of welcome publicity that the West Somerset Railway received during the year was the announcement in a number of newspapers, at both local and national level, that it would be 'business as usual' on the West Somerset Railway during the strike by members of the ASLEF union which brought the national network to a standstill. It did not escape the notice of the journalists who reported this event that the services on the WSR were being operated by many members of the same union disrupting the services on BR.

Another article that appeared in the local press during the year gave an insight into the occupations of the many new volunteers appearing on the line. Two were drivers on the London Underground, who drove diesel railcars on the WSR during their holidays and rest days, a retired farmer who was a trainee driver on the Class 14 loco, a (fire brigade) fireman working as a guard, a heavy plant diesel fitter who had been a fireman, and one of the directors of the company, working as a waiter on the Quantock Pullman.

Other volunteers working on the line during the summer period included young soldiers who were apprentices at the Army Catering School at Aldershot attending a weekend exercise, which involved lifting track in the vicinity of Bishops Lydeard Station, loading it onto works trains to be carried to Minehead where it was unloaded and relaid to form a much-needed siding. The idea for the exercise came from 2nd Lieutenant Christopher Russell, who lived at Taunton, who unfortunately could not participate in the weekend exercise because he was involved in a car accident. His place was taken by Captain Paul Lindsay-Scott (also a volunteer in the Somerset and Dorset Museum at Washford), who with Harold Blackmore supervised the work as it was carried out. It is best not to ask how a weekend exercise of this kind was supposed to improve the cooking skills of the soldiers involved.

Another task that was undertaken during the summer months was the creation by the S&D Trust of a non-working replica of the small signal box that had been at Midford on the Somerset & Dorset Railway. This was located in the cabin at the east end of the platform at Washford, which had originally housed the ground frame controlling the sidings at this location.

Following the chairman's remarks at the AGM that trains that proving unprofitable would not be run in future, it came as no surprise to anyone when it was announced that the early morning and late evening trains would cease to operate at the end of the winter timetable. Commenting on the decision Mr Portman stated, 'Historically the early morning and late night services are the loss-making ones. The services best supported by the holidaymakers are those operating after 9. 30 a.m. and those operating in the early evening. So we are cutting about 20 per cent of our summer services. The new timetable will suit our army of volunteers better because it calls for less unsociable hours working.' Admitting that the board realised that this action would probably result in a reduction in the number of people travelling on the line, he said, 'Not everyone will transfer from an early train to a later one, but we think our action will enable the company to break even, or possibly make a small profit at the end of this financial year.'

I do not know who wrote the following interesting article that appeared in the *Shopping Extra* edition of 30 March 1982, but I think you will agree that the much-improved passenger figures that were recorded later in the season should in large part be attributed to the writer. For this reason, I have taken the liberty of reproducing the article in full.

GO BACK TO THE DAYS OF STEAM – AND LET THE WORLD GO BY

Do you remember the days when trains had character? When the old steam engines at the front made such a noise as they wheezed and puffed along? When most steam engines had names.

Well down in the heart of West Somerset on the on the old Great Western Minehead branch, trains still go 'di-dum- di -dum'. Well cared for locos bustle along and smoke drifts past the windows just like the old days.

At the little country station of Bishops Lydeard, trains wait as passengers arrive -some by car, others travelling up from Taunton on the special link bus. Youngsters stand goggle-eyed at the strange sight of a steam engine, while granddads nod in approval whilst Dads buy tickets from one of those quaint little booking office windows of old. The intercom calls out in the tradition of railway termini, ' This train will stop at Crowcombe, Stogumber, Williton, Watchet, Washford, Blue Anchor, Dunster, and Minehead... and the announcer then hurries latecomers along. Passengers for the 12.15 train to Minehead, kindly board as this train is now ready to depart.'

DEPART

The twenty mile journey to Minehead takes about 1 hour 15 minutes (the West Somerset is Britain's longest independent railway) so there is plenty of time for a picnic lunch. The buffet car is often included in the train – and the sandwiches really are home made and fresh. Then again some trains include first class Pullman dining cars complete with waitresses, wine waiters, and stewards where you can enjoy a full four course lunch prepared in the kitchens of the Pullman cars en route and, on the return trip in the afternoon teas are served to guests at their reserved tables. A little bit of luxury really does linger on in West Somerset.

The grand reopening, Blue Anchor, 1976. (M.E.J. Deane, courtesy Ian Bennett)

Full steam ahead for the grand reopening, Minehead, 1976. (M.E.J. Deane, courtesy Ian Bennett)

3 Reopening day at Blue Anchor in 1976. (Chris Osment)

4 Blue Anchor Station in 1976. (Chri Osment)

5 Bagnall 2996 approaching Blue Anchor, 27 August 1976. (John Yeo)

Victor on reopening day in 1976. (Chris Osment)

Park Royal DMU at Sea Lane crossing, Dunster, in 1976. (Simon Whittingham)

8 Dunster Station in 1976
(Chris Osment)

9 Pannier 6412 at Mineh
27 August 1976.

10 Crowcombe Station in
1977. (Peter Coventry)

View of Stogumber Station in 1977, looking north. (Peter Coventry)

12 Looking towards Watchet and its footbridge in 1977. (Chris Osment)

13 Looking west towards Washford in 1977. (Chris Osment)

14 Blue Anchor Station at the start of the blizzard, in 1978. (Chris Osment)

15 First up train to arrive at Bishops Lydeard in 1979. (Chris Osment)

16 DMU at Kentsford in the blizzard of February 1978. (Stephen Edge)

17 Cravens in BR blue at Williton 1982. (Brian Hart)

D7017 with D9551 at Williton, in 1982. (Brian Hart)

19 D7017 at Williton, 1982. (Brian Hart)

20 *Jennifer* on Quantock Belle duties, Bishops Lydeard, 1982. (Brian Hart)

21 Cravens DMU at Kentsford in the 1980s. (Robin White)

TERMINUS

There is so much to see out of the window of a West Somerset train, with the Quantock Hills on the up side and the Brendons on the down side, all the way to Williton. Then quite out of the blue, the railway rounds a bend to run along the coast to Watchet Harbour. The line then heads for the hills again, but soon returns to the sea again at Blue Anchor. With Exmoor brooding over Dunster Castle on one side, and the Bristol Channel and Wales on the other, the train finally arrives at the terminus at Minehead with the popular beach but a few yards from the platform.

ATMOSPHERE

The railway is there because people like travelling on steam trains, particularly when the trains actually go to an interesting town; because people enjoy wining and dining aboard a steam-hauled Pullman train; because people like the volunteers from the West Somerset Railway Association give up their spare time to drive a loco, guard a train, or check the permanent way, or pull a signal lever, or paint a carriage, or serve a luncheon. These people will never let the atmosphere of the 'old railways' fade and pass away.

VOLUNTEER

You can help the railway and enjoy yourself at the same time, so why not come along to take a trip on the Minehead line and maybe become a volunteer.

This free publicity was probably more beneficial to the railway than all the publicity they paid for during the remainder of the season. Certainly the results were impressive enough for the Committee of the Quantock Pullman to instruct their secretary to write the following letter to the manager of the newspaper on 22 March 1983:

Dear Sir

Since the article on the Quantock Pullman appeared in your newspaper, advanced bookings have rocketed from 5% to 50%.

This year we are running ten Sunday lunch time and five Saturday evening 'Belles', and already some of the trains are fully booked!. Indeed, the amount of interest generated by the 'Shopper' article has prompted our committee to consider putting on relief trains.

Well done and thanks 'Shopper'.

Yours Faithfully,

Stephen Edge

At last the railway received a response to their numerous appeals to hire additional motive power and in November 1982 they were able to announce the arrival of a 0-6-0 tank loco, built by Hudswell Clarke (works No.1731), named *Jennifer*. The locomotive came from the North Yorkshire Moors Railway, who must have been relieved to be rid of it. It was the subject of a three-year hire agreement and although the engine was claimed to be working order, and a spokesman for the WSR expressed the hope that the railway would be able to start the next season with four working locos, the signing of this agreement proved to be an unmitigated disaster for the WSR. At a time when the company was facing a severe cash flow problem, considerable sums of money were spent in an attempt to keep the locomotive in service. The expenditure of this money on the locomotive did not prevent the engine spending long periods in the workshops, undergoing still more repairs. Eventually the locomotive was the subject of a lengthy legal battle that was only finally resolved at great expense to the WSR in the year 2004.

In spite of the decision taken earlier in the year to reduce the number of trains operating by almost 20 per cent, thanks to the type of publicity referred to earlier the passenger numbers had remained similar to the previous year. At the AGM early in 1983 the chairman was able to inform the shareholders that the losses for the year were only £4,279, a substantial improvement on the previous year's loss. It is more remarkable when, as will be revealed later, the company not only managed to pay the rental charges due in the year but also repaid £4,000 of the outstanding loan when due.

18

1983: The Recovery Continues

The company had operated only a skeleton service during the winter months so very little news was generated in the local press during the first three months of 1983. Two items which did appear, and gave fresh hope to all supporters of the company, came early in the new year. The first item appeared in February in the *Somerset County Gazette*.

CIDER FOR THE SCOTS SAVES RAIL LINK

West Somerset will not, after all, lose its link with the national railway network at Taunton, thanks, surprisingly, to a taste for Somerset cider in the north country and Scotland.

Taunton Cider company, whose brewery stands alongside the line at Norton Fitzwarren, has signed a three year freight contract with BR which gives them (Taunton Cider) a 'right-of use' over the line. The effect of this will be to scrap BR's plans to tear up more than £100,000 worth of track, so severing the main rail network from the West Somerset's privately owned branch railway.

WSR trains at present terminate at Bishops Lydeard. The company has now abandoned the long cherished ambition of extending services into Taunton even though BR were prepared to co-operate, because of the cost of such an operation. The branch line track at Norton Fitzwarren has been unused for many years. 'We thought that we could make use of that track rather than see it pulled up' said a cider company spokesman. 'Our contract is to everyone's benefit, and we are delighted. We will reconsider our rail freighting in 1986 when this contract expires'.

Meanwhile from March the cider company will dispatch its products to the north direct from the factory in railway wagons, which will be loaded by day to be picked up by an engine from the main line at night. At present the traffic is taken by road to Bridgwater and transferred there to the railway.

Cider sales in north-east England and Scotland now account for some thirty to thirty five per cent of the company's turnover, which is now in excess of £30 million.

The new deal may still leave a small gap between the WSR and the main network as BR plans to lift about 500 yards of track at Norton Fitzwarren. 'But we can recover from that' said Mr Portman, chairman of the WSR. What we could not afford was to pay our share of maintaining the junction with the main line'.

Mr Portman said that the WSR had abandoned all hopes of ever linking up with Taunton, 'but this is great news. We now have a chance of reversing our fortunes, and being in a position to retain the link,' he said. The National Union of Railwaymen which for many years has opposed any suggestion of a link up, have now withdrawn their objection. Any future connection with the main line could mean big business for the private railway company through day excursions to Minehead from other parts of the country. Special trains could also be run to carry visitors to the Butlins holiday centre at Minehead.

The news that the WSR had decided to abandon its efforts to run a commuter service appears to have been one of their best-kept secrets, because I have been unable to find any previous indication that this decision had been taken, prior to this announcement.

The second item was in the *West Somerset Free Press* on 11 March.

WAGONS ROLL AS NUR BLOCKADE IS LIFTED

The National Union of Railwaymen's blockade of the West Somerset Railway was finally lifted last weekend.

Since opening in 1976 the privately owned line has had to ferry in everything by road. But it was allowed to take delivery of five coaches and two wagons by rail on Saturday.

Said the WSR general manager Mr Doug Hill, 'It was a marvellous moment. We have had to pay a fortune for road shipments. But a new era has begun with the NUR and we hope a close relationship will evolve'.

The NUR had decided to lift its ban on rail cargoes because the WSR had given up all plans to run commuter services into Taunton. It was union fears over the job security of bus driver members that led to the blockade being imposed. Said Mr Ron Squire Taunton branch secretary, 'The situation which led to the ban no longer exists. We look forward to happy relations with the WSR 'The five passenger coaches travelled from Bristol, Thornton Fields on the Eastern Region, and Castle Cary. The WSR also took delivery of a specially designed wagon for carrying sleepers, and a wagon fitted with a hand crane.

Added Mr Hill, 'BR staff brought the rolling stock to Norton Fitzwarren and then transferred them to our charge. It was so easy. If the carriages and wagons had come by road it would have cost us a fortune'.

Because of the large numbers of shareholders that had arrived for the AGM the previous year and the further £31,890 worth of shares had been issued during the twelve months since, it was decided to change the location for the 1982 AGM, which was held on Saturday 26 March at 2.30 p.m. The location this year was to be the Minehead and District Social Club Hall. The fact that only 200 shareholders attended the meeting this year was possibly an indication that they were happier with the performance of the board.

When the accounts for the twelve-month period up to 31 October 1982 were presented a number of interesting facts were brought to light. Earlier in the year, when the decision was made to reduce the number of trains operating by 20 per cent, the directors forecast, quite reasonably, that this would adversely affect the number of people travelling on the line, together with fare receipts. Their fears proved to be unfounded, because the income from fares rose to £80,639 from £75,403 the previous year. The railway's other activities, platform tickets, rental income, television fees, wine-and-dine trains, all increased their profits on the previous year. The exception was the shop whose profits were down by approximately one third. The main reason for this appears to have been because the accounts for the shop were combined with the train catering services (not wine and dine trains), which, as were revealed later in the meeting, had not been profitable.

In reducing the wage bill by 50 per cent and holding all other charges below those of the previous year with the exception of the coal and diesel fuel bills, the company managed to reduce the loss for the year to £4,279 from £24,310. What makes these figures even more remarkable is that the company had paid Somerset County the £17,550 annual rent, whereas in the previous year a concession had been obtained and the rent had not been paid.

After the accounts had been adopted by the meeting, Chairman Portman outlined the plans for the remainder of the 1983 operating season. He stated that the forthcoming year's timetable would be a 'fine-tuning' of the year previous when revenue had increased, despite a reduction in the number of trains, and that passenger levels were maintained. A swing towards the number of steam trains operated and a sharp drop in the number of trains cancelled had helped.

He continued, 'The aim this year is to have two steam locomotives in operation with one in reserve, instead of only one in use'; a state that he claimed, 'limited revenue to £85,000 per year, which was no way to make a profit.' Then came the customary appeal to shareholders in which he outlined a three-pronged approach to further this policy: first was a large cash injection and for this reason he was appealing for everyone to purchase more shares; secondly, there was the need for more helpers to assist the railway's full-time staff of only four; thirdly, there was a backlog of maintenance work (the maintenance bill for 1982/3 had been very severely cut back). More passing loops were wanted on the single track line, he stated, together with more motive power and rolling stock.

He confirmed the earlier report that more rolling stock had been obtained and he admitted for the first time that the company now had three serviceable locomotives available. Confirming that the on-board catering services (with the exception of the wine-and-dine trains) had not made a profit he stated: 'The company should learn from other private railways how money was made from non-railway activities and work out how they could be developed.'

Confirming that the decision of the board not to pursue the Taunton link had been a bitter disappointment to many of the supporters of the railway, he said that the decision had only been made after long high-level discussions with BR. The cost involved would have been completely out of reach, and the additional income would have been very small. If BR's terms had been accepted, he said that it would have been financial suicide for the company.

Outlining the problems in some detail, he explained that BR required £175,000 by July for the capital costs of works on the track, to which they might be prepared to contribute £15,000. Thereafter, there would be an annual charge of at least £25,000 for the use of the section of line between the Norton Fitzwarren and Taunton Stations. If the WSR was unable to meet BR's proposals, there would be an annual holding charge of £12,000 a year to keep the option open.

Although work had begun to lift the track between Silk Mills crossing and Taunton as soon as the WSR had announced their decision, the chairman still hoped that they would not lift the 400 yards of track between the cider factory and the start of the WSR track, because the cider company had recently signed a freight agreement with BR. Mr Portman also welcomed the change in attitude on the part of the NUR and their co-operation in transferring coaching stock and wagons to the WSR. He also expressed the hope that the enhanced co-operation between the two parties would continue, although it was unlikely that if negotiations with BR over the link were reopened, that the WSR would confer fully with the NUR.

The response to the chairman's appeal for extra funds from the assembled company was immediate. At the end of the meeting a cardboard box was placed on the table in front of the directors. Following the directors' example – they had all placed £1 notes in the box, as a 'bonus' for the new share issue that was about to be launched – many of those present in the hall also decided to contribute to this 'bonus'. The directors interpreted this as a vote of confidence and with this sort of backing the board considered that they had the support of the shareholders.

The first of the non-railway activities referred to by Mr Portman in his address to the AGM took place between 2–4 April and was the Easter Fair & Preservation Rally, held at the Doniford Bay leisure centre. The advertised attractions included: preserved buses; classic cars; stationary engines; commercial and military vehicles; farm implements and tractors; together with trade stands and other attractions including the Taunton and Watchet Carnival Queens and the Taunton and Watchet Majorettes. There was also a childcare facility, together with a restaurant and bar service on the site.

The event was open from 11 a.m. to 6 p.m. daily and admission cost 75p for adults and 40p for children. Special train services operated to Williton Station. (Doniford Beach Halt had not been opened at the time.) Special Rover tickets were also issued, which gave unlimited train travel on the day of purchase, and included travel on the bus link from the station and admission to the rally. These tickets cost £5 for an adult and £3 for a child for one day, or £15 for an adult and £5 for a child for all three days.

I have been unable to find out how successful this event was financially, but a similar rally eventually became an annual event held on the first weekend in August and the location was moved to Bishops Lydeard.

Another non-railway event planned for the year under review was the decision to hold a raffle to support the locomotive 6412, otherwise known as the *Flockton Flyer* appeal. The tickets cost 5p each, with a first prize of £100, with four runners-up prizes of £25 each. The draw was to be held on 17 September at Williton Station. This appears to be the first draw organised by the Association that was not promoted by Mr Steve Martin.

The first report of what was to become a persistent problem for the railway in this area was written in the *West Somerset Free Press* of 20 May. It stated that persistent trespass on the railway line on both sides of Watchet Station led to ten boys being summoned at court.

It was stated that adults, especially mill workers, were setting youngsters a bad example by trespassing on the track.

In March, the WSR experienced the first of a number of problems in the Watchet area that year. A Mr Den Ruddy of Watchet was driving a fourteen-ton forklift truck towards the local docks when he collided with the parapet of the bridge over the railway to the west of the station. He managed to hit it with such force that a large section of masonry was sent crashing down onto the track below. Services on the line were suspended for twenty-four hours until the debris could be removed. Further sections of the bridge becoming dislodged by passing road traffic were avoided by making the weakened part of the bridge safe. It is just as well that this incident happened before the problems outlined in the next paragraph occurred, otherwise the railway would have probably been blamed by the town council for this incident as well.

The West Somerset Railway was blamed by Watchet Town Council for seven grass fires started in the area around Helwell Bay. The railway was also accused of sending clouds of black smoke over the nearby Kingsland housing estate, and that fumes from railway engines had stained the newly painted footbridge at the station that the council had recently overseen at a cost of £1,000. At the council meeting in May it was agreed that the clerk should write to the WSR asking them to ensure that their drivers to try to minimise the inconvenience and damage caused by the trains.

This action was taken after Mr Stephen Barrass, whose house overlooked the railway, had stated that he wished that, 'Drivers would end the habit of firing up as they entered Watchet.' Cllr Jean Howe added that, 'Last year the company stated that they had instructed all drivers to close the dampers of their engines between Doniford and Watchet.' She also claimed this was not being done, and the result was disgusting because many residents on the Kingsland Estate were regularly being 'smoked out'.

Further complaints came from Cllr Tony Knight, who claimed that as the emissions from the WSR locomotives were responsible for the 'smearing' of the newly painted footbridge and that the WSR should be asked to repaint the bridge when the time came for it to be redone. The letter of complaint brought an immediate response from Mr Hein Burger, who was the assistant general manager of the railway at that time. Possibly miffed because he had been addressed as 'Mr Henry Burger', he replied 'the steam trains are a major tourist attraction in West Somerset, drawing thousands of tourists to the area. Where you have steam trains fuelled by coal, you are bound to get smoke and smuts.'

The following week a letter appeared in the same paper from Mr Dave Rouse, who was one of the most experienced drivers on the line at that time. It read:

Sir,

From the remarks made by local councillors on 13 May (Black mark for smoky engines), it would seem that none of them can remember the days when steam power ruled the railways of this country. The stone bridge beyond Watchet Station has been there for over 100 years and has the black marks of all these years imprinted in it, so why cavil at the new paint being marked?

Fires have to be made up on steam engines, and Watchet Station stands at the foot of the climb to Washford. If any one of the councillors can fire one of our locomotives without creating smoke he or she is very welcome to have a go. I would suggest that their time might be better spent looking at the inside faces of their new paintwork, which the local idiot fringe have already commenced to deface with their brainless scribble.

We are trying to establish a useful means of transport between various places in West Somerset, and the use of steam locomotives gives a great deal of pleasure to young and old. Smoke, engines may emit at times, but it is nothing compared to the poisonous filth that is thrown out by the heavy lorries that crawl up the hill out of Watchet with their puny loads. If this traffic were where it should be – on the rail – the roads would be much safer and cleaner.

I suggest that the councillors think more about this, rather than smoke on a bridge that has been there since before they were born.

Another letter on similar lines was sent by Mr Cedric Dunmall, who was a fireman on the WSR for many years.

A decision was made to change the livery on all the company's passenger coaches. Until that point, the colours had been maroon and cream, rather similar in appearance to the original 'blood and custard' colours adopted by BR when it was formed. Announcing that the new colours were to be chocolate and cream – similar to the colours used by the former Great Western Railway – Mr Douglas Hill said, 'With an increased timetable this year it will take a little more organising to get the stock repainted. Two coaches have already been repainted in the old GWR colours, four are still in the company's previous colours, and the remainder are still in BR plain blue. But we will get it done and reflect even more nostalgia of the age of steam.'

In June, the railway announced that it had run its longest train on a Sunday. The train was in fact the same length as the boat train that had been run a few years earlier on a Saturday, consisting of seven coaches hauled by two steam engines with a 2-car DMU attached at the rear to serve other passengers. The special charter train was organised to carry 470 members of the Birmingham Society of Model Engineers Ltd who travelled by rail to Taunton, where they were met by a fleet of buses which brought them to Bishops Lydeard Station, where they joined the train for the trip to Minehead. Whilst as I have explained the claim for the longest train was perhaps a little dodgy, there was no doubt that this was the largest number of passengers in any one group that had been carried by the railway at that time.

Another innovation on the line this season was, as far as I have been able to discover, the first private (not group) charter train to be operated on the line.

Under the headline 'Trip Down Memory Lane', the *Western Daily Press* informed its readers on 8 October:

The family of the world famous science fiction writer Arthur C. Clarke is giving the West Somerset Railway a helping hand. Mr Clarke, a former pupil of the Richard Huish College Taunton, now lives in Sri Lanka, but retains strong Somerset connections.

His brother Fred Clarke who lives in Bishops Lydeard, near Taunton has agreed to pay about £200 to hire a diesel train for a special occasion on the railway, and the train is due to run the 22nd of October.

On that day a plaque will be unveiled at Bishops Lydeard Station in memory of Brigadier Sir Frank Medicott, an enthusiastic supporter of the railway who helped fund the refurbishment of the station.

Mr Clarke is hiring the train to take Sir Frank's widow, Lady Helen Medicott from Bishops Lydeard to Minehead and back, along with several invited guests, and twenty pupils from Bishops Lydeard primary school. Railway spokesman Mr Ken Roberts said 'the Clarke family have a keen interest in the railway and Fred Clarke is one of the shareholders. This type of exercise helps promote the railway, keeping it in the public eye, and increasing its popularity.' Private charter trains hired to celebrate wedding receptions, golden weddings, and other events now form a very important source of income for the railway.

In October 1983, another appeal was launched, this time for the purchase of a former Great Western 2-8-0 No.3850 heavy goods engine from Barry scrap yard. The appeal stated that to buy the locomotive from Barry and finance a three-year restoration programme, the group needed to increase their '£5-a-month-for-three-years' membership' to three hundred people. The group were successful in obtaining the locomotive from Barry, but unfortunately their three-year restoration programme proved to be a little optimistic. In November 2003, the rolling chassis was moved from Minehead to Tyseley, where it was hoped to reunite the boiler to the frames in 2004 and, the group then forecast that the loco would be returned to steam on the West Somerset Railway in 2005.

In July, the hope that the motive power problems that had plagued the railway in the past had been overcome was proved to be optimistic. A rather embarrassed Mr Doug Hill confessed to the *West Somerset Free Press* that owing to a string of breakdowns, the railway had only one engine in service that week, which was an improvement on the previous week! He continued, 'It is a bit of a headache, we pride ourselves on the fact that we are a steam railway, and that is the romantic element that woos passengers to us, but when we have to explain to intending passengers that the only trains that are running are diesel-hauled, many turn round and leave the station. When the trading figures are out at the end of the month we expect them to be substantially lower than the corresponding month last year.'

He went on to explain that when the railway's *Victor* engine went in for a re-tube the operation took weeks longer than had been expected. Whilst that engine was under repair, *Vulcan* developed similar problems and had to be laid up, then the third engine developed a 'hot box' and had to be pulled out of service for a major overhaul. The fourth engine was being restored before being put into service.

Finally he admitted that the railway had not operated any steam services for ten days. When these facts became known, a number of the supporters of the line started to feel uneasy because it was obvious that disruptions to the service like this, at the height of the summer timetable, would have an adverse effect on the financial forecasts, which a reduction in overheads would be insufficient to offset.

Better news came with the announcement that Minehead Station was to receive a major facelift. A sum of £25,000 was to be spent on the installation of the booking office that had been recovered from Cardiff Central Station, together with the provision of restaurant facilities. Said Mr Portman, 'It might sound like a lot of money, but we are applying for a grant from the West Country Tourist board – we have to develop the commercial aspects of the railway in order to boost our income.'

'We want a restaurant with a spanking reputation. We also want people to visit the station simply to savour what the Victorians accepted as commonplace. At the moment we only run a buffet selling sandwiches and the occasional hot snack.' (It would appear that the bid for funds was unsuccessful, because the sort of restaurant facility envisaged then is still not available at the station twenty years later.) Fortunately the installation of the new booking office was completed.

As the summer season drew to a close, it was announced that several 'special' trains would run through the winter months, including the Santa Specials which ran on 17 and 24 December, but that year's Santa's grotto had been relocated to Blue Anchor Station, and the trains ran from Minehead, instead of Bishops Lydeard. A DMU service from Williton ran to connect with the Santa Special trains, which left Minehead at 2.45 p.m. and returned at 3.45 p.m.

Extra Shopper trains ran on 20, 22 and 29 December and they also ran from Williton to Minehead. The Quantock Pullman dining trains, which had now been renamed the Quantock Belle service (the name it retains to the present day), now advertised as the 'restaurant on wheels', was booked to run on 11, 18 and 27 December and 1 January.

The first indication to outsiders that all had not gone well on the railway during the season was the first of several alarmist reports in the local press that would appear between September and December. The *West Somerset Free Press* of 23 September, under the headline 'End of Line in Sight for W.S. Railway', claimed:

> The West Somerset Railway may have reached the end of the line. The board of directors is ready to recommend that shareholders close it down after a slump in business.

The article went on to claim that business had fallen by 20 per cent since the previous year and a loss of between £10,000 and £15,000 was expected. Mr Portman was quoted as saying:

> The only saving we can make is on our annual £17,500 rental, and we have therefore asked the county council to waive all rental charges until 1988. We have slashed all other fixed costs, and there is nothing else left to pare. We will call an extraordinary meeting of the shareholders if we fail. Our recommendation to the meeting will be that the railway is closed because there is no prospect of the railway making a profit.'

It appeared that, although staff costs had been cut by more than half, virtually all winter services had been axed and early-morning and late-evening services had been suspended, these actions were not enough to enable the railway to balance the books. It was claimed that the exceptionally wet spring had resulted in a fall in the number of passengers using the line, and that during the heatwave visitors had shied away from the railway to sunbathe on the beach.

It came as no surprise to anyone when it was learnt that the finance sub-committee of the county council had rejected the request from the railway for the suspension of rental charges until 1988. After this rebuff, a rather dejected Mr Portman said, 'Despite the position taken by the finance sub-committee the board feel that when the railway's application is considered by the full council, the wider social and economic circumstances will be taken into account – and a that a different view will then be taken'. He then continued, 'The board lays great emphasis that the railway generates some £200,000 of trade in West Somerset each year.'

Although the assets of the company were greater than at the same time the previous year, and the company still continued to receive share applications, the chairman warned that the board considered that it was wrong to rely on that sort of financing indefinitely. He went on to claim that the shareholders had put up and lost some £200,000, and the directors who had agreed to underwrite the railways bank overdraft from their own personal accounts were no longer prepared to do so in future, unless they were convinced that the business was viable.

In the next edition of the same paper, of 29 September, a glimmer of hope appeared under the headline 'Buy the Line Proposal to Save Railway'. It was stated that at a board meeting held on 24 September, the directors had accepted a proposal that the landlords of the railway, the Somerset County Council, should be approached to see if they were prepared to allow the board to purchase the line outright, instead of paying an annual rent. Although the county council had paid BR £245,000 for the line ten years before, some of the land surrounding the railway had since been sold. Because the price of scrap metal had fallen in the period since the purchase of the line, members of the board were authorised to approach the county council to see if they would be prepared to accept an offer in the region of £100,000 for the line.

In October, a plea came from Mrs Meigan Lyons in the form of a letter that was sent to all members of the county council. She urged all councillors to consider the wider implications of the railway's closure: 'Without the railway the number of visitors to our area will quite obviously decline. Equally obviously, this will have an effect on those engaged in our tourist industry, such as hoteliers, and caterers. Inevitably this will have a further long-term effect on employment, and so make less spending money available in West Somerset. Somerset County Council has devoted much time, energy, and money, in promoting tourism. Surely such a major tourist attraction cannot be allowed to disappear without trace.'

Later in the same month came the announcement that an Extraordinary General Meeting of the shareholders would be held in the Beach Hotel opposite Minehead Station on 5 November. The meeting was called to seek the shareholders' approval for the board to approach the county council with an offer to purchase the line from the Council for £140,000. This revised figure had been arrived at after consultation with professional advisers and BR.

It appeared that the board were not confident they would be able to persuade the shareholders to back their request to purchase further shares, because it emerged before the special meeting was held that the five remaining members of staff had been made redundant, with the notices to take effect from 5 November.

Two news items that it was hoped would influence the shareholders to purchase more shares came in the week before the meeting was due to be held. The first was the announcement that at a county council meeting, those present had agreed to grant a six-month rent freeze to provide the railway with a breathing space in an effort to enable them to attempt to raise the money to purchase the line. It was claimed that both parties were close to an agreement over the purchase price but that it had been decided to refer the matter to arbitration.

In the same week it was announced that the West Somerset District Council's policy and resources committee had agreed 'in principle' to make an unspecified contribution towards the following year's rental of the line, but only after detailed discussion with the county council and the railway regarding the overall position and future running of the line. The committee chairman, Mr Tony Holman, later revealed that this decision had been taken after a meeting between the chief executive of the county council, Mr John Whittaker, and the chairman of the District Council's finance committee Mr M. Trehearne.

The meeting had originally been called because of the District Council's concern regarding the possible effects the closure of the line would have on the local economy, and the need for both parties to try to find a solution to the problem. In response to their concerns, the county council had responded by asking the representatives of the District Council what they were doing to assist the WSR, and they (the county council) were surprised to learn that no approach had been made to the WSDC by the railway company.

Informing the full meeting of the District Council held on 2 November of the outcome of the discussion, Mr Holman said: 'In short they (the county council) are looking to us for a contribution, and tomorrow's meeting at County Hall hinges on our decision.' The proposal was not carried without some opposition, Cllr Viv Brewer stated that, 'the council had to be clear that the future rail service would be tourist-based and not for commuters.' He then continued, 'I think that the railway should stop at Williton, most of the other stations are miles from the places they are supposed to serve. There are miles of track to maintain and numerous bridges. I am wondering where this money is going to come from. This fund will be a bottomless pit.'

He was supported by Cllr Dennis Merson, who agreed that the stretch of line beyond Williton was a non-starter. The directors of the WSR had announced nine months beforehand that they had abandoned their efforts to operate a commuter service. That some of their elected representatives were so out of touch with what was happening in their area did not come as a surprise to the local electorate. Fortunately, other councillors were in favour of supporting the railway.

When the special meeting of the shareholders was held at the Beach Hotel, Mr Peter Rivett, the financial director of the company, outlined the proposals to the meeting, and then added, 'In addition to the appeal to shareholders it is proposed to make a door-to-door collection from householders in Minehead and also contact local businessmen, in an attempt to raise some of the money that was needed.' The directors were also writing to several millionaires who were known to support 'good causes' from time to time. Informing the meeting that there were 5,000 shareholders, of whom only 2,000 were active, he claimed that if they could contribute £30 per head – £60,000–£70,000 – the company could remain in business. He remained confident that the balance of the money required could be obtained, possibly through a Government small business loan. He then reminded the shareholders that the future of the railway was in their hands and he hoped that their response would ensure that the railway was in with a good chance of survival.

During a question and answer session, Mr Portman was asked by one shareholder if the company could attract more visitors by purchasing more steam engines and he replied that the problem of borrowing or hiring engines was that owners were reluctant to do business with a company whose future was in doubt; most owners wanted their locomotives stabled under cover. Moreover, the cost of running a steam train was almost ten times as much as operating a DMU.

Another shareholder asked if the company was prepared to borrow money to purchase steam engines if necessary. Mr Portman replied, 'Yes, up to a sum of £30,000, although there was no question of taking out a twenty-year bank loan to cover the cost.' Other questions were asked, including whether the board was prepared to cut costs further by shortening the line and just running between Minehead and Williton, to which Mr Portman replied, 'Not at all, but if driven to it we will save what we can.'

Questions about running into Taunton, obtaining grants for capital work from the Tourist Authorities, or even the EEC, were met with the response 'no available cash' and it was pointed out that tourist grants had to be matched by putting down an equal amount of money.

When the question and answer session had finished, the board put three resolutions before the shareholders for their approval. The first resolution stated:

> The directors should be authorised to purchase the freehold of the line, either in whole or in part, at the earliest opportunity, provided that by midnight on November 15th, the directors consider that the company is able to continue trading.

Resolution No.2 as amended read:

> If in the opinion of the directors, the company cannot continue its business by reason of its liabilities, to authorise the directors to request the Somerset County Council to appoint a receiver under its debenture.

Resolution No.3 authorised an increase in the share capital of the company to £500,000. The three resolutions were carried with almost complete unanimity. Mr Portman then closed the meeting on a note of confidence saying, 'We have now got the best opportunity we have ever had of getting this thing right.'

His final question to the shareholders of 'Do you have confidence in your board?' brought forth a vociferous 'yes' in reply.

Shortly afterwards it was announced that a number of local businessmen had been approached and that the door-to-door collection was under way in Minehead. Subscribers and members were being asked to donate sums between £5 for a railway sleeper up to £100 for a complete 60ft length of track.

Towards the end of November the directors announced that an emergency board meeting had been held at a motorway service station on a Sunday. At this meeting the directors agreed to keep the company going by offering to buy part of the line from Somerset County Council. It was claimed that although shareholders had rallied round with financial aid there was still a deficit of cash to purchase the whole of the line. They were, however, in a position to make a fairly substantial and meaningful purchase offer for part of the line.

After explaining that the decision to hold the meeting at the rather unusual venue was simply because it was convenient for those directors who lived in various parts of the country to meet beside the motorway, he continued, 'Accordingly we shall approach the county council towards the end of this week and make an offer. I am fairly confident that they will agree to a part-purchase, with the deal being completed over a period in two parts, but until we get that in writing, nothing can be done.'

In early December the troubled company was able to announce that the shareholders had contributed £30,000 towards the sum needed to purchase the line, but as Financial Director Mr Peter Rivett said, 'The board could not proceed with negotiations to purchase the line from the county council until all the rent arrears had been paid.'

It must have come as a great relief to the board when the West Somerset District Council announced that it had agreed to give a sum of £5,833 to the railway to enable the company to clear the outstanding rent that was overdue. The resolution was not carried without some strong objections by a number of the councillors. In her reply to those objecting to the proposal, Mrs Lesley Pring, chairman of the finance committee on the council, pointed out that this was the first time that the railway company had approached the council for funds in the railway's twelve-year history as a private company, and it had been made clear that no more funds would be forthcoming.

It was her next remark, when reported in the local press, which aroused the greatest interest among the supporters of the railway, because she went on to say, 'It has been made clear that the company intends to purchase only the section of line between Minehead and Williton', implying that the company would not be contemplating the purchase of the remainder of the line. She continued, 'Agreement has been reached on the price for the northern section of the line (between the railway and the county council?), but independent valuers (sic) were still working on a price for the metals.'

This was the first indication that I have been able to find from any source that negotiations on the purchase of the line had even started. After 90 minutes of discussion, the motion was carried by 16 votes to 6.

Before the year ended it was announced that Mr Derek Portman had resigned and left the board because of other business commitments. His place as chairman was to be taken by Mr David Morgan, a Grays Inn solicitor who was already on the board. Financial Director Mr Peter Rivett was appointed vice-chairman and managing director. As he left the emergency meeting at Williton, which had been called to discuss these changes, Mr Rivett said Mr Portman would be missed for his strong leadership and that the policy of the company would remain unchanged, in that an immediate purchase of part or the whole of the line was the key to profitability.

At the next company AGM on 7 April 1984, many of the supporters of the railway were to learn that the losses for the year ending 31 October 1983 had not been as heavy as had been forecast.

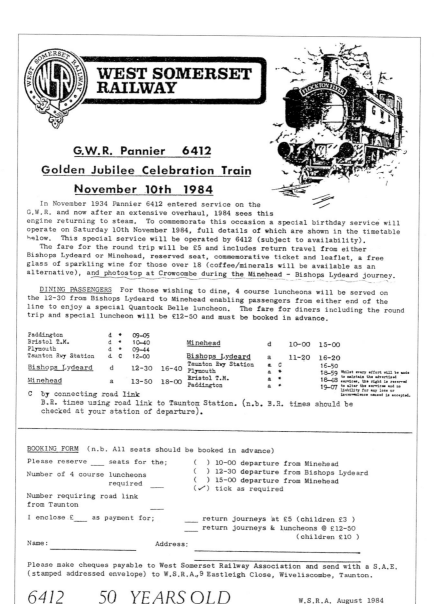

WEST SOMERSET RAILWAY

G.W.R. Pannier 6412

Golden Jubilee Celebration Train

November 10th 1984

In November 1934 Pannier 6412 entered service on the G.W.R. and now after an extensive overhaul, 1984 sees this engine returning to steam. To commemorate this occasion a special birthday service will operate on Saturday 10th November 1984, full details of which are shown in the timetable below. This special service will be operated by 6412 (subject to availability).

The fare for the round trip will be £5 and includes return travel from either Bishops Lydeard or Minehead, reserved seat, commemorative ticket and leaflet, a free glass of sparkling wine for those over 18 (coffee/minerals will be available as an alternative), and photostop at Crowcombe during the Minehead - Bishops Lydeard journey.

DINING PASSENGERS For those wishing to dine, 4 course luncheons will be served on the 12-30 from Bishops Lydeard to Minehead enabling passengers from either end of the line to enjoy a special Quantock Belle luncheon. The fare for diners including the round trip and special luncheon will be £12-50 and must be booked in advance.

Paddington	d	*	09-05				
Bristol T.M.	d	*	10-40	Minehead	d	10-00	15-00
Plymouth	d	*	09-44				
Taunton Rwy Station	d	C	12-00	Bishops Lydeard	a	11-20	16-20
				Taunton Rwy Station	a	16-50	
Bishops Lydeard	d		12-30 16-40	Plymouth	a	*	18-59
				Bristol T.M.	a	*	18-48
Minehead	a		13-50 18-00	Paddington	a	*	19-07

Whilst every effort will be made to maintain the advertised services, the right is reserved to alter the services and no liability for any loss or inconvenience caused is accepted.

C by connecting road link
   B.R. times using road link to Taunton Station. (n.b. B.R. times should be checked at your station of departure).

BOOKING FORM (n.b. All seats should be booked in advance)

Please reserve ____ seats for the;   ( ) 10-00 departure from Minehead
                                          ( ) 12-30 departure from Bishops Lydeard
Number of 4 course luncheons   ( ) 15-00 departure from Minehead
                required ____   (✔) tick as required

Number requiring road link
from Taunton   ____

I enclose £____ as payment for;   ____ return journeys at £5 (children £3)
                                    ____ return journeys & luncheons @ £12-50
                                                         (children £10)

Name: _____   Address: _____

Please make cheques payable to West Somerset Railway Association and send with a S.A.E. (stamped addressed envelope) to W.S.R.A., 9 Eastleigh Close, Wiveliscombe, Taunton.

6412   50 YEARS OLD   W.S.R.A. August 1984

19

1984: A New Start

When January 1984 arrived, many people, including volunteers, were still wondering if the WSR would be operating trains during the coming year. During January it was announced that a BR expert would be visiting the line at the end of the month to carry out an assessment of the line's scrap value. It was claimed that this figure was the missing ingredient that would enable the county council to fix a final price tag for the purchase of the line.

An official of the company said, 'If the valuation is too high then the railway could be struggling for its life. There already appears to be an acceptance of the fact that the original bid of £135,000 was pitched too low'. Now he claimed, 'The railway hopes to do a compromise deal with the county – to buy the most profitable half of the line between Minehead and Williton, and lease the remainder.'

Replying to concerns that the purchase of this section of line, including the stations at Minehead, Dunster, Blue Anchor, Washford, Watchet and Williton, as well as signal boxes could cost more than had been offered for the whole line, Mr Rivett replied, 'We have every confidence in the future. The railway is solvent for the first time in four years. If the purchase price is near the company's valuation then we shall shortly be in a position to buy a large slice of track, say from Williton to Blue Anchor. The remainder of the track from Blue Anchor to Minehead could be paid for in a phased deal next year, as long as the county is prepared to let us lease the section of track from Williton to Bishops Lydeard.'

Mr Rivett gave the impression that the company would be able to pay out around £55,000 during 1984 for the track purchase. The remainder, and the larger slice because it contained the Minehead Station complex, would be handed over the following year. He added that the terms of any sale would be 999 years' leasehold and that the county council would insist that should the company cease trading at any time the southern end of the line (Williton–Bishops Lydeard) would automatically revert back to the council.

In the event that the company ceased trading, the northern section of the line would be inherited by the company's successors. It appeared that the county council were prepared to lease the southern half of the line for around £6,000 per year, compared with the existing rent of £17,500 per year for the whole line. Finally, Mr Rivett stated, 'We hope that the county will agree to a purchase and lease deal. Renting half the line would be well within our pocket. Owning the other half will make all the difference, because it will reduce our annual outgoings sufficiently to put us safely in the black. But this presupposes that the final purchase price is right from our point of view.'

On the motive-power front, it was announced that *Victor* was expected back in steam in March, that *Vulcan* would be running shortly, as soon as minor repairs had been completed, and that extra help had been obtained in an attempt to accelerate the return of No.6412 to service. It was also announced that the company had purchased the 2-car Craven DMU from the consortium from whom they had previously leased the unit. This meant that the company now owned two 2-car DMUs.

Another locomotive to arrive on the railway at this time was No.3850, a former Great Western 2-8-0 heavy freight loco, but this was to become a very long-term restoration project for the owning group. Later in the year the No.3850 group were able to announce that they had acquired a second ex-GWR locomotive from the Gwilli Railway for £10,000. This loco, No.7820 *Dinmore Manor*, was a member of the 'Manor' class of locomotives, and was built at Swindon Works in 1950. Many members of the class had worked over the Cambrian lines in BR days and so this engine was ideal for the Minehead branch. Fortunately the group were able to complete the restoration of this locomotive in a much shorter time span than No.3850, and the Manor was able to enter service on the WSR in 1994 and has proved to be a valuable member of the fleet.

In November the company was able to announce the return to service of pannier tank No.6412 after completion of an overhaul costing £20,000. The locomotive returned to traffic just in time to celebrate her Golden Jubilee, having been built at Swindon works in 1934.

During February, an appeal was made for more volunteers. They were needed at Watchet Station because the booking office there had only been manned for nine days during the previous season, with no volunteers at all over Easter nor during June, July, and August. A company spokesman said, 'Watchet has a big potential earning power and the WSR needs to make the most of all its assets.' Volunteers were also needed to man the station buffet at Minehead, which had now been named The Railway Inn.

In March, an article in the *County Gazette* claimed that there was a possibility that the finances of the company could be helped by a lucrative freight deal, The article claimed that Tarmac Roadstone Western was contemplating shipping up to 1,000 tons of stone from its newly acquired Triscombe Quarry, and that exploratory talks between the two companies would start shortly.

Many years before stone from this quarry had been an important source of income for the Great Western Railway, with stone brought to a stone crushing plant near Crowcombe Station by means of an aerial rope way, and after the stone had been crushed it was propelled in narrow gauge tipper wagons onto a loading dock adjacent to a siding, near the station, where it was tipped in to the standard gauge wagons standing on the track below.

But, as so often in the history of the WSR at this time, the good news was followed by bad news, when Mr Peter Rivett confirmed that an independent assessor had valued the line at £224,000, to this sum there had to be a further £100,000 that the county council required for the land, making a total of £324,000. Commenting on this news Mr

Rivett said: 'We find the valuation still hard to believe. It varies so widely from that of our own technical advisors. The operation to lift the line is very labour intensive and in itself would cost £100,000. We thought that a £124,000 scrap value was more realistic, but we agreed to this arbitration. We will continue negotiations with the county, and if, and when, a satisfactory agreement is reached, any proposal will be put before an Extraordinary General Meeting later in the year.'

Also in March, the company announced its plans for the new operating season, stating that it would be operating steam or diesel railcar services, every day from the beginning of April until the end of September. Special services would operate over the Easter weekend; the company also announced that it would be operating a through DMU service between Minehead and Bishops Lydeard on Saturdays only. On other days, passengers would have to change at Williton as in the past. Special reduced fares of £1.90 were offered for this Saturday service from Minehead to Bishops Lydeard or £2.10 from Minehead to Taunton, using the connecting bus service operated by buses hired from Berry's coaches.

The innovation for the coming year was described as a 'pub on wheels'. A team (led by Phil Weaver, at that time the railway's shop manager, and who is still active on the railway) had converted a Mk 1 TSO coach into a travelling pub, complete with the appropriate pub sign, and had painted it in the new GWR-style livery. It was planned that this coach would be attached to all the steam services operating that year. Mr Doug Hill observed, 'It is all part of our drive to keep the railway in the black. The lads have made an excellent job of the bar; it should be a real attraction for our passengers.'

Another innovation, which was rather surprising in light of events that were to happen later in the year, was the introduction of the 'Roadrailer' tickets, a combined rail and bus ticket. These tickets were available from the bus station in Taunton on weekdays and were the result of a joint promotion by the Southern National Bus Co. and the West Somerset Railway.

In April, it was announced that the WSR had entered negotiations with BR and the NUR regarding the possibility of running excursion trains from various locations on the main rail network through to Minehead.

Shortly before the AGM was to be held, the railway's hopes of a lucrative contract to haul stone from Crowcombe Station to the main line at Norton Fitzwarren were dashed when Mr Eric Barnett, the county council planning officer speaking for the Quantock Hills joint-advisory committee, claimed that the proposed deal was not a sound proposition. Speaking to a meeting of the West Somerset District Council, he stated, 'The possibility of Tarmac using the WSR seems unlikely. Most markets for the stone would be local and the quarry output would be relatively small. In any case, movement of the stone by rail would not overcome lorry movements from the quarry to the A358. The stone has to be transported to Crowcombe by road where it has to be loaded onto trains.'

During the meeting it was revealed that Tarmac was proposing to spend £4 million to extract 250,000 tons of hangman's gravel per year from Triscombe Quarry. It was after these figures that West Somerset District Cllr Mr Sydney Brown, who was vice-chairman of the aforementioned Quantock Hills joint-advisory committee, said to the same meeting, 'The size of the shipments does not appear to be large enough to create any major problems. As it means that the lorries would have to use the A358 to get to the railhead at Crowcombe any advantage looks slim indeed.'

After further discussion the committee decided that freighting by rail was not a sound proposition. The reason that Tarmac had originally entered into discussions with both the WSR and BR, was obviously because they thought that they might experience difficulties with the local or the county council if they wished to transport this amount of stone by road. Because of the attitude of the local authorities, Tarmac no longer had any incentive to pursue the talks with the railway companies (BR and the WSR). Shortly afterwards, a spokesman for Tarmac stated that the talks with the two bodies had uncovered considerable practical difficulties, and although discussions would continue, he was not hopeful of a favourable outcome.

Once again, the shareholders attending the AGM found that the venue had been changed and this year it was to be held in the St John's Ambulance Hall, which happened to be next door to the social club. Some 150 shareholders (down from 200 the previous year) attended the meeting. Some of those shareholders who had travelled from the Home Counties and the London area, together with others who had made an early start, were no doubt glad of the excellent meal that had been served on the special train that had been provided from Bishops Lydeard. They also commented on how impressed they had been by the courtesy and attentiveness of the volunteer catering staff. Some were surprised by the welcome they received when, on arrival at Minehead Station on a grey cold day, they were welcomed by the new chairman of the company, Mr David Morgan, who was splendidly attired in a gold-braided frockcoat of the 1890s and a splendid top hat, a fitting reminder of the Victorian steam era.

As soon as the meeting started, and the chairman rose to inform the meeting of the first item on the agenda, which was the accounts and the directors' report, it was obvious that the tensions that had been present at the two previous meetings in 1982 and 1983 had eased. The shareholders were somewhat surprised, and no doubt relieved, to learn that the loss for the financial year ending 31 October 1983 had been £4,056, compared with a loss £4,279 for the previous year. These figures appeared to be in complete contrast to the anticipated losses of £15/20,000 for the same period.

As Mr Rivett explained how the figures had been calculated, it became obvious that the directors had not been guilty of exaggerating the difficult financial situation that the company had been facing at the end of the previous financial year. If it had not been for the action of the association, who agreed to convert a loan of £11,250 to the company into a gift; the trading loss for the year would have been over £17,500. This gesture had reduced the trading loss to £6,202, and other extraordinary income had further reduced the loss to £4,056. It was also disclosed that in spite of two fare increases during the period under review of 10 per cent and 15 per cent, the income from fares had risen by only 1 per cent. It was considered that the poor figures were not due to the fare increases, but to the weather conditions during the year. It was also revealed that turnover had increased from £97,148 to £102,119 but staff, diesel and coal costs had all increased over the previous year.

It had also been necessary to increase the number of people employed by the company from six to eight.

During the chairman's report, Mr Morgan started by pointing out that he had not been the chairman for the period that he was about to review. He then paid a warm tribute to Mr Portman, who, as readers will recall, had been forced to resign in December, because of business commitments. Recalling the days in 1981 when the company was faced with liquidation, he said that without the efforts of Mr Portman the West Somerset Railway would now be a distant memory. Thanks were also due to the staff and volunteers, and to the shareholders, for the support given to the board, both by physical effort and by way of 'share moneys'.

The chairman was able to inform the meeting that agreement had been reached with the county council regarding the value of the land (£100,000) and that discussions were continuing on the value of the track; he also revealed that the company had been able to pay a sum of £17,500 in rents, which included a half-year's rent that had been 'frozen' by the council the previous year.

After the proposal that the accounts be accepted had been passed by the shareholders, the chairman handed over the proceedings to Mr Peter Rivett, who informed the meeting that the recent appeal to shareholders to help pay off the remaining £9,000 of a Somerset County Council debenture loan (originally for £33,942) had already raised £7,200. He then added that perhaps if THAT HAT (the chairman's top hat) were handed around...! It was at this moment that Peter Rivett's young daughter Victoria produced her father's bowler hat, which with the assistance of one of the shareholders was soon being passed around the hall. When it became clear that a bowler hat was not going to be large enough for all the contributions, Mr Morgan's top hat started to do the rounds. After the meeting had ended it was announced that a sum of £310 had been collected in the hat(s).

In May, the newsletter produced by the Association informed its readers that the fare receipts on the line during April of £7,000 were below budget, but by careful driving and thoughtful timetabling, gross profits were maintained. Another article in the same edition of that newsletter stated that although steam services remained the major attraction on preserved railways like the WSR, there was a growing nostalgia amongst the public for the early classes of diesel power that had now become extinct on BR. For this reason the Diesel & Electric Group based at Williton would be holding the first diesel gala on the railway, during the weekend of 14–15 July when their entire fleet of locomotives would be on display.

The next blow to the board and the WSR was the announcement that once again all movements on and off the line had been 'blacked' by the NUR. The first indication of any problems came when the board started to make arrangements for the transfer of newly acquired stock from the main line to the branch line. In a statement to the *West Somerset Free Press*, Mr Rivett said, 'We found to our surprise that we were still subject to blacking. This is short-sighted because the NUR can only be the losers. We are not after their jobs, neither are they in any danger from us. We are buying redundant stock from BR but it is twice the price to haul it in by road. There is also the prospect that we shall be buying BR sleepers and bringing them in by rail, this would mean more work not less for the NUR.'

It appeared that the prospects of excursion trains from many points on the national network would also be jeopardised, again resulting in a further loss of work for NUR members. Whilst admitting that this traffic would not affect the jobs of members driving buses – the original cause of the dispute – Mr Ron Squire, the Taunton NUR branch secretary, said, 'I do not know what all the fuss is about, as far as I am concerned there has always been a union policy of non-co-operation as far as the WSR was concerned. That is still the case.' He claimed, 'The only change is that the WSR has decided not to run commuter services. Allowing rolling stock and supplies in last year was merely a one-off arrangement! It was not intended that it should continue. Only the union's national executive in London can change our policy. As far as we are concerned the blacking stays; indeed as far as we are concerned it was never lifted in the first place.'

As soon as this announcement had been made by the union the WSR directors made a move to persuade the NUR to once and for all lift the ban on the movement of through traffic on the Taunton–Minehead line. Mr Rivett stated that he had written an official letter requesting this action be taken and that he was awaiting the union's response. Tom Millman, the union spokesman in London, confirmed that the letter had been received, saying, 'It is being looked at, but it is unlikely that a decision would be made before the end of July.'

Soon, as well as using their resources to keep the trains running, staff and volunteers were able to devote a little time to planning events aimed at increasing the number of passengers. Publicity highlighting places of interest that could be seen along the line – 'Discover Dunster Go by Train' – was produced, which, among other things, informed the public that Dunster Castle was only a 20-minute walk from the station. Other notices appeared in the local press inviting readers to explore West Somerset by train every Sunday until 29 August. The explorer tour passengers could travel to Dunster for a return fare of £3.70, visit the castle and Yarn Market, enjoying a four-and-a-half-hour stay before their return train. Other explorer destinations were to Watchet, to explore the working harbour, and Minehead, each costing £4.00.

Another special event organised by the association was the first round trip from Bishops Lydeard to Norton Fitzwarren and from there to Minehead and back to Bishops Lydeard. The fare for this train, which ran on Sunday 7 October, was £5.00 for the round trip of 46 miles. Two Class 14 locomotives were booked to haul the train.

What I believe was the second private charter operated by the railway attracted the type of adverse publicity that the company had managed to avoid during the previous two years. A train was hired by members of the Quantock Round Table on Friday 3 August, called the 'Quantock Express Jazz Train'. Music was provided by the 'Quantock Jazzmen' and there was a buffet and bar on the train. The revellers were asked to dress in 1930s style and the charge for the evening's entertainment was £4 per head.

The train was booked to leave Minehead Station at 6.10 p.m., called at all stations to pick up passengers and was due to return to Bishops Lydeard at 11 p.m. before commencing its return journey to Minehead at 11.30 p.m. The entire area had enjoyed a spell of fine sunny, dry weather for some weeks prior to this day, but on the section of the journey from Bishops Lydeard to Williton the heavens opened and a downpour of almost monsoon proportions started. Between Crowcombe and Bishops Lydeard, on the return leg of the journey, the locomotive failed because, as the embarrassed railway officials had to admit, the engine had run out of water. Passengers who had connections to make from Bishops Lydeard were faced with a two-mile walk along the track in the pouring rain, while those who remained continued dancing for three hours until the Class 14 locomotive arrived to rescue them. As a gesture of goodwill the buffet served free food on the return journey and the majority of the passengers stated that they had thoroughly enjoyed themselves. The friends of Williton hospital received £300 from the organisers of the event. Unfortunately this incident reached the national press when it appeared in the *News of the World* on Sunday 5 August.

During the year further problems were experienced, with the local youths in the Watchet area and once again with the town council. A number of the local hooligans ambushed two trains in the cutting to the east of Watchet Station and hurled stones. A number of windows on the trains were broken but fortunately no passengers were injured. The general manager, Doug Hill, said, 'These incidents have caused considerable concern. We are keeping a sharp look out. The police have been notified but have been unable to find the culprits.'

Other incidents in the locality included windows being broken, stones being thrown onto the roof at Watchet Station and stones being placed on the track. Commenting on these incidents Mr Hill said, 'The placing of stones on the track is a particularly foolish action, and could result in the derailment of a train, or perhaps an even worse disaster. This is the first time in three years that we have had any serious incidents of vandalism, and damage, and we hope it will be the last.' Sadly Mr Hill's optimism was short-lived – incidents of this kind have occurred frequently in this area, especially during the school holidays.

Around the same time that the vandalism occurred the WSR was once again experiencing problems with Watchet Town Council. Having recently spent £1,000 on repainting the bridge councillors were demanding that the footbridge (owned by the county council) should be demolished by the WSR at the company's expense and replaced with a pedestrian level crossing, to help mothers who had difficulties in getting their prams across the bridge.

Cllr Ronald Copp informed the council, 'Everyone wants a pedestrian crossing. There is no other way across the line apart from the bridge, but it creates much hardship using it.' Once again the local councillors appeared to have very little knowledge of the area they were supposed to represent, because there was another pedestrian level crossing at the other end of the station platform at Watchet and approximately 200 yards in the opposite direction there was a road bridge over the line. Other councillors' knowledge of their area appeared to be little better and Cllr Tony Knight said he was in support of the demolishment. A small minority of people in the town wanted to retain it and once again it was Dave Rouse, one of the most experienced drivers on the railway, who had to point out the shortcomings in the plans, when he wrote another letter to the *West Somerset Free Press*. In the edition of the paper printed on 23 November he stated:

> In the Free Press of November 16th it was stated that Watchet Town Council would like to see the footbridge removed and replaced by a pedestrian level crossing. Apparently councillors are unaware that it is the policy of the Department of the Environment, to replace level crossings

with bridges, as they are not the obvious safety hazard, that exists with any crossing on the level.

There is no way that the D of E would permit such a change, and even less so with the crossing being at the bottom of a steep climb out of the station and over the embankment.

Why should it suddenly become so important, he asked, to replace a bridge that has stood for as long as any Watchet resident can remember. To say that there is no other way across the line apart from the Bridge is just rubbish. There is a long standing crossing at the other end (of the platform) apart from the road bridge, so anyone with prams or heavy shopping trolleys can cross there, as they have always done.

The footbridge has recently been painted and so should be good for the next forty years. It would be best for the council to forget any ideas on removal of the bridge, and concentrate on more urgent problems, like vandalism.

Another local resident pointed out that four people had been killed on the footpath crossing at the other end of the platform and that not so long ago the same council had been pressing for a bridge to be erected at Govers Lane. Other fears were expressed of the limited visibility of the crossing that train drivers would have, descending Kentsford bank on the approach to the station.

In November came the announcement that the company had made an improved offer to the county council for the purchase of the line. Although details of the offer were not disclosed the revised figure was believed to have been in the region of £150,000.

The format for the Santa Specials changed again this year, with trains leaving Minehead for Santa's secret grotto, which appeared to be very similar to Blue Anchor Station. On 15 and 22 December trains left Minehead at 2.30 p.m. and Bishops Lydeard for Santa's other grotto at Crowcombe Station at 11.10 a.m., 12.10 p.m., 1.40 p.m. and 2.40 p.m. For the first time notices of these services stressed that advance booking was essential. The fare for both events was £2.50 for adults, which included a glass of sherry and a mince pie, and £2 for children, including a present, a cracker and sweets. Later the company was able to announce that record numbers of passengers had been carried on the Santa trains, that all seats had been sold, and on some occasions trains had been strengthened to cope with the number of passengers wishing to travel. Except for the fact that more trains are now run, this format has remains unaltered. The company also operated special shopper trains from Minehead to Taunton (via bus link) on 8, 15 and 22 December.

For the first time in the history of the preserved line a best-kept station competition was held for stations along the branch, reviving a custom that went back to GWR days. In 1984 the competition was judged by Mr Ernest Walkley, a senior BR official from Taunton. Minehead Station was declared the winner, much to the delight of the volunteer stationmaster Mr John Guest.

On staff matters, the occupations of the volunteers continued to interest the local press, and when the first lady signalman (no politically correct terms like signal persons in those days!) was 'passed out' to operate the signal box at Blue Anchor Station, the local newspapers quickly picked up the story. Mrs Elizabeth Ann Shoosmith, who worked as a computer programmer in her 'day' job, lived at Radstock and, after having spent her spare time over the previous five years as a volunteer on the WSR, thought she would try her hand in a signal box. She is reported to have said, 'It might seem a far cry from my daily job but, actually, a railway system follows logical sequences and operates, in one way, rather like a computer. You have to keep an eye on what is going on, and remember to do things in the correct sequence. Some of the levers are a bit hard to throw,' she claimed, 'but you soon get the knack.' Fortunately for their marriage Elizabeth's husband was also a keen railway enthusiast and was a trainee DMU driver on the line.

With the summer season drawing to its end, the volume of complaints against the local bus services started to grow. The complaints were taken up by Minehead Town Council after a number of people were left stranded when the Rapide long-distance coach simply failed to turn up one Saturday afternoon. After waiting for 45 minutes beyond the time that the coach was due, the disgruntled holidaymakers went to the tourist information office where staff tried to telephone Taunton bus station, only to find that no one answered.

When the tourist office tried to contact Sherrins Coaches, the company's official agents in Minehead, they found that their offices were closed on Saturday afternoon. The result was that all eight intending passengers missed their onward connections and two of them missed flights from Heathrow. Before they left Minehead all the holidaymakers involved vowed that they would not be returning to the resort again, two of the party even cancelling hotel bookings made for the following year.

During the following months council officials made numerous complaints to the bus company but failed to obtain any positive response. Possibly as a result of this, and similar incidents, an attempt was made by the town council to avoid other tourists boycotting the town due to the poor bus services. In December the town council informed the *Somerset Free Press* that they had written to the headquarters of the NUR in London asking the union to reconsider its blockade of the rail link with the West Somerset private railway. This move followed a preliminary approach to the district office of the union at Taunton, which brought the standard response: the blacking could only be lifted by the union's national executive committee. The Town Clerk Don Wall announced that as yet he had not received any reply, but promised that he would continue to progress the matter.

This year also saw the introduction of a scheme that was to be of great benefit to residents in the Taunton Deane and West Somerset District Council areas. It became known as the 'Star Card' scheme, and it entitled residents to travel at half price on the railway for twelve months, once they had completed the application form, paid the fee registration of 50p and presented proof of address and a passport-type photograph to Minehead Station. Apart from the fact that passes are now issued for a three-year period and cost £3.00, the scheme continues to operate to this day.

Towards the end of the year rumours started to circulate amongst the staff and volunteers on the line – and later appeared in the local press – that there was a possibility the railway would either break even or make a small profit for the period ending 31 October 1984. Such stories were understandably greeted with some suspicion by those who had survived all the dramas besetting the company since its inception.

★ THE STARCARD SCHEME ★

★ STARCARD is available to all residents in West Somerset and Taunton Deane Districts!

★ STARCARD entitles the holder to travel at at HALF NORMAL FARES on ALL WEST SOMERSET RAILWAY trains, (except "Quantock Belle" dining cars and Special Excursions)

Examples (1983): Watchet to Minehead return Normal £1.90 Starcard 95p
Minehead to Taunton return Normal £4.00 Starcard £2.00
Watchet to Taunton return Normal £3.10 Starcard £1.55
BISHOPS LYDEARD to MINEHEAD RETURN NORMAL £3.40 Starcard £1.70

★ STARCARD is valid for one year from date of issue. All YOU have to do to obtain YOUR STARCARD is:
1. Complete the Application Form below,
2. Take it - or send it with SAE please - to The Railway Station, Minehead, Somerset,*with,
   a) 50p
   b) a recent passport style photograph,
   c) proof of your local residence.

To WEST SOMERSET RAILWAY PLC
I am a resident in West Somerset or Taunton Deane Districts. I enclose 50p and a recent photograph and I wish to apply for my STARCARD (* you may also apply in person only to Bishop's Lydeard Railway Station)
BLOCK LETTERS PLEASE

NAME...Mr/Mrs/Miss/

Address..

....

Signature.......................... Date.........................

Office Use only STARCARD ISSUED	No.	Date

20

1985: Happy Days Are Here At Last

In 1985 many railway groups in the country decided to commemorate the 150th anniversary of the founding of the Great Western Railway. BR ran a number of steam services in the West Country hauled by former Great Western steam locomotives. However, these celebrations were somewhat muted after BR Engineering announced the closure of the Swindon works of the former Great Western Railway, three weeks before the planned programme of events was due to start. The unions, not unreasonably in view of the large number of workers who lost their jobs, withdrew their co-operation, which led to problems with some of the events planned by BR.

Like all the other preserved railways, the WSR decided to go ahead with their planned events, which included the provision of a trackwork exhibition at Crowcombe Station, the opening of a GWR museum at Blue Anchor Station (both still in situ), the pannier tank No.6412 (the only GWR locomotive available) operating on the line at the start of the summer season for the first time since 1979 and a newly painted chocolate and cream set of five coaches which had been restored 'to the finest Great Western standards'. This set, which was to be hauled by No.6412, would operate on Sundays only and would be known as the 'Great Western Limited'.

Other planned events included a special 'Quantock Belle' service in which both the diners and staff dressed in Victorian costumes, a steam-hauled train from Bishops Lydeard to Norton Fitzwarren, and goods train demonstrations. The WSR also assisted the Taunton branch of the Great Western Society to stage two exhibitions in Taunton at this time. The first, known as the 'Great Way Round', was held in conjunction with the Somerset County Museum and the second exhibition, called 'God's Wonderful Railway', was held in the Abermarle Assembly Rooms before moving to other locations in Somerset – Bridgwater, Wellington and Taunton Library – during the summer.

In February a firm called Hover West announced that it would start to operate a hovercraft service between Barry in South Wales (where many steam locomotives were awaiting recovery in Dai Woodham's scrap yard) and Minehead. The plans were for the hovercraft to arrive on the beach opposite Minehead Station. Mr Clive Griffiths, the owner of Hover West said, 'The railway has agreed to act as our main agent in the town, and at the same time allow the station to be used as our terminal. The WSR will handle all bookings and ticket sales, with both companies determined to boost trade for each other. Our customers can travel the most modern way by hovercraft, and then transfer to ride – the Victorian way – on a steam train.' It appeared that under the agreement reached between the two parties, couriers would shepherd travellers from the hovercraft to the station and back again, and the travellers would be able to use the station's buffet and waiting room facilities. Talks were also stated to be underway to obtain combined hovercraft and steam train tickets throughout the summer. Other reports claimed that the Southern National bus company and other coach operators were vying to operate excursions over Exmoor in conjunction with the hovercraft services. Because the crossing only took 25 minutes from Barry it was claimed that an hourly service could be operated if there was sufficient demand.

The refusal of the board of the WSR to consider the request by the Watchet Town Council to install a pedestrian crossing at Watchet provoked fury amongst the councillors. Deputy chairman of the council, Cllr Malcolm Brown, claimed that the council had been promised a report on the crossing by the railway and it was not even going to get that. Warning the council that the line was up for sale and likely to be purchased by the WSR, the chairman Cllr Alec Damby said, 'We should write to the County insisting that a piece of land should be reserved for a crossing. A clause should be written into the sale terms safeguarding a crossing.' Cllr Tony Knight attacked the railway for not putting the crossing idea to the Railway Inspectorate, adding that the railway was breaking an undertaking given three years previously to do so. Still continuing on this theme he said, 'Trains come into Watchet at a very slow speed; it is not like a main line with expresses. I cannot understand the logic that says a crossing would be dangerous.'

Continuing the attack on the WSR Cllr Mrs Eileen Woods proposed that the county should be asked what its proposals were for the present pedestrian railway bridge over the line at Watchet Station. Showing the same remarkable ignorance of the area as many of her colleagues, she continued, 'If the line was purchased by the WSR the town could end up with no bridge or level crossing. We could find ourselves in the situation where neither the county nor the railway claims responsibility for the bridge.' Ignoring the advice given by people with a far greater knowledge of the problems of railway level crossings than the councillors, a proposal that the council should write to the county asking them what they proposed to do about the crossing was carried unanimously.

In March it was announced that work had started on building a new station on the branch, to be known as Doniford Beach Halt; it was situated between Williton and Watchet stations, and was intended to serve the nearby holiday camp and caravan site. The halt was to be built by a Manpower Services work force using materials rescued by the volunteers. It was hoped that the work would be completed in three months, and that it would be open in time to cope with the peak summer traffic.

After admitting that when the station was opened, the WSR would have more stations than BR in Somerset at that time, the railway company director Mr Ken Davis said, 'It will be quite a simple halt in the Great Western tradition, but it will be long enough to take four coaches.'

Other plans that were intended to increase the income of the railway during the summer season were announced in March. These included mail trains which, by arrangement with the Post Office, meant trains could pick up letters from any of the stations on the line. Only first-class letters were accepted, and after being franked with a special 20p WSR stamp they were dropped in to the nearest postbox to Minehead Station. Obviously aware of the problems with the NUR Mr John Nash, the railway's postmaster, was quick to point out, 'There is no possibility of us being in competition with the Post Office. The letters we shall be carrying are for onward transmission by the Post Office. What we are hoping is that stamp collectors will rush to obtain samples, if they do so, the railway could raise as much as £2,000 in the coming year.' I rather think that this was not one of the most successful ventures carried out by the line, as I can find no further mention of the project.

Another idea that was to prove more successful was the operation of 'Sunset Specials' for the first time during this year. These trains which operated every Wednesday evening from 19 June until 1 September, leaving Minehead Station at 20.15 hours, arriving at Blue Anchor Station at 20.30 hours, allowing passengers to stroll along the nearby beach for 45 minutes, before the train returned to Minehead at 21.30 hours. All services, it was stated, would be steam-hauled, and the timetable claimed that advance booking was essential. This venture was more successful and Sunset Specials have been included in the timetables up to the present time.

The association also played its part in the attempts to increase the number of passengers using the line by operating more dining trains. In addition to the special Victorian train already mentioned they operated a total of ten Sunday luncheon trains, and a further four Saturday evening dinner trains. The fares on the luncheon trains were now £12 and included afternoon tea, as well as the lunch and round trip. On the Saturday evening trains the price was £10 for dinner and the round trip. It was hoped that all services would be steam-hauled by pannier tank 6412 and, once again, it was stressed that advance booking was essential.

On Saturday 23 March the Annual General Meeting of the company was held. Although the venue for the meeting remained the same as the previous year (the St John's Ambulance Hall), the starting time of the meeting was brought forward to 2 p.m.

Having enjoyed their lunch on the by-now-customary shareholders special train they arrived at the venue in good time for the chairman to start the meeting promptly. In view of the rumours that had been circulating, the first item on the agenda, the company's financial statements, was eagerly awaited. When it was announced that the company had made an operating loss of £566 there was a stunned silence, followed by an audible sigh of relief when Mr Rivett announced that thanks to the donation of £5,833 received from the West Somerset District Council the company had achieved a trading profit of £3,342 before tax.

Other interesting facts to emerge showed that income from fares increased from £81,804 in the previous year to £84,052. The income from all other sources, with the exception of the shop and buffet services, was down with the result that turnover had only increased from £137,257 to £139,078 during the year. Although problems, due to the prolonged miners' strike, had been experienced with coal supplies, which were also of variable quality, the company had managed to hold the fuel costs down to below those of the previous year. It was also disclosed that a further £41,711 shares had been issued, compared with £13,853 the previous year, and all loans that had fallen due during the same period had been paid, as had all rental charges that were due. The financial report was adopted by the meeting.

In his report the chairman stated that he thought that the company 'had turned the corner', and paid tribute to the 'Herculean' efforts of the staff and volunteers. Admitting that the small profit was only due to the generosity of West Somerset District Council and that the position of the company was still extremely 'fragile', he proclaimed, 'At least we have stemmed the flow of blood.' He informed the meeting that discussions on the purchase of the line were continuing, that an improved offer had been made to the county and as soon as a firm price was fixed, all the shareholders would be circularised. In the meantime the appeal for funds for this project remained open. It was stressed that it was essential that agreement on the purchase of the line be reached as quickly as possible because rent was due to increase by a further £5,000 at the end of the financial year. He concluded by saying that during the year under review, all the directors' efforts had been concentrated on keeping costs under control, but during the coming year the efforts of directors, staff, and volunteers must be concentrated on attracting more visitors to the line. He set a target of 10,000 extra passengers during 1985.

This is the first year, I believe, that the shareholders were not exhorted to purchase more shares during the meeting, although no doubt the board hoped that the improving financial figures would persuade them to do so.

In spite of fears expressed by fishermen about the possible danger to their livelihood – because fish stocks would be driven away from the area by the noise of the hovercraft – and worries expressed by other parties that the craft would be a danger to bathers and people on the beach, who could be injured by flying gravel and sand, the service won the approval of the transport inspectors – the service was cleared to start in May. After two false starts, when representatives of the WSDC arrived to welcome the hovercraft only to be left standing on the beach because it failed to arrive on both occasions due to a combination of low water and rock ridges showing, it finally arrived on 23 May. After cracking a bottle of champagne over the bow of the craft, Mr Sydney Brown, the chairman of the district council said, 'We give the hovercraft a warm welcome' and added: 'It could be one of the most beneficial additions to our holiday trade.'

Unfortunately, these hopes were soon to be dashed; only a month later on 28 June, Mr Griffiths of Hover West admitted that no services had operated during the previous week due to the lack of passengers and the bad weather. Worse news was to come, when he admitted that although he had tried to obtain the help of a wealthy backer to assist him in running the service, if he was unable to attract further capital before the end of the week, then the venture would collapse. His forecast was accurate and the thirty-eight-seat hovercraft was returned to the Isle of Wight the following week.

In August came the inevitable news that the WSR directors had not been successful in obtaining the contract to move stone from Triscombe Quarry by rail. When the news was announced, Mr Rivett admitted that the contract would have required the railway to put in a lot of investment up front and that pay-off time would be a long way in the future.

The long-running problems with the NUR continued. The chairman was not best pleased when, having written to the NUR asking the reasons for the blacking and asking them what action they wanted the WSR to take to overcome their disagreements, he had received a reply that the NUR could not agree to the WSR suggestions. The WSR had not made any suggestions. The chairman then announced that, as the NUR appeared not to know the reasons for their action, he would write to the TUC asking them to intervene in the dispute. The extent of his anger became apparent when he continued, 'We are fed up with petty dictators telling us what we can and cannot do.' He added, 'I know of several members of the NUR who are out of sympathy with their union view. They have tried to bring this matter up at the annual conference of the NUR, but cannot even get it on the agenda. We know that this is a London-based decision and that nothing can be done locally.'

Mr Rivett later disclosed how badly the problem with the NUR affected the company when he stated the WSR had recently purchased a number of coaches from BR, that were surplus to BR's requirements, for the sum of £1,500 each, which included the cost of delivery to the WSR by rail. Because of the attitude of the union the company had been forced to pay a further £1,500 for each coach to be delivered by road.

Despite the need to make every effort to maximise their income the general manager Mr Doug Hill admitted in June that the company was losing valuable income. The problem was caused by there not being enough volunteers to man the booking offices at the many stations along the line. Although guards and travelling ticket inspectors tried to ensure that all passengers paid their fares they were not always successful; the railway had to rely on the honesty of their passengers. As Mr Hill said, 'A lot of passengers are honest and pay when they have completed their journey, but there is an unknown number slipping through our fingers. We could do with at least another two booking office clerks a day, particularly at Blue Anchor, and Watchet.'

On the locomotive front, in July it was announced that the Somerset & Dorset Railway Trust, owners of 2-8-0 locomotive No. 53808, had awarded a contract to the WSR to complete the restoration work that had been started by the Trust, in exchange for a hire agreement permitting the WSR to use the locomotive on their line for a period of eight years from the time when the work was completed. Photographs of *Jennifer* being lifted (at a cost of £300 for the hire of the crane) to enable fitters to carry out much-needed work on the wheels and bearings coincided with the news that *Vulcan* had been 'failed' in service with broken roller bearings, which it was estimated would cost around £5,000 to repair.

Steadily increasing numbers of passengers using the line during the summer timetable, combined with the problems outlined above, forced Mr Rivett to write the following letter to the *Steam Railway Magazine* in July:

May I, through the medium of your correspondence column, test the spirit of co-operation said to exist between the various preservation groups in the UK.

Over the last three years the board of the West Somerset Railway has striven to make sure this line did not go under. We have had some measure of success. Our shareholders have stood by us and pumped in more money, the staff have responded to the leadership given, and the volunteers have commenced projects long shelved through lack of encouragement.

If a company is measured by the progress from continual losses, insolvency, and debt to solvency, lack of debt, and profitability then very real progress has been made down in Somerset.

In one area however progress has been slow. We inherited two Bagnall tank engines that were not designed for the long journeys demanded of them. To these have been added pannier tank no 6412 out shopped by Minehead late last year.

We desperately need to buy or hire another good quality locomotive of at least 15,000 lbs TE, and an axle weight not exceeding 17 tons 12 cwt. It need not be an ex-GWR engine although that is clearly preferred. In spite of comments bandied about in the past, we are a responsible railway, quite capable of buying or hiring another locomotive and looking after it.

At the risk of sounding immodest, the actions of our past Chairman Derek Portman, and latterly David Morgan, and the board in saving the WSR, did in fact save the railway preservation movement from sustaining its first casualty. We now need someone to show the same faith in the WSR that we showed, by making available a suitable locomotive for a period of two years. After that there is string of restored locomotives coming on stream.

If you have a suitable locomotive trapped in a preservation siding, or if you wish to sell a 'runner' to raise funds for another project, kindly contact the undersigned.

To avoid misunderstandings, principals only are invited to apply.

Fortunately for the WSR this appeal was successful and the board was able to announce later that Collett 0-6-0 No. 3205 would shortly be coming to the line from the Severn Valley Railway. This engine performed sterling service on the railway for many years until it was transferred to the South Devon Railway.

Towards the end of the season came the first indication of a possible change in attitude by the councillors on the county council towards the WSR. Until now they had been aware of the problems between the NUR and the railway but had appeared unwilling to intervene. Cllr Glyn Court, a member of the council's newly created transport committee, said that the county council wanted to break the deadlock that was keeping the WSR out of Taunton and it was therefore seeking urgent talks with both BR and the unions. After announcing that the county council was also prepared to consider giving grants to enable the WSR to carry freight traffic, he said, 'We are turning our attention more creatively towards the development of West Somerset – and in particular its tourist trade. We want to get the WSR into Taunton because of its vital contribution to the prosperity of the area. It is a major tourist attraction but also capable of handling freight. We hope to arrange tri-partite talks to resolve the present impasse with an agreement acceptable to all sides.'

The spirit of co-operation did not, however, extend to the West Somerset District Council whose planners turned down an application by the WSR to lease part of the station area to concessionaires. The company hoped to obtain extra income by renting a small area to a firm hiring out bicycles and Sinclair C5 electric cars. District planning officer Mr Colin Russell informed the councillors, 'We are not opposed to tourist facilities; on the contrary, we would wish to promote them, but after all the railway is a tourist facility in itself, do we want to see it cluttered with bikes and things?' The council rejected the application.

A test of the strength of the new attitude to the WSR from the county council came when, after the meeting arranged between the county council, BR and the NUR, the council learned that BR required £300,000 to reinstate the link between the main line and the branch. Announcing this after the meeting had ended, Cllr Humphrey Temperley explained that the reason the link had become so expensive was because BR had completed a major re-signalling project in the area, together with the need to install extra track. Explaining that the council had set up a technical working party to look at all the problems and prepare answers and costings. He continued, 'The current county council's policy is to work towards a rail connection, the investment we have in the WSR as a responsible landlord must be enhanced. A successful link will boost the economy and tourist facilities in the area. BR has shown a positive and caring attitude towards the passenger and freight needs of West Somerset.'

Evidence that the new-found goodwill did not extend to all the members of the council came when, in another interview, Cllr Mrs Pat Morley stated that, 'Assurances would have to be given to the bus unions about the future of existing bus services. I think the WSR's future is mainly as a tourist attraction rather than as a public transport service.' Yet another councillor who appeared to be unaware of what was really happening. It was also learned that the NUR had agreed to further talks but a spokesman for the union stated that he saw no new criteria to persuade the union to lift its ban on reaching Taunton. At last it seemed that the county council was starting to become aware of the problems that the WSR directors had faced for almost a decade. When asked for his reaction to the outcome of the talks Mr Rivett replied, 'There is no way we can afford that sum ourselves, we are a bit surprised at the figure, which frankly we find rather high.' If there was to be any chance of footing that kind of bill then other parties, such as the county council, West Somerset and Taunton Deane Council, together with BR, would have to share the costs.

After the summer season had ended the winter timetable, with Santa Specials, Christmas shopper and Quantock Belle trains, followed a similar form to that of the successful previous year. By the end everyone involved with the railway felt that passenger figures had been buoyant and like the chairman believed the railway had indeed turned the corner.

21

1986: We Have Turned the Corner

Further evidence of the improved relations between the county council and the WSR came in January 1986 when both parties were able to announce that agreement had been reached on the new rent structure. The directors of the West Somerset Railway had asked the council to reduce the annual rent for the line, which was due to be increased from £17,500 p.a. to £22,000, to a more realistic level of £10,000 p.a., and to remove the index-linked rent clause, together with the railway company's responsibility for coastal erosion. Explaining that the rent increase was due to be implemented the following week, Cllr Humphrey Temperley said, 'This increase will not only wipe out the estimated profit of £3,000 to £4,000 for this year, but would also place the WSR in severe financial problems. In short it could mean the end of the company.' He then urged the committee to accept the revised format for the lease of the line, in which it was proposed that the WSR would be expected to pay an annual rent of £12,500 p.a. for the next three years. Although the index-linking problems were removed, the council refused to accept responsibility for the coastal erosion problems. The move, he explained, was intended to give the railway a breathing space to get on a sounder financial footing.

Confirming that the council saw the line as a major tourist attraction they were anxious to promote, Cllr Temperley then went on to say, 'We are concerned that the railway is not properly observing its maintenance responsibilities. The fencing is seriously out of repair in many places, and we are concerned about the legal and insurance implications should an accident occur.' He did go on to praise the efforts being made to overcome this problem by the staff and the volunteers, saying, 'The company fully appreciates the problems, and is taking steps to remedy them in time, but we shall be carefully monitoring their efforts.' The revised lease agreement was accepted by the sub-committee and later by the full council. Mr Peter Rivett, the managing director, expressed his delight at the outcome of the negotiations and added, 'This agreement will enable us to get our act together and put sufficient money into keeping the fabric of the railway in good repair.'

In January came the expected announcement from the board of the WSR that they had rejected the offer from BR to create the link up between the main line and the branch for between £250,000 and £300,000. In addition to the initial charge, BR was also asking for a further £20,000 for piloting WSR trains over the BR line between Norton

Fitzwarren and Taunton and another £10,000 for inspecting the stock belonging to the WSR. Peter Rivett confirmed that talks were continuing to persuade BR to retain the link between the two lines for the purpose of stock transfers and special trains if the outcome of the talks with the NUR were to prove successful. He then added, 'We are interested in developing Bishops Lydeard as a rail/bus interchange, and will be starting talks on this aspect of operations. We recognise that to some, this is regarded as an essential thing to the company's success. It is quite possible that sometime in the future, the railway may become so overwhelmingly popular, that BR may consider a deal in which they may agree to share some of the cost.'

This answer seemed to disappoint Cllr Glyn Court, who said that the county was very supportive of an energetic policy concerning the railway and would be discussing the matter with the West Somerset Railway Panel at a meeting on 2 February. It also resulted in a large amount of correspondence in some of the local papers, many of the letters coming from 'knockers' claiming that the railway should pay an economic rent, should not be subsidised by the county, that it should be closed and the track bed converted to a bypass road, that it did not provide a useful transport service and only existed to keep a lot of railway 'nutters' happy playing trains. Other letters, not all of which came from volunteers, pointed out the benefits that the line brought to the area and the local tourist industry. In an attempt, as he described it, to separate fact from fiction, Peter Rivett wrote a long letter to the *West Somerset Free Press* in which he admitted that if the railway had not 'taken the wrong route some years ago it might have been in a position today, where it was financially strong enough to enter Taunton'. He then outlined in great detail why many of the suggestions that had been made in the letter columns of the local papers could not be followed. As all these matters concerning freight traffic, new locomotives, rolling stock and the question of the link have been dealt with in detail already, I do not propose to reiterate the statements made in the letter.

The Annual General Meeting of the company on 26 April was again held in the St John's Ambulance Hall. In contrast to the situation a few years previously the first item on the Agenda, to consider the company's financial statements and the report of the directors and auditors, was awaited with great anticipation by the shareholders, many of whom had by now become volunteers on the line.

After observing that the weather in West Somerset during the review period had been rather indifferent, which had not helped the railway in its efforts to attract more passengers, he was delighted to report that the turnover for 1985 had increased from £139,673 during the previous year to £174,432 for the period ending the 31 October 1985. Income from fares, he stated, had also increased from £84,052 to £105,798. This had resulted in an operating profit of £3,093 and a trading profit of £3,180. Although the trading profit was slightly less than the previous year, this year's figures were more remarkable because the company had not received any donations from local authorities or other outside sources. With the exception of donations, all other sources of income showed increases on the previous year. The other most noticeable change was the income from the shop and buffet facilities, which rose from £38,660 to £54,496 in the current year.

The chairman, Mr David Morgan, then informed the meeting of the negotiations that had taken place on the Taunton link, the rent review and the need to maintain the fabric of the railway, and closed by thanking all the staff and volunteers for their help during the year. Although the shares issued during the period had been rather disappointing compared with the previous year, no appeal was made to the shareholders to obtain more shares.

The problems encountered in the previous year with Watchet Town Council continued. As recounted in the previous chapter, despite expert advice from various sources the town council had written to the county about the replacement of the footbridge, without much success it seems, because the councillors later instructed the town clerk to write to the county council demanding that they should withhold help with the railway company's rent.

Following the council meeting held in August the clerk to the council, as instructed, had later written to the West Somerset Railway complaining that the councillors considered that the road bridge to the west of the station was dangerous and had been so for the past three years. Another complaint concerned the standard of the repairs to the wall on the bridge, which were necessary after the parapet had been damaged by a forklift truck. The councillors were also dissatisfied with the standard of the repairs that had been carried out to the section of wall near the footbridge.

In his reply to the council, Mr Peter Rivett denied that the bridge was unsafe, although he conceded that perhaps it could be considered unsightly, furthermore he disagreed with the councillors' view that the repairs to the wall near the footbridge were 'an eyesore'. After informing the councillors that they would have to live with the repairs, he then went on to accuse the council of using 'empty words' when they claimed to support the railway. 'Not only was no support forthcoming when the railway's fate hung in the balance, but you have lost no opportunity since to slate us in the press and complain to the county council!'

After pointing out that some of the directors were beginning to wonder if it was worthwhile trying to carry on in the face of such criticism, he pointed out that if the railway were to close, Watchet stood to lose some 17,000 visitors who came to the town by rail each year. Finally, he stated, 'I must point out that some of the things expressed in this letter are my own opinions, arrived at after four years of hard slog in what I often feel is a lost cause. The members of the railway company's board are not railway nuts, but are all volunteers receiving no expenses, attendance or travelling allowances (unlike the councillors).' He continued, 'We do it because we believe that it is a worthwhile project and necessary for someone to save the WSR. After four years I think we are all beginning to have our doubts.'

In conclusion, he added out that he had a secure job and earned a salary in excess of the total wage bill of the WSR. He continued, 'So its demise would only bring me more time with my family. It is you who should be worrying – but then, one never misses the water until the well runs dry.' The letter was read by the clerk to a stunned silence at the subsequent council meeting. Afterwards Councillor Major Alex Gordon misquoted Hamlet when he said 'methinks he doth protest too much', but the contents of the letter were noted in the council's minutes without further comment.

As might be imagined, this letter provoked a considerable amount of correspondence in the local press. Some letters supported the attitude of the council, claiming that the 'success' of the WSR had only been achieved because of huge subsidies, from the Manpower Services Commission and the Somerset County Council, and that no more money should be provided from public funds to support the WSR (S.A. Bircham, *West Somerset Free Press*, 21 November). Another letter of support came from a local pensioner, who pointed out that the WSR was run by volunteers, and that perhaps the town council should organise a group of volunteers to rectify the work on the walls that were causing the councillors so much concern.

Other letters were written by Chris van den Arund, who was now the chairman of the association, attacking those critics claiming that the line would never be profitable unless the section from Williton to Bishops Lydeard was abandoned, and from Mrs Pauline Rivett, the wife of the managing director, who criticised the county council for spending a further £8,000 on yet another survey. She claimed: 'It doesn't really matter what the report says, since the contents of a six-hour visit is bound to carry more conviction than the six years experience of the present board, but because it will be nicely typed and bound in a pretty cover, it will be accepted by those who have paid for it.'

This correspondence was to continue in the local press for some time, eventually the competence of the directors and the management of the railway became the subject of considerable criticism. The results that were to be achieved by the railway over the next few years were to prove just how out of touch many of these critics were.

On the locomotive front, the WSR was able to attract a welcome visitor from the Great Western Society at Didcot, in the form of a small prairie tank No. 5572 on loan for the season.

Evidence that the WSR was at last starting to attract the plaudits of the critical enthusiast magazines came in an article in the *Railway World* in November 1986. Remarking on the operation of the small prairie tank engine during the season the article stated, '"It's magic," said the junior visitor to the line. The occasion was 7 September, with the operation of Didcot's 4575 class 2-6-2T on the West Somerset Railway as part of the railway's tenth anniversary celebrations. For once during a dismal summer the sun shone warmly, and the day was a great success. The West Somerset Railway has a lot to offer, potentially it could be one of the great restored railways, with some of the most "genuine" atmosphere of any; particularly the delightful stations. The present management and the contributing society's volunteers have achieved one of the most remarkable turn round in the fortunes of any private railway. Congratulations, too, are in order for the D&EG for diesel preservation, and Hymek D7017 lifted an 11 coach train on 7 September to good effect.' The 'magic' of the day was the way in which the Great Western Society's small prairie seemed so at home on the WSR. As with several other visiting engines this season, a lot of goodwill and planning went into the transfer and the way in which preservation groups have worked together is an encouraging development. It must also have been encouraging to the directors of the WSR at a time when they were facing so much adverse publicity in the local press.

More encouraging news came in September when the *West Somerset Free Press* reported: 'The wet summer has had a silver lining for the WSR. The weeping skies have brought passengers to Britain's longest preserved railway in their hordes.' Announcing that cash receipts were 25 per cent up on the same period last year, Peter Rivett said, 'We are delighted with the business we have been doing. While everyone else has been bewailing the misfortunes brought by the weather, we've been basking in another season of success. We have carried more passengers and on occasions have been amazed at the number of passengers who have boarded our trains when the heavens opened.'

Commenting further, he observed that the aspect of the passenger boom which had pleased the board most had been the large numbers of passengers boarding the trains at Bishops Lydeard. 'In the main,' he said, 'They have been holidaymakers from Dorset and Avon who have specially come for a ride on the West Somerset and its steam trains. Most trains have left packed to capacity bound for Minehead, and other stations en route. In fact, at times we have had passenger capacity problems. Our trains can only haul a maximum of six coaches at the moment. But business has built up so rapidly, that we are now hoping to be able to pull seven or eight coaches next year.'

Confirming that the railway was likely to record a profit for the third year running, he announced that the board was planning a huge maintenance and repair programme for its track, rolling stock and stations during the coming winter months. To meet this programme, hundreds of sleepers were due to arrive in the next few days for the relaying of large sections of track.

Party bookings on the line were becoming more commonplace, but in May there came confirmation that this practice was now spreading to the Quantock Belle services, when Mr and Mrs Cutbill of Wiveliscombe invited eleven members of their family, two of whom had flown in from America, to join them for lunch on the train.

As often happened in the past, good news was accompanied by bad news. In October, fears about the future of the WSR were expressed when it was announced that there was a possibility that Minehead would be designated a 'primary road route'. Cllr Sidney Brown, the chairman of the West Somerset District Council, speaking to the district's leisure and tourism committee, warned that the county council would simply not be prepared to foot the huge bill for improving three bridges spanning the A358. Instead the county would demolish the bridges and close the railway: 'It is pointless improving the road only for the county to say they will have to take down the bridges and close the railway. We want Primary Route designation into Minehead, but not at the cost of the railway. The road link is important as the tourist trade increases, but so is the railway. We want both road and rail links if the area is to be served properly. I know that West Somerset is considered to be in the backwoods, but it is about time someone from County Hall spent some time here looking at our problems.'

After pointing out that Wiltshire had managed to improve roads and retain railway bridges in the Swindon area, he said, 'But our county council's philosophy is that the railway makes the A358 improvements impossible.' Emphasising his point he finished by reiterating, 'We must not stand for any arguments that the bridges should come down. We want to see the WSR pushing through to Taunton so that excursion trains can travel direct to Minehead, from the Midlands, the North and London.'

In reply, Mr Michael Ireland, the chief technical officer, agreed that there was no question West Somerset needed a primary route. After admitting that the railway bridges were perfectly capable of an engineering solution, he confirmed that the real difficulty was the cost of resolving the problems and trying to determine where the necessary funds would come from. Other councillors again claimed that if the bridges were demolished, the WSR would not be put out of business and that if services were terminated at Williton (from Minehead), the line would be profitable.

Once again the local councillors appeared to be out of touch with the events happening in their area. The line was profitable (just) and the majority of passengers were boarding the trains at Bishops Lydeard and if services were terminated at Williton, much of this traffic could be lost. This appeared to have escaped their notice. At the end of the debate the members agreed to raise the future of the bridges at top level talks on primary route designation at a meeting that was to be arranged with county council officials.

Other special events that were run during the year included the vintage transport rally, held at Bishops Lydeard Station on 17–18 May, and the Santa Specials – both these events were now starting to operate to a proven formula.

The news that John East, head of the English Tourist Board, was to visit the WSR, prompted speculation that he might be persuaded to intervene in the dispute between the railway and the NUR. After spending an hour on the WSR when he visited the area in November and before leaving to visit other tourist attractions in the area, he announced, 'The link-up with the main line could be considered for some of the £10 million plus that we expect to get from the government to dish out in capital grants next year. We have money to invest in West Somerset, and are looking for projects to be put forward. The more that we can get people to think positively about tourism here, the more resources we will make available.'

Mr David Morgan, the chairman of the WSR, announced that he was delighted at the prospect of tourist board funding, adding, 'Although we welcome any form of assistance, the ETB always attaches strict conditions to their grants and would obviously want to see some improvements in facilities. Any project would have to slot into any action they laid down, therefore every aspect must be looked at before action can be taken.'

The fears expressed by Mrs Rivett in her letter to the *West Somerset Free Press* in early November proved to be only too accurate. The county council had commissioned a firm of tourism consultants called John Brown to prepare the report. When their report was published the consultants made sweeping criticisms of the management of the West Somerset Railway, which it claimed amongst other observations was 'weak and poor'.

After waiting in vain for the county officials to disassociate themselves from the remarks made by their consultants, Peter Rivett announced his resignation from the board. Giving the reason for his resignation as political interference in the management of the WSR, he announced:

> Somerset County Council's unwillingness to disassociate itself from the sweeping criticisms of the railway management team, in the specially commissioned report from tourism consultants John Brown had actually made things worse. I felt particularly aggrieved by the consistent

political interference and comments made by certain politicians regarding the railway's management team. I have given the council time to distance themselves from the report, but to date I have received no response. Therefore I must assume that they concur with the comments made by Mr Brown. I am a professional manager. The management of the railway has been questioned and under the circumstances I have no alternative but to resign.

In the press release from the board that accompanied the announcement, it was stated that the decision by Mr Rivett, who was a much respected management accountant in the City of London, had come as a 'bombshell'. It also pointed out that during the four years that Mr Rivett had been on the board he had turned trading losses of £24,000 per annum into profits between £3,000 and £5,000 per annum largely due to his efforts.

Thus, what had until then seemed a promising year, came to a rather miserable end.

FROM 8 JULY 1986 to 28 AUGUST 1986

VISIT

TAUNTON

THE COUNTY TOWN OF SOMERSET

MANY SHOPS!   MUCH TO SEE!

day excursion by
STEAM
train

EVERY TUESDAY, WEDNESDAY AND THURSDAY

Depart Minehead at 10.15 by STEAM train.
Arrive Taunton at 12.30.

Depart Taunton at 5.05 p.m.
Arrive Minehead at 6.32 p.m.

FARES: (Return)   Adults   £ 5.50
                   OAP's   £ 4.50
                   Children   £ 2.75

Family Return (2 Ad + 2 Ch) £ 13.00
3rd, 4th and 5th Child at £ 1.00 each

WEST SOMERSET RAILWAY

SUNSET
SPECIAL
TO
BLUE ANCHOR

DEPARTS MINEHEAD 20.15

EVERY WEDNESDAY

18 JUNE to 27 AUGUST 1986

Allows approx 45 minutes at BLUE ANCHOR for a stroll on the beach, enjoying a view on DUNSTER MINEHEAD and NORTH HILL, a quick pint on the train's RAILWAY INN Bar or a visit to the excellent BLUE ANCHOR RAILWAY MUSEUM.

RETURN TO MINEHEAD by 21.30

RETURN FARE £ 1.50 ---- CHILDREN £ 0.75

ADVANCE BOOKING RECOMMENDED

ENJOY AN EVENING OUT WITH THE

 WEST SOMERSET RAILWAY

THESE SPECIAL FARES ARE AVAILABLE ONLY ON THE TRAIN SPECIFIED

22

1987: Full Steam Ahead

The new year started full of promise when the Minehead Chamber of Trade appointed a liaison officer, Mr Richard Perkins, to deal directly with the railway management in providing assistance from town businessmen and women. The chamber's chairman, Mr Brian Meedon, stated that chamber members were also being encouraged to purchase shares in the railway, to a minimum value of £20 each, and they were also being prompted to advertise in WSR publications:

> We think that for the economic benefit of this particular community of West Somerset there needs to be a link, therefore all traders are being encouraged to throw their weight behind a campaign to restore the rail link. This is an attraction that is good for Minehead. The density of traffic on the A39 and A358 roads, which is likely to get heavier this year because of the added attractions of Somerwest World (Butlins by another name) make it essential that the railway should be able to work jointly with BR in arranging through trains from various centres direct to Minehead.

Other initiatives by the chamber included suggestions that the traders should provide volunteers to help the railway by painting the sides of WSR goods wagons with the traders' names, as had been the custom in the past. At the same time, the WSR offered advertising space on billboards at their stations in their publicity leaflets and timetables.

An attempt to restore a meaningful dialogue with the WSR after the breakdown in communications caused by the incidents that led to the resignation of Peter Rivett was made by Cllr Humphrey Temperley. He announced that the county was planning to intervene in the dispute between tourism consultants John Brown and the WSR. Three weeks later, it was obvious that some progress towards a reconciliation had been made, when David Morgan announced that informal talks had taken place between the railway management team and council officials, and added, 'Once agreement has been reached with the council on matters of mutual interest, Mr Rivett would return.'

As he left the same meeting Cllr Temperley was also reported to have said, 'I am very appreciative of the sterling work Mr Rivett has done for the WSR over the past few years. It is largely due to his efforts that the finances of the railway are now on a sound footing.'

West Somerset Railway

santa specials 1987

Travel to Santa's Grotto by Train! Christmas with a difference!
Once again we have arranged our popular STEAM hauled SANTA SPECIALS, which will run from

BISHOPS LYDEARD to CROWCOMBE

on

SATURDAYS 12 and 19 DECEMBER 1987,
SUNDAYS 6, 13 and 20 DECEMBER 1987,
TUESDAY 22 DECEMBER 1987.

MINEHEAD to BLUE ANCHOR

on

SUNDAY 20 DECEMBER 1987

		X			
BISHOPS LYDEARD d	10.45	12.05	14.00	15.20	
CROWCOMBE a	11.00	12.20	14.15	15.35	
		X			
CROWCOMBE d	11.45	13.05	15.00	16.20	
BISHOPS LYDEARD a	11.55	13.15	15.10	16.30	

MINEHEAD	d	14.30
BLUE ANCHOR	a	14.45
BLUE ANCHOR	d	15.30
MINEHEAD	a	15.45

Note: X = NOT on Tuesday 22 December 1987.

Santa will be in his Grottoes at Crowcombe and Blue Anchor and will give a present to all children up to 12 years of age. On the return journey to Bishops Lydeard or Minehead they will also receive a cracker and sweets. For adults the ticket includes a glass of Sherry and a Mince Pie.

Further refreshments can be obtained in the Buffet Coach on the train.

Fares: Adults: £ 3.00   (including Sherry and Mince Pie).
       Children: £ 2.50   (including present, cracker and sweets).
       Parties of 20 or more: 10% discount on the above rates.

Bookings: By post or in person at Minehead Station, using the attached Booking Form.

Parking: There is ample free parking available at both Bishops Lydeard and Minehead Stations.

- -

SANTA SPECIALS 1987   BOOKING FORM

Name :
Address:

Telephone:

Postcode:

Please send the following tickets:

TRAIN PREFERRED:

BISHOPS LYDEARD to CROWCOMBE

    Children @ £ 2.50   = £
    Adults   @ £ 3.00   = £

         TOTAL   £

	DECEMBER					
	6	12	13	19	20	22
10.45						
12.05						XXXX
14.00						
15.20						

Please indicate ages of children requiring presents from Santa:

Boys					
Girls					

MINEHEAD to BLUE ANCHOR

14.30 on 20th December 1987

Please use "1" or "2" to indicate first or second choice.

Please send this Booking Form (plus Cheque or Postal Order made payable to "West Somerset Railway Plc") to:

West Somerset Railway Plc
The Railway Station
M I N E H E A D
Somerset, TA24 5BG

PLEASE ENCLOSE A STAMPED ADDRESSED ENVELOPE TO ENSURE DESPATCH OF YOUR TICKETS BY RETURN POST

We regret that telephone bookings can not be accepted.

West Somerset Railway

SPECIAL TRAINS SPECIAL TRAINS SPECIAL TRAINS

FRIDAY 9th DECEMBER: Late night Shopping in Minehead

Special trains from Williton at 17.00   18.30   20.35   for all stations to Minehead.
Return trains from Minehead at 17.50   20.00   21.30.
Special Return Fares from Williton/Doniford/Watchet/Washford £1.00.
From Blue Anchor & Dunster 50p. Children under 14 FREE.

SATURDAY & SUNDAY 17th/18th DECEMBER
Santa Steam Specials from Minehead to Santa's Grotto at Blue Anchor

From Minehead at 10.45   12.05(Sunday)   14.00   15.15(Sunday)
Sherry & Mince Pies for Adults and a Present for the Children.
All-in fares Adults £3.50   Children £3.00

MONDAY 19th DECEMBER: Late night Shopping in Williton

Washford dep. 18.10   Watchet dep. 18.20   Doniford dep. 18.25.
Return from Williton at 21.00. Fare: Adults 50p Return. Children FREE.

MONDAY & TUESDAY 26th/27th DECEMBER
Steam Trains from Minehead to Williton

at 11.00 and 14.15. Returning at 11.55 and 15.10.

SUNDAY & MONDAY 1st/2nd JANUARY
New Year Steam & Diesel Trains
& Model Railway Exhibition at Bishops Lydeard

Trains depart Minehead at — 10.15   11.55   13.45   15.35
Trains depart Bishops Lydeard 10.35   11.55   13.45   15.30

Full details from **West Somerset Rly., Minehead Station. Tel: 0643 4996**

It was noticeable that although Mr Rivett had resigned, the board had not yet named anyone to take his place. The reason for this apparent omission became clear in late January when Mr Morgan admitted that not only the council but also the board were trying to persuade Mr Rivett to return. It was also revealed that Peter Rivett had continued to help the board with financial matters since his resignation.

On 20 February it was announced that Mr Rivett had rejoined the board of the WSR. After thanking all those people who had worked so hard on his behalf to enable him to return he said, 'We are now something of a major employer in the area, something we forecast we would be, when we started to climb out of the doldrums. Our turn round has been such a startling one that even some members of the trade press have been singing our praises. We promised to create jobs and wealth for West Somerset, and to become profitable. We are achieving all three and prospects have never looked better.'

This optimism spread to the motive power department although the Bagnall 0-6-0 ST was confined to the workshop undergoing firebox and piston valve repairs and the second Bagnall, *Vulcan*, was no longer available because it had been sold to the North Shields Land Transport Museum. New tyres had been ordered for the pannier tank No.6412, so that it was available for the start of the new season. The return of the small prairie No.5572 to Didcot in January had been delayed due to bad weather, but arrangements had been made by the WSR management for the engine to reprise for a second season, as soon as a visit to the Keigthly & Worth Valley Railway was completed.

As a result of the appeal by Mr Rivett, the Collett 0-6-0 No.3205 was due to arrive from the Severn Valley Railway in March and it was confidently expected that the ex-S&D 2-8-0 locomotive No.53808 would be steamed in time for the start of the summer. With the exception of the S&D loco, which did not return to steam until September, the remaining predictions were accurate and so not only did the WSR have four ex-main line locos available during the season for the first time, but in 53808 they had a locomotive capable of pulling the 8-coach trains that were becoming necessary at times, to carry all the passengers wishing to travel. Ample demonstration of the power of this locomotive was shown on 13 September when it hauled eleven packed coaches from Minehead to Bishops Lydeard and returned: the longest train to run on the WSR at that time.

Although all the volunteers unconnected with the accounts department were confident that the railway had achieved its best financial results to date, many were still surprised when they attended the shareholders' meeting on 9 May, held at the St John's Ambulance Hall. Dealing with the first item on the agenda, the financial statement, Peter Rivett announced that the number of passengers carried on the line had increased from 57,000 in 1985 to 67,000 in 1986. This had resulted in an increase in turnover from £174,432 to £240,773. During the same period the income from fares had increased from £105,798 to £147,643. Another valuable contributor to the profitability of the company was the retail sales department, so long the 'Cinderella' department of the railway, which recorded a profit of over £11,000.

These figures resulted in a total operating profit for the period of £24,147 (£3,093 the previous year), later reduced to an operating profit of £14,147 after £10,000 was transferred to a deferred maintenance account. These results came as a pleasant surprise, even to those who had been at the 'sharp end' of the activities on the railway during the previous summer. After some members of the audience had congratulated the board on their achievements, a resolution that the accounts should be adopted was quickly passed by the meeting.

In the next item on the agenda, the chairman's report, David Morgan, after dealing with the problems caused by the John Brown report, informed the meeting that discussions were continuing with the county council following the establishment of a joint-working party comprising members of the WSR board and the council's railway panel, with a view to agreeing a development plan and to explore areas of mutual benefit.

Another matter for discussion would be the renegotiation of the company's lease with a view to extending its term and obtaining a more realistic appraisal of the obligations imposed. He also referred to a number of new appointments to the board. Mr Harvey Cox had replaced Mr John Whittaker as the county's representative. Other appointments included Dennis Taylor, who had a responsibility for commercial matters, Dr Cattermole, Mark Smith and Andy Forster. D.W. Myland had retired from the board. It was also announced that a new staff appointment had been made when Malcolm Kershaw had been appointed Chief Mechanical Engineer.

After thanking the staff and volunteers for their efforts during the year, the chairman spoke optimistically of the future of the railway. In conclusion, he made no apologies to the shareholders for drawing their attention to the new stock loan issue, details of which accompanied the report that they had received. Explaining that the money was needed to build up the company's fleet of operational locomotives, he said, 'Your support for this issue is essential if we are to realise the railway's tremendous potential. Now we have shown the world at large that the railway is a going concern, please reward us with a positive response to our appeal, even if you can only afford a small amount.'

In June came the usual 'good news–bad news' scenario the WSR had become accustomed to over the many long years. On 19 June, Mr Ian Smith, the NUR branch secretary, was quoted as saying, 'There is new wind blowing in the union.' He could see no reason for the boycott and he also felt that a reasonable agreement could be negotiated for linking the line to Taunton. He emphasised that he was referring to excursion traffic and stock movements, but not commuter services.

The following week it became obvious that the 'wind of change' had not reached the union's rank and file members. Mr Ian Smith was forced to admit, 'We (the union members) are a lot more moderate than we used to be and there would be some support for the ban to be lifted, but I cannot prejudge what the outcome of the vote will be at the meeting called to discuss the matter.' Later the branch secretary announced that his members had voted in favour of continuing the ban.

Although BR refused to be drawn into the conflict, claiming that it was in no position to 'encounter' the union members, a spokesman revealed, 'This is something for the union people to sort out themselves, we cannot dictate to the union members.' The national executive of the NUR also refused to discuss the matter, claiming that it was 'a local decision'. The action of the NUR members brought condemnation from all sides.

Cllr Les Jowett of the West Somerset District Council approached the West Country Tourist Board, the English Tourist Board, the Association of District Councils and Somerset County Council, asking them to also exert pressure on the union. He also demanded that BR should order its staff to let the West Somerset Railway into Taunton. At a press conference, Cllr Jowett said, 'It is very serious and ridiculous, that six or seven members of the NUR should be holding up the economy of the whole of West Somerset.' Cllr Temperley of the county council stated, 'The NUR are pursuing this rather childish blacking and it is simply not in anyone's interests, including theirs. There may be ways of overcoming this problem, and we have confidence that it will be sorted out in the long term. What is so sad about the current situation is that a link would in fact mean more jobs for the NUR members.' Later, tourist board officials were also reported to have taken the matter up with BR and union officials. No one on the board of the WSR was prepared to comment on the situation that was developing, in case their observations jeopardised any progress that might have been made.

Further bad news came in June when Peter Rivett disclosed that there was a serious threat that the line could be cut in half because of the serious cliff erosion that had taken place in the Watchet area. Speaking from his London office he said, 'Everything is now thrown into the melting pot by the erosion of the sea cliffs at Watchet. The line could be completely severed there, and I fear that it will be sooner than later. Mr Rivett was certain that the Somerset County Council, as owners of the line, would not meet the heavy cost of carrying out the sea defence work to avoid further cliff falls.' He continued, 'They (the county council) say it is the WSR's liability, but there is no way that we can entertain paying for the work, it will be a tragedy for Somerset if the line is severed.'

When asked if the alternative was to operate a 'fun railway' between Minehead and Watchet, Mr Rivett explained that this was not possible, because there were no facilities at Watchet for turning trains. 'We would have to operate between Minehead and Blue Anchor, which would hardly be worthwhile, my own choice as an accountant would be to operate a service between Bishops Lydeard and Williton.'

Mr Rivett's fears for the future of the railway proved to be unfounded when, following a series of meetings between Tom King, the MP for the area, Watchet Town Council, the West Somerset District Council, and the Somerset County Council, it was announced that a £140,000 protection scheme for the cliffs at Splash Point had been drawn up, and rushed through the WSDC Technical Services Committee, and unanimously passed by the full council at a special meeting in less than a week.

Cllr Viv Brewer was understandably pleased at the outcome: 'It is a job that has to be got on with, and if the work started tomorrow it would not be too early.' Cllr Tony Knight, chairman of the Watchet Town Council said he was delighted at the news, and without the slightest touch of irony, he added, 'I am sure that all the members of the council and the townsfolk are delighted that action is to be taken so swiftly, following our meeting with Mr Tom King, the railway, district and county officials. We feared that our alarm bells would be ignored so it is gratifying that the campaign has been rewarded for the safety of Watchet.'

The work, believed to have been funded jointly by the Department of the Environment and the Somerset County Council, was due to start in November and involved constructing a rock armour barrier using scores of six-ton blocks of stone, brought in lorries along a specially constructed access road from the town's Harbour Road to the beach to the east of the port. The vehicles would drive alongside the branch line, before emerging onto the beach at a specially constructed break in the cliffs between the seafront recreation ground and the coastguard lookout field.

At the end of the summer timetable the company was able to announce that the passenger figures for the financial year had increased by 8,000 to over 75,000. That year a further 1,000 local residents had joined the 'Star Card' scheme operated by the railway, which offered them reduced fares. Owing to demand, the railway also proposed to operate extra trains on Saturday 31 October and Saturday 7 November to Taunton, via the bus link. Additional Santa Special and Christmas shopping trains would also be operating.

News that the pannier tank had returned to traffic following the fitting of replacement tyres was followed by the shock announcement that the railway was putting the remaining Bagnall, *Victor*, up for sale and that, if possible, they wished to dispose of it by 30 November. Although groups and individuals associated with the WSR were offered first refusal, the decision caused outrage among many of the volunteers who had grown quite attached to the loco, despite of her frequent 'tantrums'.

On 29 October, in what was the most serious accident to have occurred on the line since it was reopened, two elderly ladies escaped unscathed when their car was hit by pannier tank No.6412 at the Roebuck Lane crossing when it was hauling a special train. The driver of the engine was Dave Rouse, who said, when he had recovered from the shock of the accident, 'When I came around the bend I was surprised to see the car stopped on the crossing ahead of me. There was nothing I could do. The engine just brushed the car aside like a matchbox. The two women in the car were extremely shocked and upset, but they are extremely lucky to be alive.'

The driver of the car, Mrs Catherine Leonard-Williams, aged seventy-two, confirmed that both she and her companion in the car, Mrs Lillian Routh, aged eighty-seven, were lucky to be alive, and claimed that she, 'had stopped on the line to see what was coming and before we knew what was happening there was the train. The car was just brushed aside with us in it, and we were buffeted around. It was very frightening, a split-second later and we would have been killed.' Still under the impression that the best place to stop if you want to see if a train is coming is on the railway track, she announced that she was going to complain to the railway company, because she claimed that the lights controlling the crossing were not working.

23

1988/9: The End of the Beginning

At the start of 1988, there appeared to be growing confidence among the members of the board, from which came a determination to ensure that the problems that had beset the railway for a number of years should be resolved quickly, if the long-term future of the line was not to be jeopardised.

The first of the problems to be tackled was the attitude of the unions towards the link-up with the main line. Early in the new year, Peter Rivett announced that along with the backing of the Somerset County Council, who were providing £3-5,000 to assist the project, the board was about to enter into negotiations with BR. Agreement had already been reached with Taunton Cider, who were prepared to allow the WSR to use a link-up through their sidings for stock transfers, and for up to eight excursions a year from the main line.

When announcing the decision of the board, Peter Rivett said, 'We don't think the NUR will man the barricades when it comes to the crunch. We think that they will not want to be seen as being that unreasonable. After all, the link, which will enable day excursions to be run to Minehead from cities like London and Birmingham, will provide work for their own members. The volatile nature of the local NUR branch has to be taken into account, but we are pressing ahead.'

The change of attitude by the board did not meet with universal approval; the Local Trades Council was stated to be shocked at the proposals. Claiming that they had made overtures to the local branch of the NUR to try getting the ban removed, they understood that the union branch had undergone a change of heart, which could be jeopardised by the attitude of the board.

Replying to these concerns, Mr Rivett stated, 'We consider that the confrontation is worth the risk because if the union does react, the cost will not be embarrassing. The hook-up is cheap enough and if the move does not work it will not be the end of the world. We have no reason to renege on the agreement we have reached with Taunton Cider and Somerset County Council.'

Shortly afterwards, the LCGB (Locomotive Club of Great Britain) announced that on Saturday 23 April it would be operating 'The Minehead Marauder Rail Tour'. The first ever rail tour to Minehead planned to leave Manchester Victoria at 7 a.m., calling at

Bolton, Wigan North Western, Earlestown, Warrington, Crewe, Stafford and Birmingham; it would then run to Minehead via Taunton, using preserved steam and diesel locomotives on the WSR, enabling the visitors to spend a whole afternoon in Minehead before their return journey. The fares for this excursion were £23 for adults and £20 for members, with concessions for children.

In February, the company admitted that it was expecting to experience overcrowding on some trains during the peak summer timetable, which they could do little about in the immediate future. The length of the trains was no longer a problem – now that No. 53808 had entered service it was capable of pulling an 11-coach set over the length of the line and often did. The line capacity limited the company to the use of a maximum of three trains on the line. The directors announced that they were studying the possibility of reopening the passing loop facility at Crowcombe Station, which would increase the capacity of the line by a third.

The cost of such a project was going to be considerable, requiring a new signal box to be built with capacity for full signalling facilities. The fact that the board had been able to consider the idea gave an indication of just how much progress had been made over the previous two years.

The other problem that had beset the railway for some time was the renewal of the lease and it seemed that the board were anxious to ensure that this matter was resolved during the next twelve months. The annual general meeting was held at yet another venue in Minehead at the Avenue Church School Hall, on 23 April. For those shareholders who had started to become used to steadily increasing profits, the year was to prove rather disappointing. Whilst the turnover during the year had increased from £240,773 to £280,535, with the bulk of this increase coming from higher fare income – an increase from £147,643 to £180,587 – generated by the increased number of passengers carried, which had risen by 8,000, there was a considerable increase in expenditure.

Of this increase, the largest was incurred by staff costs, which rose from £58,205 to £83,127; a reflection of the increase in the number of staff employed which had risen from fourteen to twenty. These increases resulted in the operating profit being reduced to £943 and a trading loss of £403 compared to £24,147 the previous year. The financial report was adopted by the meeting after Peter Rivett had answered a number of questions from the floor asked by shareholders concerned that the bad old days might be returning.

Because David Morgan had resigned as chairman earlier in the year, although he retained his seat on the board, Dennis Taylor gave his first report to the shareholders as the new chairman. He started by taking the opportunity to express both his own and the board's appreciation of the work that David Morgan had undertaken and how grateful both he and the other members of the board were that he had agreed to remain involved. He informed the meeting that following the successful completion of the restoration work on locomotive No. 53808, the company had reached agreement with the association that they would undertake the restoration work on the small prairie No. 4561. To enable this work to be undertaken, the company had raised £23,400 by means of fixed-interest redeemable stock. This money would also be used to fund the building of a new shed at Williton as a workshop for the diesel units on the line.

He also confirmed that talks were ongoing with the county council on the subject of the new lease, but refused to give any indication how these talks were progressing. After thanking shareholders for purchasing a further £11,165 of shares during the period under review, he appealed to the audience not only to purchase more shares in the line but asked them to persuade their friends to travel on the line.

When the managing director gave his report, he said that the timetable for the coming season would be similar to the previous year, but that the Saturday and Santa Special services would be recast following disappointing results during the year under review. At no time during his speech did Peter Rivett give any indication that he was about to resign, initially as managing director, and later from the board on 27 June. The reasons given for both resignations were disagreements with the remainder of the board on a number of issues, including the way negotiations were being conducted on the proposed lease. Following his resignation, Mark Smith, who had a seat on the board as the WSRA representative, was appointed managing director.

Shortly after Peter Rivett's resignation, on 15 August, the directors announced, that an EGM would be held at the Hobby Horse Hotel in Minehead on Saturday 24 September to discuss the following resolution: that the authorised share capital of the company be increased from £500,000 to £1,500,000 by the creation of an additional 10,000,000 ordinary shares priced at 10 pence each.

The shareholders attending the meeting soon learned that the reason the increased share issue was needed was because agreement had been reached with the Somerset County Council on the terms of a new lease. The county proposed to sell the lease to the WSR for £210,000 and thereafter charge a nominal rent of £1 per annum for ninety-nine years. SCC immediately reinvested £50,000 in the WSR so that the true cost to the WSR was really £160,000. At what must have been one of the shortest shareholders' meetings in the company's history, the resolution was quickly passed.

Probably because for the first time in its history, the company had three main line engines in service, loading on the passenger trains during the season were heavy and sales in the recently extended retail outlet at Minehead were encouraging.

The newly built halt at Doniford was opened in time for the summer season by Cllr Humphrey Temperley, who had done so much to help the WSR in the discussions with the county council on the new lease.

Although some people had been disappointed by the previous year's profits, an indication of how much money had been put aside for maintenance purposes became apparent as passengers travelled along the line, with part of the canopy at Minehead Station re-roofed, a considerable amount of restoration work carried out at Stogumber Station and at Crowcombe, work had started on rebuilding the signal box as part of stage one of the reopening of the passing loop. At Bishops Lydeard both platforms had been resurfaced and the car parking area had been tidied up.

On 1 January the board was able to announce that the share issue, which had been opened on 23 September, had closed on 31 December, some 3,835,410 shares (£383,541)

West Somerset Railway

EVENING STAR

Built Swindon 1960. Hauled last S&D line Pines Express 1962. Now BR's last steam loco is back in Somerset on Britain's longest preserved line. Join us for a 40 mile Steam Spectacular as 92220 tackles the WSR gradients NON–STOP. This you can't afford to miss, be sure of a seat – BOOK NOW!

NON-STOP SPECIALS, SUNDAY 19th MARCH

Dep. Minehead	11.15	14.30		Dep. Taunton	12.30 *	—
Arr. Bishops Lydeard	12.25	15.40		Dep. Bishops Lydeard	12.50	15.55
Arr. Taunton	—	16.00 *		Arr. Minehead	14.00	17.05

* by bus link with BR connections at Taunton from London, Reading, Swindon and Bristol, etc.

NON-STOP SPECIALS, SATURDAY 1st APRIL

Specials will dep.Minehead at 11.00 and 16.00. on Saturday 1st April.
Return workings from Bishops Lydeard at 12.38 and 17.18 with bus link from Taunton BR at 11.55 and 16.40.

Bar/Buffet Car on all Special Trains. We strongly advise that all tickets are booked in advance.
Return Fares: Bishops Lydeard – Minehead £6.50. Taunton – Minehead £7.50. Children Aged 5 – 15 Half Fare.

This is just one of the exciting events planned for 1989 so this year why not take a break in West Somerset, it really has a lot to offer — from Exmoor to sea-shore.

● For Special Train tickets in advance send remittance plus stamped addressed envelope to:
West Somerset Railway plc. The Station , Minehead, TA24 5BG

● For 1989 colour timetable brochure send s.a.e. to above address. Telephone enquiries 0643 4996

WEST SOMERSET RAILWAY ASSOCIATION

Bringing Evening Star to Somerset is costing a lot of money and the WSR Association is footing the bill. **YOU** can help **US** by joining the Association **NOW**. You will be kept in touch with all the exciting developments, such as the imminent return to steam of 4561, by four information and photo. packed Journals a year. You will receive generous travel concessions **AND** have the chance to really enjoy yourself by helping as a volunteer if you so wish. We believe our subscriptions offer very good value for money so please **DON'T DELAY, JOIN TODAY.**

Please complete and send to:
**John Greenslade, WSRA Membership Secretary (SR),
7 Park St., Stratton St. Margaret, Swindon, SN3 4LL.**

I would like to support the WSR by becoming a member of the West Somerset Railway Association.

NAME _____

ADDRESS _____

_____

_____ POST CODE _____

Single Adult £8 ☐   Senior Citizen or Student £6 ☐

Family £12 ☐   Senior Citizen Husband & Wife £9 ☐

I would also like to donate £ _____
to 92220 expenses ☐   4561 restoration ☐

Please tick as appropriate and make all cheques payable to:
West Somerset Railway Association.

appearance courtesy National Railway Museum

92220

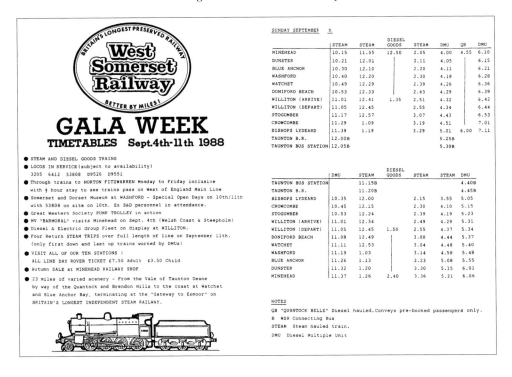

having been issued. This had enabled the company to complete the ninety-nine-year lease from the Somerset County Council, thus saving the WSR some £22,000 in rent for 1990.

In contrast to the results of earlier years, the shareholders learned during the annual general meeting, held at the Hobby Horse Inn on Saturday 22 April, that in 1988 the turnover for the company had risen from £280,535 to £357,476 during the year. The number of passengers carried on the line had increased to over 89,000 with a resultant increase in fare income from £180,587 to £232,316. The improved layout of the retail outlet resulted in a profit of £17,487, which in turn contributed to a operating profit of £47,392 and a trading profit of £39,392 after £10,000 had been set aside for maintenance provisions.

In 1989, these figures were to be surpassed. A 9F locomotive No.92220 *Evening Star*, the last steam locomotive to be built at the Swindon works in 1960 and owned by the National Railway Museum, had been operating trains on the BR main line for seven years. Although it had a ten-year boiler certificate, it was no longer allowed to operate on the main line, but could operate on preserved lines.

In 1988, the National Railway Museum announced that it would consider any application from a preserved line, who felt they could operate this locomotive for a season. Because this engine was capable of hauling even more coaches than No.53808, the length of the trains being determined by the length of the passing loops, the directors thought that this locomotive might ease their overcrowding problems.

A quick check revealed that although this locomotive was by far the largest to ever travel on the branch, it was within the axle loading for the line. After taking the plunge, the directors' efforts were rewarded when the National Railway Museum announced that the locomotive would be spending the 1989 season on the WSR. The restoration of the small prairie tank No.4561 was also completed during the year and for the first time, the railway had five main-line steam locomotives in service. They were all needed as thousands of extra passengers flocked to the line to see the first 'named' locomotive to run on the WSR.

The number of passengers carried on the trains during the 1988/89 season was 116,493: an increase of 27,000 over the previous year. The increased level of passenger traffic resulted in a rise of over 50 per cent in fare receipts up from £232,316 to £357,523. Increases in the income from the retail outlet and the on-train buffet facilities from £97,092 to £138,174 meant that the operating profit for 1988/89 was almost double that of the previous year: £84,889 against £47,392.

After a further £15,000 had been transferred to a deferred maintenance provision the net-trading profit was £65,414 after payment of taxes. The net worth of the company was now £574,524 and as the deficit brought forward from previous years had been almost eliminated, shareholders were reminded at the AGM that the company would be expected to pay tax on future profits.

Any doubts about the financial stability of the WSR were dispelled when these results were announced and the many people involved in the railway preservation as a whole were convinced that for the West Somerset Railway, this really was the 'end of the beginning'.

In 1990, shortly after the period covered in this book, Mr Whittaker informed the members of the finance sub-committee of the county council that, by selling off some of the land and buildings the council had bought from BR before the transfer of the lease to the West Somerset Railway, the council had achieved an 8 per cent return on the money they had originally paid for the line. Thus, the purchase of the branch line ultimately proved to be beneficial to Somerset ratepayers.

ON SATURDAY 22nd APRIL 1989 A

SHAREHOLDERS SPECIAL

HAULED BY 9F 2-10-0 92220 EVENING STAR, BRITISH RAILWAYS' LAST STEAM LOCOMOTIVE
or S.& D.J.R. 7F 2-8-0 53808

INCLUDING THE LUXURIOUS QUANTOCK BELLE DINING CARS

WILL RUN BETWEEN

BISHOPS LYDEARD & MINEHEAD

IN CONNECTION WITH THE 17th ANNUAL GENERAL MEETING OF THE WEST SOMERSET RAILWAY COMPANY

TIME TABLE

DOWN			UP		
CONNECTING SERVICES FROM:			Minehead	dep.	5.10
London Paddington	dep.	*9.35*	Bishop's Lydeard	arr.	6.22
Reading	dep.	*10.01*	Bishop's Lydeard	dep.	6.30 B
Birmingham New St.	dep.	*8.30*	Taunton G.W.R. Station	arr.	6.45 B
Bristol Temple Meads	dep.	*10.10*	Taunton Castleway	arr.	6.50 B
Taunton Castleway	dep.	11.30 B	*CONNECTING SERVICES TO:*		
Taunton G.W.R. Station	dep.	11.40 B	*Bristol Temple Meads*	*arr.*	*8.22*
Bishop's Lydeard	arr.	12.10 B	*Birmingham New St.*	*arr.*	*11.24*
Bishop's Lydeard	dep.	12.25	*Reading*	*arr.*	*9.11*
Minehead	arr.	1.35	*London Paddington*	*arr.*	*9.41*

B Taunton – Bishop's Lydeard & return is by special omnibus picking up at REAR of Taunton G.W.R. Station.
For timings at intermediate stations please enquire at the Company's office at Minehead.

To book on this special train, kindly complete the form below, detach and return, with S.A.E. please, to:
COMMERCIAL DEPT., S.H., WEST SOMERSET RAILWAY, THE RAILWAY STATION, MINEHEAD, TA24 5BG

* "BELLE" and 1st Class accommodation is strictly limited and will be allocated on a first come, first served basis.
* Bookings should be made by 15th April 1989 to ensure a seat.
* W.S.R.A. membership cards and complimentary tickets are not valid for this train.
* In addition to a formal luncheon service, hot & cold beverages, sandwiches & light snacks are available in the Buffet Car.
* Persons wishing to travel who have not booked can only be carried if accommodation is available.
* Cheques/P.O.s payable to West Somerset Railway plc.

BOOKING FORM

Please send me:–   £

.... Tickets 1st Class Taunton–Minehead return (limited availability)   at   £6.50 each =
.... Tickets 3rd Class Taunton–Minehead return   at   £5.00 each =
.... Tickets BELLE Class Taunton–Minehead return   at £14.00 each =
.... Tickets 1st Class Bishop's Lydeard–Minehead return (limited availability) at £5.50 each =
.... Tickets 3rd Class Bishop's Lydeard–Minehead return   at   £4.00 each =
.... Tickets BELLE Class Bishop's Lydeard–Minehead return   at £13.00 each =

BELLE CLASS comprises travel, Luncheon en route to Minehead, with Afternoon Tea on the return trip.

Name . . . .   Remittance enclosed
Address . . . .
       . . . .
       . . . . Postcode . . . .

WE VERY MUCH REGRET THAT TELEPHONE BOOKINGS CANNOT BE ACCEPTED.
If desired accommodation is not available, will you accept next class? (with appropriate refund) Yes/No

24

Finally...

The period from 1990–2003 was regarded by many, as a period of consolidation for the WSR. Many of the dreams and aspirations of those pioneer volunteers were realised, the Crowcombe loop was reopened, excursion traffic from the main line became a regular feature and, when the sea wall at Minehead required refurbishment, the dream of the branch carrying freight from stone quarries were realised at last, when the 100,000 tons of rock required were carried via the main line, to the branch and on to Minehead. This work, together with similar work carried out again at Helwell Bay point, was only possible because the line had earlier been upgraded to take engines with an axle-loading weight of 23.5 tons.

The signal boxes at Minehead and Bishops Lydeard were both brought into service, and the station areas at both locations are now track-circuited; with all movements controlled from the signal box. In addition to the signalling of the station area at Bishops Lydeard, the section of line south towards the main line junction at Norton Fitzwarren was also signalled. The total cost of the scheme was £96,000, which included a direct line between the Bishops Lydeard box and Exeter panel on the national network main line, to control movements between it and the branch.

At Minehead the former goods shed, that for many years served as the only location where the repair and maintenance of locomotives could be undertaken under cover, had been extended to include a new machine shop. A new two-road purpose-built engine shed was built alongside the former goods shed, which is still in use. The new shed for the maintenance of the coaching stock which was being discussed in 1989 was built, and thereafter doubled in size.

Other projects being discussed in 1989 that have been completed include the maintenance shed for the D& E group and the 'tarmac' shed, both of which have been built at Williton. The company is not content to rest on its laurels, other projects being discussed at the time of writing include the replacement of the whole canopy at Minehead Station at a cost of over £100,000, and the erection of a purpose-built stabling block at Bishops Lydeard for the locomotives at that end of the line.

Following the success of the visit of *Evening Star*, it has become company policy to hire a guest engine in for galas to be held during the season. The range of engines that have visited the line since 1990 have ranged from: former GWR 14XX class tank engines;

king-class locomotives; a wide range of the BR standard-class engines, together with black fives; 8Fs from the LMS and B1 class engines from the LNER; and West Country locos from the former Southern Railway.

Ideas pioneered during those formative years, like Sunset Specials, Santa Specials, the Quantock Belle, and star cards have been honed and improved, whilst new ideas like murder mysteries, fish and chip specials, and coach tour bookings have all been started and expanded where possible. The number of steam galas held each year, often with a theme, has increased and the sight of up to six main-line engines in steam in Minehead yard must be one that the early pioneers could only dream of.

During the period 1990–2002, the railway has remained consistently profitable, with the exception of 2000. This has enabled the company to fund all the major projects without recourse to bank loans. While the annual profit levels have never reached the level of those achieved in 1989 – mainly because of the board's policy of reinvesting any surplus income into the continuing maintenance programme – at the end of 2002 the cash-in-hand balance stood at £938,857; of that sum £350,000 was already committed to capital projects.

Other figures show that during this period of consolidation, the number of passengers carried rose from 116,493 in 1989 to 172,457 in 2002 (with over 187,000 in 2003). During the same period the income from fares rose from £357,523 to £1,012,346, and turnover from £540,590 to £1,294,040.

One objective the early pioneers strove for that has not been achieved is the rail link to Taunton. Many people involved with the WSR believe that the year 2003 marked the

end of the second phase in the history of the WSR, and that a new period was about to start – the period of expansion – when at last the long-held dream of the Taunton link will be realised.

These dreams became a step closer to reality with the announcement in March 2004 that the association had purchased 33 acres of land between the West Somerset Railway line and the main line between Taunton and Exeter at Norton Fitzwarren. This area, which includes part of the track bed of the former branch line to Barnstaple, is intended for development, subject to planning permission of course. A new station, locomotive-turning facilities, locomotive workshops, and carriage shed and sidings are mooted.

The following month (April 2004), the company announced a ten-year plan that included massive improvements at Minehead Station, which it was claimed would cost more than £1 million. In addition to plans to turn locomotives on a site near the seafront, they intended to recreate a traditional Edwardian station yard, together with a purpose-built transport interchange. Other proposals included: a travel centre providing national rail bookings, as well as WSR tickets; restoration of the station canopy; increased car parking facilities for 320 visiting cars and 100-plus staff cars.

The company also predicted that the number of passengers carried would increase to 250,000 per annum by the year 2015 and this would also see the number of full-time and part-time staff increase by a third to approximately sixty. All of these plans were in addition to the expansion planned at the other end of the line at Norton Fitzwarren.

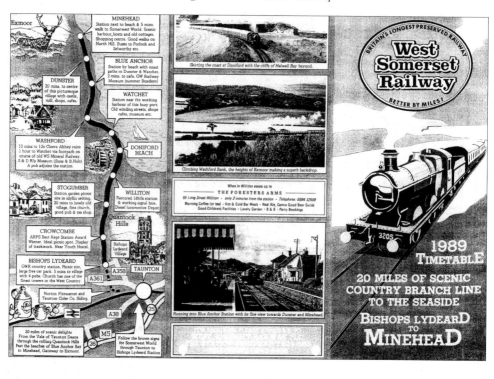

Exmoor

MINEHEAD
Station next to beach & 5 mins. walk to Somerwest World. Scenic harbour, boats and old cottages. Shopping centre. Good walks on North Hill. Buses to Porlock and Selworthy etc.

BLUE ANCHOR
Station by beach with coast paths to Dunster & Watchet. 2 mins. to cafe. GW Railway Museum (summer Sundays).

DUNSTER
20 mins. to centre of this picturesque village with castle, mill, shops, cafes.

WATCHET
Station near the working harbour of this busy port. Old winding streets, shops cafes, museum etc.

WASHFORD
10 mins to 12c Cleeve Abbey ruins 1 hour to Watchet via footpath on course of old WS Mineral Railway. S & D Rly Museum (Suns & B.Hols) A pub adjoins the station.

DONIFORD BEACH

STOGUMBER
Station garden picnic site in idyllic setting. 20 mins to lovely old village, fine church, good pub & tea shop.

WILLITON
Restored 1860s station & working signal box. Diesel Locomotive Depot.

CROWCOMBE
ARPS Best Kept Station Award Winner. Ideal picnic spot. Display of trackwork. Near Youth Hostel.

Quantock Hills

Bishops Lydeard Village

BISHOPS LYDEARD
GWR country station. Picnic site, large free car park. 5 mins to village with 4 pubs. Church has one of the finest towers in the West Country.

A361

A358 TAUNTON

Norton Fitzwarren and Taunton Cider Co. Siding.

20 miles of scenic delights From the Vale of Taunton Deane through the rolling Quantock Hills Past the beaches of Blue Anchor Bay to Minehead, Gateway to Exmoor.

Follow the brown signs for Somerwest World through Taunton to Bishops Lydeard Station

A38 **25** **26** **M5**

Skirting the coast at Doniford with the cliffs of Helwell Bay beyond.

Climbing Washford Bank, the heights of Exmoor making a superb backdrop.

When in Williton steam up to
THE FORESTERS ARMS
55 Long Street Williton - only 2 minutes from the station - Telephone: 0984 32508
Morning Coffee (or tea) - Hot & Cold Bar Meals - Real Ale, Camra Good Beer Guide
Good Childrens Facilities - Lovely Garden - B & B - Party Bookings

Running into Blue Anchor Station with its fine view towards Dunster and Minehead.

BRITAIN'S LONGEST PRESERVED RAILWAY

West Somerset Railway

BETTER BY MILES!

3205

1989 TIMETABLE

20 MILES OF SCENIC COUNTRY BRANCH LINE TO THE SEASIDE

BISHOPS LYDEARD TO MINEHEAD

1989 TIMETABLE

Trains run to Timetables shown as indicated by key below. No trains run where a dash – is shown against the date.

	Mar	Apl	May	June	July	Aug	Sept	Oct	
1	–	D	C	A	B	B	B	A	1
2	–	A	A	A	B	C	D	A	2
3	–	–	A	D	B	C	G	A	3
4	–	S	A	B	B	B	G	–	4
5	–	–	A	A	B	D	G	A	5
6	–	S	D	A	B	C	G	–	6
7	–	–	A	A	B	G	D	7	7
8	–	D	–	A	D	B	G	A	8
9	–	A	A	A	B	C	G	–	9
10	–	–	A	D	B	C	G	A	10
11	–	A	A	B	B	B	A	–	11
12	–	–	A	A	B	D	C	A	12
13	–	A	D	A	B	C	C	–	13
14	–	–	A	A	B	B	D	A	14
15	–	D	–	A	D	B	A	A	15
16	–	A	A	A	B	C	D	–	16
17	–	–	A	D	B	C	A	A	17
18	S	A	A	B	B	B	A	–	18
19	S	–	A	A	B	D	A	A	19
20	–	A	D	B	B	C	A	–	20
21	–	–	A	A	B	C	D	A	21
22	–	S	–	B	D	B	–	A	22
23	S	A	A	A	C	C	D	A	23
24	A	–	A	D	B	C	C	A	24
25	D	A	A	B	B	B	A	A	25
26	B	–	A	A	C	D	A	A	26
27	A	B	D	B	B	C	H	A	27
28	A	–	H	B	B	H	A	D	28
29	A	D	H	B	D	B	–	A	29
30	A	C	A	A	C	C	A		30
31	A		A		B	C			31

G Gala Week – Special Service and attractions.

H Special Bank Holiday Service with extra trains.

S Special Service. Please contact Minehead for details of G H & S.

(R) A Request Stop – Crowcombe, Stogumber, Doniford Beach and Dunster are all request stops. To board a train please give a clear hand signal to the driver. If you wish to alight, please inform the guard on joining train or during the journey.

FARES: Family Fares available between principal stations for a minimum of 2 adults + 2 children. Round Trip Tickets offer excellent value – travel the whole line from any intermediate station. Senior Citizens are given 20% discount off the normal fares. Children under 5 travel free, 5–15 half fare and over 15 full fare. Party Bookings for 10 or more Children/Adults.

REFRESHMENTS: Bar/Buffet Car on most steam trains.

SOUVENIRS: Large shop at Minehead, wide selection of gifts etc.

DISABLED VISITORS: Wheelchair bound visitors are usually able to remain in their chairs on most trains. Flat access to Minehead platform with Disabled Toilets 100 yards from the station.

SUNSET SPECIALS: Each Wed. evening during main summer months. Steam Train with Bar, Minehead–Blue Anchor & back.

GALA WEEK: Special events/attractions. Sept.3rd–10th.

SANTA SPECIALS: During December –Steam Trains to Santa's Grotto. Advance booking essential! For details of all these events and attractions please contact Minehead! (s.a.e. appreciated)

WEST SOMERSET RAILWAY ASSOCIATION: Become a WSR volunteer or supporter! Quarterly Journal, travel concessions etc. Details: WSRA 7 Park Street, Stratton St. Margaret, Swindon.

Table A — OFF PEAK SERVICE SUNDAYS TO FRIDAYS

		Steam	Diesel	Steam	Diesel	Diesel
Minehead		10.15	12.10	2.05		4.30
Dunster	(R)	10.21	12.15	2.11		4.35
Blue Anchor		10.30	12.21	2.20		4.41
Washford		10.40	12.28	2.30		4.48
Watchet		10.48	12.36	2.38		4.54
Doniford Beach	(R)	10.52	12.39	2.42		4.57
Williton		11.05	12.47	2.47	2.52	5.01
Stogumber	(R)	11.17	12.56		3.01	5.10
Crowcombe	(R)	11.29	1.03		3.08	5.17
Bishops Lydeard		11.39	1.13		3.18	5.27

		Diesel	Steam	Diesel	Steam	Diesel
Bishops Lydeard		10.35	12.10	2.15		3.25
Crowcombe	(R)	10.45	12.25	2.25		3.35
Stogumber	(R)	10.54	12.34	2.33		3.42
Williton		11.05	12.47	2.41	3.05	3.52
Doniford Beach	(R)	11.08	12.56		3.09	3.55
Watchet		11.12	1.00		3.14	3.59
Washford		11.19	1.11		3.24	4.06
Blue Anchor		11.26	1.22		3.34	4.14
Dunster	(R)	11.32	1.29		3.42	4.19
Minehead		11.37	1.35		3.48	4.24

Table D — SATURDAYS ONLY DIESEL SERVICE (REDUCED FARES APPLY)

			(i)			(ii)	
Minehead		9.30	11.00	12.30	2.15	4.00	5.10
Dunster	(R)	9.35	11.05	12.35	2.20	4.05	5.15
Blue Anchor		9.41	11.11	12.41	2.27	4.12	5.21
Washford		9.48	11.18	12.48	2.35	4.20	5.28
Watchet		9.56	11.26	12.56	2.42	4.27	5.34
Doniford Beach	(R)	9.59	11.29	12.59	2.45	4.30	5.39
Williton		10.07	11.37	1.07	2.49	4.34	5.47
Stogumber	(R)	10.16	11.46	1.16	2.58	4.43	5.56
Bishops Lydeard		10.24	11.54	1.24	3.06	4.51	6.03
Taunton BR Station		11.15	12.45	2.00	3.45	5.30	Bus
Taunton Bus Station		11.25	12.55	2.10	3.55	5.40	

			(i)			(ii)	
Taunton Bus Station	Bus	10.15	11.45	1.00	2.45	4.30	
Taunton BR Station		10.25	11.55	1.10	2.55	4.40	
Bishops Lydeard		9.38	11.18	12.38	1.38	3.30	5.28
Crowcombe	(R)	9.48	11.18	12.48	1.48	3.30	5.28
Stogumber	(R)	9.56	11.26	12.56	1.56	3.38	5.36
Williton		10.06	11.36	1.06	2.06	3.47	5.46
Doniford Beach	(R)	10.10	11.40	1.10	2.10	3.50	5.50
Watchet		10.13	11.43	1.13	2.13	3.54	5.53
Washford		10.21	11.51	1.21	2.21	4.01	6.01
Blue Anchor		10.28	11.58	1.28	2.28	4.13	6.08
Dunster	(R)	10.34	12.04	1.34	2.34	4.19	6.14
Minehead		10.39	12.09	1.39	2.39	4.24	6.19

(i) June 17–Sept.30 (ii) May 13–Sept.30

Table B and Table C — PEAK SERVICE

		Steam	D/S	Steam	Diesel	Diesel
Minehead		10.15	12.00	2.05	4.00	6.10
Dunster	(R)	10.21	12.06	2.11	4.05	6.15
Blue Anchor		10.30	12.15	2.20	4.11	6.21
Washford		10.40	12.25	2.30	4.19	6.29
Watchet		10.48	12.34	2.38	4.24	6.35
Doniford Beach	(R)	10.52	12.38	2.42	4.27	6.38
Williton		11.05	12.48	2.53	4.35	6.44
Stogumber	(R)	11.17	1.01	3.06	4.43	6.53
Crowcombe	(R)	11.29	1.14	3.19	4.50	7.01
Bishops Lydeard		11.39	1.24	3.29	5.00	7.11
Taunton BR Station	12.00		Bus		5.25	Bus
Taunton Bus Station	12.05				5.30	

		Diesel	Steam	D/S	Steam	Diesel
Taunton Bus Station		11.15				4.40	Bus
Taunton BR Station		11.20		Bus		4.45	
Bishops Lydeard		10.35	12.10	2.15	4.00	5.05
Crowcombe	(R)	10.45	12.25	2.30	4.15	5.15
Stogumber	(R)	10.54	12.34	2.39	4.24	5.23
Williton		11.05	12.47	2.51	4.39	5.33
Doniford Beach	(R)	11.08	12.56	3.00	4.48	5.37
Watchet		11.12	1.00	3.06	4.53	5.41
Washford		11.19	1.11	3.16	5.03	5.48
Blue Anchor		11.26	1.22	3.26	5.13	5.55
Dunster	(R)	11.32	1.29	3.33	5.21	6.01
Minehead		11.37	1.35	3.39	5.27	6.06

D/S
The same times apply for Table B and Table C but during the High Peak service (Table C) the 12.00pm from Minehead and the 2.15pm from Bishops Lydeard are Steam Trains.

TAUNTON LINK
Services shown between Bishops Lydeard and Taunton are by specially chartered bus which meets trains and on which WSR and BR through tickets are valid. Certain Southern National buses MAY also connect with some trains but WSR tickets are NOT valid on these services. Please telephone for full details – Southern National, 0823 272033.

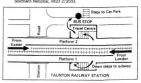

TAUNTON RAILWAY STATION

Steps to Car Park · BUS STOP · Travel Centre · Platform 2 · From Exeter · From London · Platform 1 · Down steps to subway · Road · Station

Note: Whilst every effort will be made to maintain the advertised services, the Company does not guarantee that trains will depart or arrive at the times stated and reserves the right to cancel, alter or suspend any or all of its service without notice and accepts no liability for any loss, inconvenience or delay thereby caused.

DESIGN & ARTWORK: PETER BARNFIELD   PRINT: DOVETON PRESS BRISTOL

MERRYMAKER

Minehead and the
West Somerset Railway
(inc. Blue Anchor, Dunster, Watchet)

| Wednesdays | 2 June to 22 September |
| Sundays | 4 July to 26 September 1982 |

An opportunity to visit the attractive north Somerset seaside resort of Minehead and to ride on the delightful West Somerset Railway - 20 miles of beautiful scenery. It's Britains longest private railway and there's the chance of a trip on a steam-hauled train. The W.S.R. trains also call at Watchet, Blue Anchor and Dunster, so you can break your journey a while - train service permitting. It is a lovely day out at bargain prices.

Combined charges
inc. BR train fare, bus
and West Somerset Rly.

		2nd Class	
		Adult £	Child £
Paddington	Ealing Broadway	9.90	4.95
Slough	)		
Reading	)	9.50	4.75
Oxford	)		

Tickets may be purchased in advance or up to time of departure from those stations listed. Also from B.R. London Town Offices at 407 Oxford Street, W.1 Lower Regent Street, SW.1 170b Strand, WC.2 87 King William Street, EC.4 Victoria Street, SW.1 and selected B.R. Travel Agents.

This is the age of the train ⇒

A rare example of co-operation with British rail at this time (1982).

Appendix

Numbers of passengers carried each year on the West Somerset Railway from 1976–2003:

Year	Annual Total	Cumulative total
1976	50,300	50,300
1977	54,700	105,000
1978	85,037	190,037
1979	89,379	279,416
1980	84,203	363,619
1981	72,833	436,452
1982	58,056	494,508
1983	51,537	546,045
1984	52,406	598,451
1985	57,339	655,790
1986	66,910	722,700
1987	75,075	797,775
1988	89,476	887,251
1989	116,493	1,003,744
1990	121,859	1,125,603
1991	116,513	1,242,116
1992	113,341	1,355,457
1993	120,103	1,475,460
1994	127,177	1,602,737
1995	128,378	1,731,115
1996	144,947	1,876,062
1997	146,883	2,022,945
1998	144,160	2,167,105
1999	153,832	2,320,937
2000	154,421	2,475,358
2001	169,275	2,644,633
2002	172,457	2,817,090
2003	187,201	3,004,291

Santa Special Trains:
Summary of passengers carried

Year	Adults	Children	Total
1983	336	341	777
1984	N/A	N/A	683
1985	562	479	1,041
1986	974	838	1,812
1987	1,047	1,014	2,061
1988	N/A	N/A	N/A
1989	N/A	N/A	N/A
1990	N/A	N/A	5,115
1991	2,198	1,747	3,945
1992	2,692	2,233	4,925
1993	2,549	2,004	4,553
1994	2,881	2,249	5,130
1995	2,949	2,284	5,233
1996	3,256	2,596	5,852
1997	3,316	2,623	5,939
1998	3,391	2,749	6,140
1999	3,473	2,503	5,976
2000	3,780	2,734	6,514

Addendum

Summary of Recommendations from *The Future of the West Somerset Railway* (The Brown Report, see page 134):

3.6 Summary of Recommendations for Council Action

1   The Council should continue to accept that the West Somerset Railway has no significant role to play as a public transport link.

2   The Council should review its policies and aspirations for the railway; in particular, it should consider the extent to which it requires it to function in the wider public interest as:
    – a generator of tourism
    – a working museum
    – a recreational facility
    – an educational facility
    – a conserved piece of heritage.

3   If the Council wishes it to perform any or all of these wider public roles, it should review its relationship with the present railway company, whose objects (given its lack of resources) must perforce be more limited, and which in practice serves primarily the interests of its directors and shareholders.

4   If the railway is to perform the above tasks, or even if its future as a commercially viable attraction is to be secured, significant additional investment in capital works, track renewal, motive power and rolling stock will be required. A technical survey should be carried out, by or in consultation with, suitably qualified persons who have direct experience of preserved steam railways, to determine what these costs would be.

5   If these costs are not prohibitive, the Council should take steps to provide or secure the necessary funds, not least to secure the future of its own longer-term investment.

6   The Council should consider the following course of action:
    (i) The Council should establish, in partnership with the district councils and others, an independent trust on the lines of established museum trusts.

(ii) The Council should transfer the land and track to the Trust, and provide it with core funding.

(iii) The Trust should raise funds for a major programme of capital works, track maintenance and acquisition of rolling stock and locomotives; and for subsidising on-going operations.

(iv) The railway company's lease should be renegotiated, in consideration of the extra investment. One condition of the new terms should be that the management team and board of directors should be strengthened. The Trust should have the right to appoint directors.

(v) Further study should be carried out on the wider costs and benefits of maintaining operations over the southern section, prior to major expenditure. This should take account of the development potential of Bishops Lydeard Station.

(vi) Schemes for developing Minehead and Bishops Lydeard stations as major visitor attractions should be produced, with costs and benefits.

(vii) For the time being, no action should be taken on the Taunton link, at least until the future of the southern section is known. If in due course it is still felt necessary to pursue the question, a feasibility study should be commissioned.

7   The Council should embody its policies for the railway into a rational long-term development plan.

8   A possible phasing of the line's further development might be as follows:

Phase One: Coastal Consolidation (1987/88)

-        concentrate available carrying capacity on northern section; consolidate financial position.
-        concentrate manpower and capital resources on developing product quality on northern section, especially on the trains themselves and at Minehead and Williton.
-        develop major visitor facility at Minehead Station.
-        reinvest revenue heavily in marketing.
-        retain track to Norton Fitzwarren.
-        re-establish physical link with BR through Taunton Cider sidings.

Phase Two: Southern Reopening (1989/90)

-        gradually install signalling and passing loops on southern section.
-        acquire additional rolling stock and motive power in readiness for re-extended services: prepare to high quality of finish.

– redevelop Bishops Lydeard (or another site) as southern terminus and major visitor facility.
– major marketing relaunch.

Phase Three (subject to review): Taunton Link (1991/92)

– acquire additional stock required to operate Taunton link.
– develop physical link.

The above summary was extracted from the *West Somerset Railway Follow on Study of its Tourism Potential.*

This report, which was published in November 1993, was forty-three pages long and became known as the second Brown Report. Because it deals with matters outside the time period covered by this book it does not feature in these pages.

Bibliography

Bristol Evening Post

Somerset County Gazette

West Somerset Free Press

West Somerset Railway Association Journal

West Somerset Railway PLC

Western Daily Press

Other titles published by The History Press

Somerset Railways
TED GOSLING & MIKE CLEMENT

This book gives the reader a chance to look back at the scenery and stations of Some
beautiful railway network. Historic stations such as Chard Junction, Milborne Por
Binegar are depicted, as well as classic steam trains the Devon Belle and the Pines Ex
A fitting tribute to railway workers and their vibrant rail network, this title is a must
railway historians and those with an interest in the local area.

978-0-7524-5212-8

The Chiltern Railways Story
HUGH JONES

This is the story of the most successful rail company that came into existence afte
privatisation of British Rail in 1996. Through the personal memories of staff and custo
as well as many previously unpublished images from the archives, this modern ra
history celebrates the past and present success of Chiltern Railways, while explaining
the company means to so many.

978-0-7524-5454-2

The Metropolitan Line: London's First Underground Railway
CLIVE FOXELL

Built in 1863, the world's first underground passenger railway helped to create the B
suburban landscape we are all so familiar with today, and was once part of an optir
Victorian plan to link Manchester with Paris by rail. This fascinating illustrated histo
London's first tube line and the people involved in its evolution tells its story right t
plans for the railway in connection with the London 2012 Olympics.

978-0-7524-5396-5

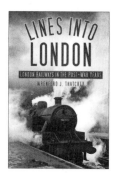

Lines into London: London Railways in the Post-War Years
WRENFORD J. THATCHER

A nostalgic journey through the last years of steam and the early diesels around Lor
this collection of evocative photographs is divided into eastern, southern, western
midland regions, revealing the post-war changes on the London railways. The dying
of steam power and new era of diesel traction is chronicled in this selection of previ
unpublished images from the 1940s, '50s and '60s.

978-0-7524-5892-2

Visit our website and discover thousands of other History Press books.
www.thehistorypress.co.uk

The Histo Press